BEST OF THE BEST

Editor in Chief **Judith Hill**

Art Director **Perri DeFino**

Managing Editor **Miriam Harris**

Project Manager **Dana Speers**

Designer **Elizabeth Rendfleisch**

Editorial Associate **Colleen McKinney**

Production Coordinator **Stuart Handelman**

Chief Marketing Officer, Publisher **Mark V. Stanich**

Vice President, Marketing **Bruce Rosner**

Director, Retail Sales **Marshall Corey**

Operations Manager **Catherine A. Bussey**

Business Manager **Doreen Camardi**

ISBN: 0-916103-69-2   ISSN: 1524-2862

FOOD & WINE
annual cookbook-awards collection

BEST
OF THE
BEST

THE 100 BEST RECIPES FROM THE
BEST COOKBOOKS OF THE YEAR

American Express Publishing Corporation
New York

FOOD & WINE
BOOKS

contents

other main dishes

vegetables & side dishes

desserts

Every recipe in this book was carefully tested in the FOOD & WINE kitchens and was chosen with you in mind. From the hundreds of cookbooks published in 2000, we selected the dishes that we thought our readers would pick for themselves—if they could spend the time to read 700 books and test 300 recipes.

Of those hundreds of cookbooks, we judged just 27 to be outstanding. For every three recipes that we tested, only one made the cut, joining the ranks of the 100 best recipes from the best cookbooks of the year.

The recipes are presented here in the style used in their own books: If the steps in the method were numbered, they're numbered here. If a recipe was broken into main and sub recipes, that's the way it appears here. If there were lots of tips or chatty intros, that's what you get here. So if you find yourself gravitating toward recipes from a certain author, you'll know that there's a cookbook out there that really suits you and that the recipes in it are written just as they are in these pages.

We include a new feature in this, our fourth volume of *Best of the Best.* Along the bottom of the pages, you'll find tips that we used or discovered as we tested and considered each recipe—such as techniques that will help you cut time, information on how far ahead the dish can be made, or suggestions for ideal accompaniments. In the same space, we recommend a wine for each of the first courses and main dishes.

We think these are the most delectable, accurate, usable recipes in all the original, hardback cookbooks published in the United States this year. We hope you agree. Let us know what you think by e-mailing bestofbest@foodandwine.com.

Judith Hill

Judith Hill, Editor in Chief
FOOD & WINE Books

As we read and reviewed, tested and tasted, we became particularly impressed with certain books that were published this year. The winners of our fourth annual editor's choice awards are bestowed on the best of the best of the best.

best cookbook of the year

Rick Bayless: Mexico One Plate at a Time by Rick Bayless
published by Scribner

best cookbook of the year: runner-up

Tom Douglas' Seattle Kitchen by Tom Douglas
published by William Morrow and Company, Inc.

most beautiful book of the year

Hot Sour Salty Sweet by Jeffrey Alford and Naomi Duguid
published by Artisan

best recipe of the year: savory

Mushroom-Studded Tortilla Soup with Chipotle Chiles and Goat Cheese
Rick Bayless: Mexico One Plate at a Time by Rick Bayless, page 154

best recipe of the year: sweet

Chocolate Snowball
Anne Willan: From My Château Kitchen by Anne Willan, page 250
published by Clarkson Potter/Publishers

roll call of winners

Alfred Portale's 12 Seasons Cookbook by Alfred Portale
The perfect recipes for each month of the year from one of America's best chefs.

Anne Willan: From My Château Kitchen by Anne Willan
Drool over the beauty of château living and get a taste of it, too. The acclaimed founder of Ecôle de Cuisine La Varenne lets us in on her life in Burgundy and her delicious yet do-able personal repertoire.

Cookies Unlimited by Nick Malgieri
Basic, reliable, and complete—from all-American oatmeal raisin cookies to short-bread to French tuiles to a holiday gingerbread cottage.

Cracking the Coconut *Classic Thai Home Cooking* by Su-Mei Yu
The wake-up-your-mouth flavors of authentic Thai cooking are demystified in this collection of tantalizing recipes.

Death by Chocolate Cakes *An Astonishing Array of Chocolate Enchantments* by Marcel Desaulniers
The recipes are luscious, they're unfailingly reliable, and they're chocolate. Need we say more?

The Dessert Bible by Christopher Kimball
All the basic desserts we know and love, along with lots of information on how baking works and what to do if yours doesn't.

The Farmer's Market Cookbook *Seasonal Recipes Made from Nature's Freshest Ingredients* by Richard Ruben
An unpretentious little book that's heavy on fresh fruit and vegetables, from a passionate farmer's-market aficionado.

50 Chowders *One-Pot Meals—Clam, Corn & Beyond*
by Jasper White
The king of Boston seafood deftly expands the definition of chowder.
Vegetable, meat, and poultry inventions join the ranks of his definitive fish
and shellfish renditions.

The Foods of the Greek Islands *Cooking and Culture at the Crossroads of the*
Mediterranean, Including Recipes by New York's Acclaimed Molyvos Restaurant
by Aglaia Kremezi
Your favorite Greek-restaurant favorites show up here, plus dishes in the same
spirit that will be happy new discoveries.

Gordon Ramsay: A Chef for All Seasons by Gordon Ramsay
A celebrated English chef's take on what U.S. critics often call New American
cooking. Mouthwatering recipes with photos to match.

The Herbfarm Cookbook by Jerry Traunfeld
Herbs galore make for a garden of good ideas for every flavor-filled leaf and
flower you can grow or buy. Plus an exhaustive section on growing, keeping, and
using them all, from angelica to violets.

Hot Sour Salty Sweet *A Culinary Journey through Southeast Asia*
by Jeffrey Alford and Naomi Duguid
A gorgeously photographed and produced book with carefully researched
recipes from Southeast Asia. A stunning accomplishment in every way.

How to Cook Without a Book *Recipes Every Cook Should Know by Heart*
by Pam Anderson
The basics, carefully thought through and arranged to work as a cooking course
in a book. A great confidence builder for any new cook.

The Japanese Kitchen by Hiroko Shimbo

This is the real thing. If you want to try your hand at sushi and all the other wonders of Japanese cuisine, here's the place to start.

Julia's Kitchen Wisdom *Essential Techniques and Recipes from a Lifetime of Cooking* by Julia Child

A slim volume that manages to include all the basics, infused with Julia's fine wit (and, of course, wisdom).

Mario Batali: Holiday Food *Recipes for the Most Festive Time of Year* by Mario Batali

A cute little book with a popular chef's personal renditions of Italian holiday favorites. Lots of simple dishes here, and they're good year-round.

My Mother's Southern Entertaining by James Villas

Southern home cooking at its finest. The always-reliable Villas recipes show us once again how well Mr. Villas and his mother, Martha Pearl, know the meaning of yummy.

Nancy Silverton's Pastries from the La Brea Bakery by Nancy Silverton

Treads the golden mean with recipes that are neither so homey that you've seen them a million times nor so professional that you can't take them on yourself.

The Olives Dessert Table *Spectacular Restaurant Desserts You Can Make at Home* by Todd English, Paige Retus, and Sally Sampson

Luscious, wildly extravagant desserts with many components. Here's the beauty of it: each component is among the best of its kind and well worth making for its own sweet self.

1,000 Jewish Recipes by Faye Levy

The be-all and end-all, complete compendium of Jewish dishes. You will need no other.

Rick Bayless: Mexico One Plate at a Time by Rick Bayless
Rick Bayless can do no wrong so far as we're concerned. He exhaustively
researches authentic Mexican food and makes sure all the recipes will work in
the U.S. Every recipe's a winner. Bravo, Rick!

Savoring the Spice Coast of India *Fresh Flavors from Kerala* by Maya Kaimal
In recipes passed down from her family and other southern Indian cooks, Maya
Kaimal brings to life the tropical state of Kerala.

Simple to Spectacular *How to Take One Basic Recipe to Four Levels of
Sophistication* by Jean-Georges Vongerichten and Mark Bittman
The inspired Jean-Georges Vongerichten fills another book with stimulating ideas.
Even the simple recipes are pretty spectacular.

Simply Tuscan *Recipes for a Well-Lived Life* by Pino Luongo
Tuscan Pino Luongo delivers the authentic article with delicious recipes that will
be new to most Americans.

Staff Meals from Chanterelle by David Waltuck and Melicia Phillips
The staff at New York's renowned Chanterelle restaurant clearly eats very well
indeed, but also simply, which makes the recipes perfect for the home cook.

Tom Douglas' Seattle Kitchen by Tom Douglas
Sophisticated, yet down-to-earth. Restaurant quality, yet easy. Original, yet not
over-the-top. Douglas's recipes embody contradictions we adore.

Wildwood *Cooking from the Source in the Pacific Northwest*
by Cory Schreiber
Dedicated to the Northwest, *Wildwood* is a must-have for those who love salmon
and oysters, hazelnuts and berries, Walla Walla onions and wild mushrooms.

hors d'oeuvres & first courses

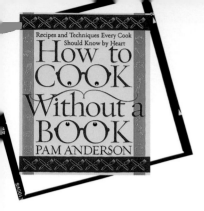

Recipes and Techniques Every Cook
Should Know by Heart
How to
COOK
Without a
BOOK
PAM ANDERSON

sweet pea spread with bacon

from *How to Cook Without a Book*

MAKES ³⁄4 CUP (ENOUGH FOR ABOUT 36 TOAST ROUNDS)

If you have time, spread this green pea puree on toast rounds, garnishing each with the crumbled bacon bits. If not, simply transfer the spread to a serving bowl, sprinkle with the bacon bits, and serve with pita or bagel crisps.

3   slices bacon, cut into ¹⁄4-inch pieces

2   garlic cloves, lightly crushed and peeled

1   cup frozen green peas, cooked following package instructions and drained

Fry the bacon along with the crushed garlic cloves in a medium skillet over medium heat until bacon is crisp, about 5 minutes. Transfer the bacon with a slotted spoon to a paper towel–lined plate; set aside. Combine the garlic and 2 tablespoons of bacon drippings, the cooked peas, and salt and pepper to taste in the workbowl of a food processor fitted with a steel blade. Process until puréed. With the machine still running, add 2 tablespoons of warm tap water to thin the mixture. Transfer to a small bowl and top with crumbled bacon or spread on toast rounds (see note above).

FOOD&WINE test-kitchen tips

- This spread is so tasty that you may want to make a double batch, which works out well because boxes of frozen peas generally contain 2 cups.

- Essentially a vegetable puree, this could be served as a side dish or garnish as well as a spread.

smoked whitefish spread

from *1,000 Jewish Recipes*

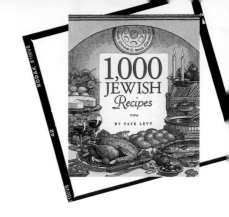

MAKES ABOUT 6 SERVINGS

In many homes smoked fish is a favorite food on the break-the-fast table, and so are bagels. This spread is a perfect topping for bagels, but is also good on rye bread or on crackers that aren't very salty such as water crackers.

8	ounces whipped cream cheese
1/3	cup flaked smoked whitefish
2	teaspoons chopped fresh chives

2 to 3 tablespoons sour cream (optional)
Freshly ground pepper to taste
Cayenne pepper to taste

Mix cream cheese with whitefish and chives in a small bowl. If spread is too stiff, stir in sour cream, a tablespoon at a time. Season with pepper and cayenne. Refrigerate until ready to serve.

hors d'oeuvres & first courses

FOOD&WINE test-kitchen tips

- If you're making the recipe as an hors d'oeuvre (our favorite use for this yummy spread), try toasting thin slices of baguette to go with it. Serve the toast warm or at room temperature.

palace olive poppers

from *Tom Douglas' Seattle Kitchen*

MAKES 6 TO 8 SERVINGS

This slightly "retro" appetizer has been served at Palace Kitchen since the day we opened. Executive Chef Eric Tanaka was inspired by a recipe in a fifties cookbook he found in a used-bookstore—he updated it by using Kalamata olives instead of pimiento-stuffed green olives. The poppers make a great appetizer or party snack, especially when accompanied by a full-bodied ale like Redhook ESB.

If you want to make a lot of poppers for a party, double or triple the recipe and use a pastry bag with a plain $\frac{1}{4}$-inch round tip to fill the olives. Soften the cream cheese first by beating it lightly with an electric mixer.

24 "colossal size" Kalamata olives

3 tablespoons cream cheese

1$\frac{1}{2}$ cups grated sharp Cheddar cheese

9 tablespoons all-purpose flour

$\frac{3}{4}$ teaspoon Tabasco sauce

$\frac{1}{2}$ teaspoon kosher salt

3 tablespoons unsalted butter, melted

1 to 2 tablespoons milk, as needed

Herb Sour Cream Dressing (recipe follows)

1 Pit the olives with an olive pitter, keeping them as whole and unbroken as possible. Place the cream cheese in a small bowl and beat it with a spoon to soften it slightly. Using your fingers, stuff the olives with the softened cream cheese. Set aside.

2 Combine the Cheddar cheese, flour, Tabasco, and salt in a bowl, using a wooden spoon or rubber spatula. Add the melted butter and mix. Add the milk, starting with 1 tablespoon and using more as needed, and mix. Use your hands to knead the dough for a minute until a soft dough is formed.

FOOD&WINE test-kitchen tips

- If Kalamata olives aren't available, use any kind you like, whether green or black, just as long as they're good quality and firm.

- These appetizers taste great with the Herb Sour Cream Dressing as suggested, but we found they flew out of the test kitchen just as fast when we made them without the sauce.

3 Preheat the oven to 375°F. Pinch off small balls of dough about the same size as the olives. Flatten each ball of dough with your fingers and wrap each olive with it. Place the dough-wrapped olives on a parchment paper–lined baking sheet about an inch apart. Bake until golden brown, about 25 minutes.

on the plate Drizzle herb sour cream dressing on appetizer plates and serve the warm olive poppers hot from the oven, on top of the cream.

a step ahead Unbaked, these dough-wrapped olives will keep refrigerated, covered with plastic wrap, for a day or two.

in the glass Redhook ESB or a Bombay Sapphire martini, with olives of course

herb sour cream dressing This also makes a delicious dip or dressing for raw vegetables. We leave salt out because the olives can be salty, but you will probably want to add some to taste if you use the dressing in other dishes.

MAKES ³⁄₄ CUP

- ½ **cup sour cream**
- 3 **tablespoons heavy cream**
- 1 **teaspoon chopped fresh flat-leaf parsley**
- ½ **teaspoon chopped fresh thyme**
- ½ **teaspoon chopped fresh rosemary**
- **Pinch of freshly ground black pepper**
- **Kosher salt (optional)**

In a small bowl, combine the sour cream, heavy cream, chopped herbs, and pepper. Add salt to taste if not using with olives.

cheese coins

from *Pastries from the La Brea Bakery*

YIELD: 6 TO 7 DOZEN COINS

Most often known as cheese crackers, cheese wafers, or cheese thins, these are my version of that classic savory snack. For a more pungent flavor, I use a ripe English Stilton to replace the Cheddar. For a variety of shapes, form the dough into rectangular logs or round logs. Coat them with an assortment of seeds and spices to add color and texture. Store the logs in the freezer, ready to slice and bake whenever you like.

3 sticks plus 1 tablespoon (12½ ounces) unsalted butter,
   chilled and cut into 1-inch cubes

1 tablespoon kosher salt

Pinch of dried chili flakes

4½ cups unbleached pastry flour or unbleached all-purpose flour

1 cup crème fraîche or sour cream

1 cup (4 ounces) grated Parmesan Reggiano cheese

1 cup (4 ounces) grated white Cheddar cheese or Stilton

¾ cup (3 ounces) grated Pecorino Romano or Gruyère cheese

for the coating

1 extra-large egg white, lightly beaten

¼ cup polenta or finely ground cornmeal, optional

¼ cup coarsely ground black pepper, optional

¼ cup paprika, optional

¼ cup seeds such as fennel, sesame, or caraway, optional

FOOD&WINE test-kitchen tips

- If you don't have an electric mixer with a paddle attachment, you can make the pastry the old-fashioned way, by hand. Just stir the salt and chili flakes into the flour and then add the butter as you would to make pie dough, cutting it in with a pastry blender until the mixture is the consistency of coarse meal.

- It's such a good idea to get a variety of tastes from one batch of dough that we couldn't stop experimenting with possibilities. Try triangle and square shapes, as well as the suggested round and rectangular. Add poppy seeds, coarse salt, and chopped nuts to the list of good coatings.

In the bowl of an electric mixer fitted with the paddle attachment, cream the butter, salt, and chili flakes on low, 2 to 3 minutes, until softened. Turn the mixer up to medium and continue to mix another 2 minutes, scraping down the sides of the bowl as needed. Turn the mixer off, add the flour, and mix on low until it's the consistency of a coarse meal.

Add the crème fraîche and grated cheeses, mixing until the dough just comes together.

Turn the dough out onto a lightly floured work surface and knead a few times to gather it together. Divide the dough into three pieces and flatten it into rectangles, about 1 inch thick. Wrap in plastic and chill until firm enough to shape, about an hour.

Working with one piece of dough at a time, drop each side of the rectangle against the work surface to help compress the dough and eliminate air pockets. For rectangular crackers: Shape the dough into a rectangular bar, 1½ inches wide and 8 inches long, packing and compressing the sides. For round crackers: Working from the center out, roll the dough into tight circular logs, about 1½ inches in diameter and 8 inches long. Wrap each log in plastic and chill in the freezer for about 2 hours, until very firm.

Adjust the oven rack to the middle position and preheat the oven to 350 degrees.

Keeping each type of coating separate, spread them on a work surface. Brush the logs with egg white and roll each log in a different coating to cover. Place the logs on a cutting board and using a very sharp knife, cut into ⅛-inch-thick slices. Place them ½ inch apart on a parchment-lined baking sheet. If you don't want to slice and bake all of the dough, wrap the logs in plastic and store in the freezer.

Bake for 10 to 15 minutes, until very lightly browned and crisp.

bite-size cheddar and thyme gougères

from *The Herbfarm Cookbook*

MAKES ABOUT 72 PUFFS

Cheese puffs, really—these are miniature Cheddar versions of a savory French cream puff traditionally enriched with Gruyère cheese. Whatever you call them, fresh from the oven they make the ideal cocktail snack. Once you form the dough into mounds on the baking sheets, you can refrigerate or freeze them and bake the puffs just before your guests are ready to devour them.

³/₄ cup water

¹/₂ teaspoon salt

6 tablespoons unsalted butter, cut into ¹/₂-inch cubes

³/₄ cup all-purpose flour (spoon and level; 3¹/₄ ounces)

4 large eggs

1¹/₂ tablespoons finely chopped fresh English thyme

1 cup grated sharp Cheddar or Gruyère cheese (2 ounces)

1 dough Preheat the oven to 400°F. Put the water, salt, and butter in a medium (2- to 3-quart) saucepan and bring it to a boil over medium heat. Add the flour all at once and beat vigorously with a sturdy wire whisk, still over heat. It will form a very firm mass of dough that should pull away from the sides of the pan. Remove the pan from the heat. Crack an egg into a small cup. Pour the egg into the saucepan and immediately beat it into the dough using the whisk or a handheld electric mixer. Repeat with the remaining 3 eggs, incorporating each one thoroughly before adding another. The mixture will be satiny and sticky and have a consistency between soft dough and thick batter. Stir in the thyme and ¹/₂ cup of the cheese.

FOOD&WINE test-kitchen tips

- If it seems easier to you, use a food processor to incorporate the eggs, thyme, and cheese into the dough. As soon as the mass of dough forms, scrape it into the processor, immediately add the eggs, one at a time, and then pulse in the thyme and cheese.

- We like gougères at room temperature, too. Just be sure to serve within a few hours of baking. Fresh gougères are little puffs of heaven, but they lose their celestial quality quickly.

2 forming and baking Line 2 baking sheets with parchment paper. Using 2 flatware teaspoons, drop balls of dough (each measuring 1 teaspoon in volume) in rows on the paper, allowing 1 inch of space between them for spreading. Or use a pastry bag with a large plain tip and pipe the dough out in ½-inch mounds. Place a pinch of the remaining cheese on top of each gougère. (At this point you can cover the pans tightly with plastic wrap and refrigerate them for up to 24 hours.) Bake the gougères until puffed and golden brown, 20 to 25 minutes. Serve while still warm.

note Once the dough is formed, you can put the baking sheets in the freezer until the little mounds are solid, then transfer them to resealable freezer bags. When you want to bake a batch, transfer them to a paper-lined baking sheet and bake at 400°F for 25 to 30 minutes.

herb substitutions In place of the thyme, use an equal amount of finely chopped fresh summer savory, 2 tablespoons finely chopped fresh marjoram or oregano, or 3 tablespoons finely chopped fresh dill or chives.

baked mussels stuffed with mint pesto

from *The Herbfarm Cookbook*

6 APPETIZER SERVINGS OR 12 HORS-D'OEUVRE SERVINGS

This is a terrific hors d'oeuvre or tapas dish that you can make ahead and bake at the last minute. The mussels are first steamed, then the meat is stuffed back in their shells on a bed of flavorful firm pesto made with spearmint and parsley, but without cheese. Serve them with cocktail forks and make sure your guests scoop up the pesto as they lift each mussel from the shell.

2	pounds fresh live mussels, large if possible, washed and beards removed
½	cup dry white wine

pesto

¼	cup pine nuts
2	cloves garlic, peeled
¾	teaspoon salt
1½	cups (gently packed) fresh spearmint leaves
1	cup (gently packed) fresh flat-leaf parsley leaves
	Freshly ground black pepper to taste
¼	cup extra-virgin olive oil

1 steaming the mussels Put the mussels in a large (6-quart) pot and pour the wine over them. Cover the pot tightly, place it over high heat, and cook just until all the mussels open. Drain the mussels into a colander set over a bowl to catch the liquor. Allow the mussels to cool until you can easily handle them and reserve the liquor for another use (it freezes well and is good in chowders, bisques, or seafood stews).

FOOD&WINE test-kitchen tips

- The recipe suggests large mussels, and we found this to be important advice. Big ones come out juicy and stand right up to the pesto. If you can only get small ones, try cutting the cooking time somewhat and using less of the minty sauce.

- As the author explains in the book's admirably thorough information section, the mint generally available in supermarkets is spearmint. Its flavor is less strong than that of peppermint, which would be way too powerful here.

2 pesto Process the pine nuts, garlic, and salt in a food processor until the nuts are finely ground. Add the mint, parsley, and pepper. Pulse the machine until all the leaves are coarsely ground, scraping down the sides if necessary. With the machine running, pour in the olive oil in a steady stream and process until the mixture is a paste with some texture of the leaves remaining. You can also make the pesto with a mortar and pestle.

3 stuffing the mussels Detach and discard the top shell of each mussel. Loosen the meat in the bottom shell and check each one to make sure there is no trace of beard left inside the mussel. Lay the mussels in their half-shells on a baking sheet. Lift a mussel and place ½ to ¾ teaspoon pesto in its shell depending on its size, then lightly press the mussel back in place. Stuff the remaining shells. The mussels can be stuffed earlier in the day, covered with plastic wrap, and refrigerated until ready to bake.

4 baking Preheat the oven to 375°F. Bake the mussels just until the pesto begins to bubble and the mussels are hot to the touch, 6 to 8 minutes. Serve on plates or platters lined with mint leaves or sprigs.

warm quail salad with apple, hazelnuts, and oregon blue cheese

from *Wildwood*

SERVES 4 AS AN APPETIZER

Oregon blue cheese is produced by the Rogue River Creamery, located in the southern portion of the state. While the Rogue River blue may not be as creamy as its American and European counterparts, it's perfect in salad preparations. Pair it with quail, apples, pears, and cracked hazelnuts for a hearty appetizer that celebrates the bounty of the autumn harvest in the Pacific Northwest.

4	tablespoons olive oil
2	tablespoons balsamic vinegar
2	shallots, minced
2	teaspoons water
1	tablespoon undiluted orange juice concentrate
1½	teaspoons salt
1¼	teaspoons freshly ground black pepper
4	boneless quail or boneless, skinless chicken breasts or thighs
10	cups (10 ounces) mixed baby greens
1	unpeeled pippin apple, cored and thinly sliced
¼	cup golden raisins
¼	cup hazelnuts, toasted, skinned, and coarsely chopped
4	ounces Oregon blue cheese or other blue cheese, crumbled (about 1 cup)

To prepare the dressing: In a small bowl, whisk together 3 tablespoons of the oil, the vinegar, shallots, water, orange juice concentrate, ½ teaspoon of the salt, and ¼ teaspoon of the pepper; set aside.

FOOD&WINE test-kitchen tips

- You can tell this recipe comes from a restaurant—not that it's difficult to make, but the portions are large. At home, we'd probably serve this quantity to 8 people, cutting the quail in half after cooking to make 8 portions. Or, this hearty salad would make an excellent main dish as is.

 wine recommendation Brachetto d'Acqui, a sparkling red wine from northern Italy, would be a marvelous choice to accompany this dish. Its lush flavors will be more than a match for the blue cheese without overwhelming the quail.

To prepare the quail or chicken: Preheat the broiler. In a large skillet, heat the remaining 1 tablespoon oil over medium-high heat. Season the quail or chicken with the remaining 1 teaspoon each salt and pepper. Place the quail or chicken in the skillet and brown evenly on all sides. Transfer to a broiler pan and broil 4 inches from the heat source, turning once, for 5 to 10 minutes, or until the juices run clear when the meat is pierced with a knife; set aside and keep warm.

To prepare the salad, in a large salad bowl, combine the greens, apple, raisins, hazelnuts, and blue cheese. Add the dressing and toss.

To serve, portion the salad onto 4 plates. Top with the warm quail or chicken.

toasting nuts Preheat the oven to 325°. Place the nuts on a large jelly roll pan, spreading them out so they don't touch. Toast in the oven for 20 minutes, or until lightly browned, occasionally shaking the pan so the nuts toast evenly.

If toasting hazelnuts, remove the nuts from the oven and wrap them in a dish towel to steam and cool them. Once they have cooled a bit, roll the hazelnuts around in the towel to remove the skins. Transfer the hazelnuts to a colander with medium holes and roll them around with your hands to knock off the remainder of the skins. As the hazelnuts are skinned, remove them from the colander.

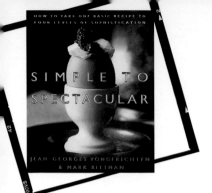

fast gazpacho

MAKES 4 SERVINGS

Nothing faster, and quite good, especially when made with high-quality vegetables. Be sure to taste and adjust the seasoning before serving.

1	medium cucumber, peeled
4	tomatoes (about 1½ pounds), cut into chunks
1	red bell pepper, cored, seeded, and cut into chunks
1	small onion, peeled and cut into chunks

Salt and freshly ground black pepper

Tabasco sauce to taste

3	tablespoons extra-virgin olive oil, or to taste
3	tablespoons sherry vinegar, or to taste

1 Cut the cucumber lengthwise in half and scrape out the seeds.

2 Combine the cucumber, tomatoes, red pepper, onion, and salt and pepper to taste in the container of a blender. Blend, but don't make it too smooth; the soup is better with a coarser texture.

3 Add more salt, if necessary, and the Tabasco, olive oil, and vinegar. Serve, or cover and refrigerate for up to 2 hours.

TIME: 10 MINUTES

FOOD&WINE test-kitchen tips

• The blender will set to work more quickly if the tomatoes, the easiest of the vegetables to cut through, go in first, right on top of the blades.

wine recommendation The herbal quality and good acidity of a Sauvignon Blanc make it the ideal candidate to accompany the zesty mix of vegetables in this soup.

asparagus soup

from *Alfred Portale's 12 Seasons Cookbook*

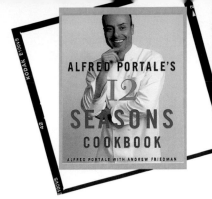

ALFRED PORTALE'S
12
SEASONS
COOKBOOK
ALFRED PORTALE WITH ANDREW FRIEDMAN

MAKES 4 SERVINGS

Does "Asparagus, Spinach, and Potato Soup" sound appealing to you? Me neither. But spinach and potatoes play crucial roles in allowing this asparagus recipe to live up to expectations.

To make soup from asparagus, the stalks must be cooked until their stringy fibers break down completely. By the time this happens, their pale green color boils away, leaving a less-than-compelling complexion. The concentrated chlorophyll in the spinach compensates for this by supplying a natural "artificial coloring" that provides the soup a familiar, comforting appearance.

The potatoes are included for textural support. When heated, they release a natural starch that is ultimately blended into the stock, providing the appropriate thick consistency.

As good as this soup is hot, I also love serving it chilled, especially outdoors on a sunny, slightly warm May afternoon. (See Variation, page 28.)

2	medium leeks, white part only
1	tablespoon canola oil
1	medium onion, chopped
2	cloves garlic, peeled and sliced
3	cups chicken stock
1	medium russet potato, peeled and cut into medium dice (about 1¼ cups)
2	bunches asparagus, cut into ¼-inch rounds (about 3½ cups)

Coarse salt and freshly ground white pepper to taste

1	bunch fresh spinach, stemmed, washed, and coarsely chopped (about 8 ounces)
2	tablespoons unsalted butter

Chop the leeks and rinse well. In a stockpot, heat the oil over medium heat. Add the leeks, onion, and garlic, and cook, stirring, for about 4 minutes, or until softened. Add the stock and potato, raise the heat to high, and boil for about 5 minutes. Add the asparagus and season with salt and pepper. Reduce the heat and simmer for 12 to 14 minutes, or until the asparagus is tender. Stir in the spinach and cook about 2 minutes longer, until it just wilts. Remove from the heat.

▼

hors d'oeuvres & first courses

Working quickly so that the soup does not cool too much, purée the soup in a blender or food processor, working in batches if necessary. Strain it through a fine-mesh sieve, pressing firmly with the back of a spoon to remove the asparagus fibers and extract as much liquid and flavor as possible. Swirl in the butter to enrich the soup and serve.

thinking ahead This soup can be made a day in advance. Allow it to cool, then cover and refrigerate it. Reheat gently, stirring occasionally, over medium heat.

variation This soup is just as good chilled as it is hot—serve it cool, but not frigid. If refrigerated, allow it to come up a few degrees before serving.

FOOD&WINE test-kitchen tips

- Spinach can harbor a lot of sand in its crinkles. Here's the easiest way we've found to wash it: Fill the sink with cold water, dump the leaves in, and swirl them around in the water. Then leave them alone for a few minutes so the sand sinks to the bottom. Lift the spinach out of the water leaving the grit behind. Spin the leaves dry in a salad spinner.

- Leeks tend to be dirty, too. The soil gets between the layers of the bulbs, and so they're much easier to wash after they've been chopped, as recommended in this recipe. Do the same as above but on a smaller scale. Put the chopped leeks in a bowl of water, swish, let settle, and skim them out.

 wine recommendation Dry fino sherry makes a traditional partner to many soups and will work well here. Another great option would be Bergerac, a white from the Southwest of France that is made from Sémillon and grassy-flavored Sauvignon Blanc to match the asparagus.

sweet butternut soup with thyme crème fraîche

from *Tom Douglas' Seattle Kitchen*

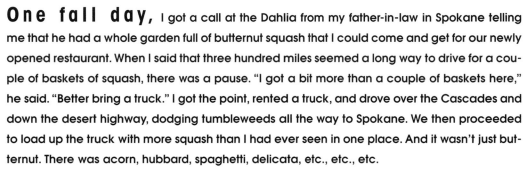

MAKES 6 SERVINGS

One fall day, I got a call at the Dahlia from my father-in-law in Spokane telling me that he had a whole garden full of butternut squash that I could come and get for our newly opened restaurant. When I said that three hundred miles seemed a long way to drive for a couple of baskets of squash, there was a pause. "I got a bit more than a couple of baskets here," he said. "Better bring a truck." I got the point, rented a truck, and drove over the Cascades and down the desert highway, dodging tumbleweeds all the way to Spokane. We then proceeded to load up the truck with more squash than I had ever seen in one place. And it wasn't just butternut. There was acorn, hubbard, spaghetti, delicata, etc., etc., etc.

That was the fall we got creative with squash—for months we cooked and served it every which way—sautéed, baked, pureed, hashed, in fritters and beignets and pies and tarts, and we made lots and lots of squash soup. This soup was the most popular of all the dishes—and we serve it today, especially if my in-laws are in town for a visit.

3½	pounds butternut squash
	Olive oil for brushing squash
1	tablespoon unsalted butter
2	tablespoons olive oil
4	cups thinly sliced onions (about 2 onions)
3	cups chicken stock
1	cup heavy cream
1½	teaspoons chopped fresh flat-leaf parsley
½	teaspoon chopped fresh sage
½	teaspoon chopped fresh rosemary
½	teaspoon chopped fresh thyme
1	teaspoon sherry vinegar
	Kosher salt and freshly ground black pepper
	Thyme Crème Fraîche (recipe follows)

1 Preheat the oven to 400°F. Cut the squash in half and scoop out the seeds. Brush the cut edges lightly with oil and place, cut side down, on a baking sheet. Roast the squash until very soft, about 1¼ hours. Remove from the oven. When cool enough to handle, scoop the squash meat from the skin and set aside.

▼

2 While the squash is roasting, caramelize the onions. Heat the butter with the olive oil in a sauté pan over medium-low heat. Add the onions and cook slowly, stirring occasionally until they are soft and uniformly golden brown, 25 to 30 minutes. Set aside.

3 In a food processor, process the squash, onions, and 1 cup of the chicken stock until smooth. Transfer the puree to a large pot. Add the remaining 2 cups chicken stock and heat the soup to a simmer, whisking a few times. Add the heavy cream, chopped herbs, and sherry vinegar. Season to taste with salt and pepper. You can make this soup a few days ahead and store it in the refrigerator. To serve, just reheat.

on the plate Ladle the hot soup into bowls and serve with a swirl of crème fraîche.

in the glass A good fruity Viognier from France or California, or a dry Riesling from Washington State or Alsace

thyme crème fraîche This slightly tart, herb-flavored cream goes perfectly with the sweet flavor of the butternut soup. You can buy commercial crème fraîche, make your own (recipe follows) or use sour cream, if you prefer.

MAKES ½ CUP

½ **cup crème fraîche**
2 **teaspoons chopped fresh thyme**
Kosher salt and freshly ground black pepper

Place the crème fraîche and thyme in a small bowl and whisk until smooth. Season to taste with salt and pepper.

FOOD&WINE test-kitchen tips

- We admit to using store-bought frozen stock when we tested this recipe. And it was still the best squash soup we've ever tasted. We're willing to bet that the special flavor you get from roasting the squash and caramelizing the onions will carry the day with canned stock, too. As the chef recommends, if you do use canned, opt for the low-sodium version. That way you can control the seasoning yourself.

- If cutting onions makes you weep, try using your food processor, fitted with the slicing blade.

crème fraîche   Use crème fraîche as you would use sour cream or heavy cream. Spoon sweetened crème fraîche over a bowl of fresh berries. Or stir chopped fresh dill, grated lemon zest, and ground black pepper into crème fraîche and serve it with smoked salmon or smoked trout. This recipe easily doubles or triples.

1	**cup heavy cream**
2	**tablespoons buttermilk**

Combine the heavy cream and buttermilk. Place in a container, cover, and leave out at room temperature for 2 to 3 days until thickened.

a step ahead   Crème fraîche will keep, covered, in the refrigerator for a few weeks.

SIMPLY TUSCAN

PINO LUONGO

artichoke, romaine, and pea soup

from *Simply Tuscan*

SERVES 4 TO 6

¼ cup extra virgin olive oil

1 medium Spanish onion, chopped

1 clove garlic, chopped

2 tablespoons chopped fresh Italian parsley

1 medium Idaho potato, peeled and finely diced

12 baby artichokes, tops and outer leaves trimmed off, cut lengthwise into 6 wedges each, soaked in 1 quart water with 1 tablespoon lemon juice

Salt and freshly ground pepper to taste

6 cups hot water

3 heads romaine lettuce, well rinsed and cut crosswise into 1-inch slices

3 cups shelled fresh or frozen peas

1 teaspoon chopped fresh mint

In a soup pot over medium heat, warm 3 tablespoons of the olive oil. Add the onion, garlic, and half the parsley. When the onion is translucent, add the potato and cook for 10 minutes, stirring occasionally with a wooden spoon.

Drain the artichokes and add them to the pot. Season with salt and cook for 5 minutes. Add the hot water, cover, and let the soup simmer for 15 minutes. Add the lettuce and the peas and cook, covered, for 15 minutes more. Remove from the heat and adjust seasoning.

Garnish each serving with mint, black pepper, and the remaining parsley and olive oil.

FOOD&WINE test-kitchen tips

- If you have a choice among artichokes, pick one with that looks like a flower bud with nice tight petals. It will be fresher than one with splayed leaves.

 wine recommendation Hearty vegetables have a tendency to give most wines a vegetal taste. Your best bet for such dishes is often a Sauvignon Blanc from New Zealand, which comes to the flavor party with some pleasant vegetal notes of its own.

lentil soup with spinach

faki soupa me spanaki

from *The Foods of the Greek Islands*

MAKES 6 TO 8 SERVINGS

For as long as I can remember, my mother has cooked this lentil soup once a week in the winter. Following a recipe in Theonie Mark's book *Greek Island Cooking,* which contains recipes from Rhodes, I've added spinach leaves.

Serve with cured fish, such as smoked trout.

2	cups brown lentils, picked over and rinsed
1/3	cup olive oil
1/2	cup chopped onion
3	garlic cloves, thinly sliced
1/2	cup grated ripe tomatoes (see Note) or canned diced tomatoes with their juice
1/2	cup dry red wine
1	teaspoon Aleppo pepper or pinch of crushed red pepper flakes
Salt	
4	cups vegetable stock or chicken stock
1	teaspoon dried thyme, crumbled
1	teaspoon dry mustard
1	bay leaf
1 1/2	pounds spinach, stemmed
Pinch of ground cumin (optional)	
2 to 3 tablespoons red wine vinegar	
Freshly ground black pepper	

FOOD&WINE test-kitchen tips

- We found that when this soup sits for any length of time, the lentils absorb the liquid, and the dish becomes more like stew than soup. Just add some water.

- We had good luck making this soup ahead of time. You can keep it for a week in the refrigerator, or you can freeze it. Add water as needed to thin it out when you reheat it.

- Heretics that we are, we sprinkled Italian Parmesan cheese on top of this Greek soup and thought it an excellent addition.

 wine recommendation A light white wine with full fruit flavors will be the ideal partner here. Luckily, one of the most readily available Greek wines, the charming, fruity Santorini, suits this soup to a tee.

Place the lentils in a large saucepan and add cold water to cover. Bring to a boil, remove from the heat and let stand for 15 minutes. Drain.

In a large pot, heat the oil and sauté the onion over medium heat until just soft, about 3 minutes. Add the garlic and sauté for 1 minute more; do not let it color. Add the lentils, tomatoes, wine, Aleppo pepper or pepper flakes and salt to taste. Bring to a boil, add the stock, thyme, mustard and bay leaf and return to a boil. Reduce the heat to low, cover and simmer for 30 minutes, or until the lentils are tender.

Add the spinach and cumin, if using, and simmer for 5 to 10 minutes more, or until the spinach is wilted. Add the vinegar and black pepper to taste. Taste and adjust the seasonings. Serve hot.

note To grate tomatoes, cut in half, remove the stem and grate on a large-holed grater, cut side facing the holes. Discard the skin.

cheese-and-mushroom quesadillas
quesadillas de queso y hongos

from *Mexico One Plate at a Time*

MAKES 8 QUESADILLAS, SERVING 8 AS AN APPETIZER, 4 AS A LIGHT MAIN COURSE

2   tablespoons olive oil (preferably extra-virgin) or rich-tasting pork lard, plus a little more for the tortillas

1   pound button mushrooms (or other flavorful mushrooms, such as shiitake, oyster, cremini or chanterelles), cleaned and sliced ¼ inch thick (you'll have about 4 cups)

Fresh hot green chiles to taste (roughly 2 to 3 serranos or 1 to 2 jalapeños), stemmed, seeded and thinly sliced

2   tablespoons chopped fresh *epazote* leaves
OR ¼ cup chopped fresh cilantro

Salt

8   fresh corn tortillas (or flour tortillas if good corn tortillas are not available)

8   ounces Mexican melting cheese (Chihuahua, *quesillo, asadero* or the like) or Monterey Jack, brick or mild cheddar, shredded (you'll have about 2 cups)

About 1 cup salsa (I love the Roasted Tomato–Green Chile Salsa on page 38)

1 the mushroom filling In a medium skillet, heat the 2 tablespoons oil or lard over medium. Add the mushrooms, chiles and *epazote* (if you're using cilantro, set it aside to add later), stir well and cover. Continue to stir every minute or so, replacing the cover each time, until the mushrooms have released a lot of juice, 4 to 5 minutes. Uncover and let briskly simmer until all the liquid has evaporated, about 3 minutes. Taste and season with salt, usually about ¼ teaspoon. Add the cilantro now, if that's what you're using.

FOOD&WINE test-kitchen tips

- We made these with oil, and they were exceptional quesadillas, no doubt about it. We decided immediately that this recipe qualified as one of the best of the year. Then we made them with lard— and they were even better. If you have access to real lard (not the white, homogenized stuff that comes in a box) and if you're not afraid of animal fat (it's only 1½ teaspoons per person, after all), go whole hog, so to speak. Look for the good stuff at Hispanic, German, or Hungarian markets.

 wine recommendation Non-European Chardonnays tend to be so oaky that they overpower most food. The bold flavors of this dish are an exception. Choose a Californian, or if you prefer a more elegant style of wine, look for a bottle from New Zealand or South Africa.

2 forming and griddle-baking the quesadillas Heat a well-seasoned or nonstick griddle or heavy skillet over medium. Turn the oven on to its lowest setting. One by one, make the quesadillas: Lightly brush one side of each tortilla with oil, then lay it oiled side down on the hot griddle. Spread with about ¼ cup of the cheese, leaving a ½-inch border all around. Spoon about 3 tablespoons of the mushroom mixture down the center of the cheese-covered tortilla. When the cheese begins to melt (but before the tortilla begins to crisp), fold the tortilla in half along the line of the filling. Cook, flipping the quesadilla every minute or so, until the cheese is completely melted and the tortilla crisps, about 5 minutes in all. As each quesadilla is done, transfer it to a baking sheet and keep warm in the oven.

3 serving the quesadillas When all the quesadillas are done, set them out in a cloth-lined basket. Pass the salsa separately for each guest to spoon on.

working ahead The mushroom filling can be made several days in advance; cover and refrigerate. The quesadillas are best when prepared just moments before serving.

▼

roasted tomato–green chili salsa *salsa de molcajete* You'll taste essence of Mexico in a bite of this salsa, though you may get more than you expect. Roasting focuses the tomatoes' sweetness and rounds out the typical green grassiness of fresh chiles, creating perfect harmony.

MAKES ABOUT 2 CUPS

1   pound (2 medium-large round or 6 to 8 plum) ripe tomatoes
Fresh hot green chiles to taste (roughly 2 medium jalapeños or 4 serranos)
3   garlic cloves, unpeeled
¼   cup finely chopped white onion
About ⅓ cup loosely packed chopped fresh cilantro
Salt
A dash of vinegar or squeeze of lime, if you think necessary

1 roasting Roast the tomatoes on a baking sheet 4 inches below a very hot broiler until they're darkly roasted (they'll be blackened in spots), about 6 minutes. Flip them over and roast the other side—5 to 6 minutes more will give you splotchy-black and blistered tomatoes that are soft and cooked through. Cool. Working over the baking sheet, pull off and discard the blackened skins; for round tomatoes, cut out the hard cores where the stems were attached.

Roast the chiles and garlic in a dry skillet or on a griddle over medium heat, turning them occasionally, until they are soft and darkened in places, about 5 minutes for the chiles, 15 minutes for the garlic. Cool, then slip the papery skins off the garlic.

2 finishing the salsa Either crush the roasted garlic and chiles to a smooth paste in a mortar or chop them to near-paste in a food processor. If using a mortar, crush in the tomatoes one at a time, working them into a coarse puree. For a food processor, add the tomatoes and pulse to achieve a coarse puree.

Scoop the chopped onion into a strainer and rinse under cold water. Shake to remove the excess moisture.

Transfer the salsa to a bowl, stir in the onion and cilantro and season with salt, usually a generous ½ teaspoon. Thin with a little water (usually about 2 tablespoons) to give it a spoonable consistency. Perk it all up with vinegar or lime if you wish.

working ahead Once the onion and cilantro have been added to the salsa, it should be eaten within a few hours. Without onion and cilantro, the refrigerated salsa base keeps for several days, though the flavors will dull.

quiche lorraine

from *Julia's Kitchen Wisdom*

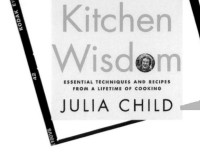

FOR A 9-INCH QUICHE, SERVING 6

6   strips of crisply cooked bacon

A partially baked 9-inch tart shell (see below)

3   "large" eggs

About 1 cup cream

Salt, freshly ground pepper, and nutmeg

Preheat oven to 375°F. Break bacon into pieces and strew in shell. Blend the eggs with enough cream to make 1½ cups of custard, and blend in seasonings to taste. Pour into shell to within ⅛ inch of rim. Bake 30 to 35 minutes, or until puffed and browned. Unmold onto a round platter and serve warm or at room temperature.

quiche proportions   Any quiche can be made with either heavy or light cream or with milk. The proportions always are 1 egg in a measuring cup plus milk or cream to the ½-cup level; 2 eggs and milk or cream to the 1-cup level; 3 eggs and milk or cream to the 1½-cup level; and so forth.

variation: cheese and bacon quiche   Follow the above recipe, but sprinkle ½ cup grated Swiss cheese into shell before adding the custard, plus another spoonful on top before baking.

all-purpose pie dough—*pâte brisée fine*   You will note the mixture of flours and fats here. Without them, our general American all-purpose flour, which is relatively high in gluten, can give you a brittle rather than a tender crust. But if you have "pastry flour," you can use that alone, along with all butter rather than a mixture of butter and vegetable shortening.

DOUGH FOR TWO 9-INCH ROUND SHELLS OR A 14-BY-18-INCH FREE-FORM SHELL

1½   cups unbleached all-purpose flour

½   cup plain bleached cake flour

1   teaspoon salt

1½   sticks (6 ounces) chilled unsalted butter, diced

4   tablespoons chilled vegetable shortening

½   cup ice water, plus droplets more if needed

Drop the flours, salt, and butter into the bowl of a food processor fitted with the steel blade. Pulse 5 or 6 times in ½-second bursts to break up the butter.

Then add the shortening, turn on the machine, and immediately pour in the ice water, pulsing 2 or 3 times. Remove cover and observe the dough, which will look like a mass of smallish lumps and should just hold in a mass when a handful is pressed together. If too dry, pulse in droplets more water.

Turn dough out onto your work surface, and with the heel of your hand rapidly and roughly push egg-size blobs out in front of you in 6-inch smears. Gather the dough into a relatively smooth cake; wrap in plastic, and refrigerate at least 2 hours (or up to 2 days), or you may freeze it for several months.

what to bake it in or on Bake your tart shell in a bottomless buttered flan ring set on a buttered pastry sheet, or in a false-bottomed cake pan or fluted pan, or on a buttered upside-down pie plate or cake pan. Or you can fashion a free-form shell on a buttered pastry sheet.

a proper rolling pin Get yourself a straight rolling pin about 18 inches long and 1¾ inches in diameter, or use an Italian pasta pin.

forming a tart shell
• **to form a 9-inch round shell in a flan ring** Have the ring and pastry sheet buttered and at your side. Cut the chilled dough in half and keep one half wrapped and chilled. Rapidly, on a lightly floured surface, roll the other half into a circular shape ⅛ inch thick and 1½ inches larger all around than your ring.

FOOD&WINE test-kitchen tips

- It depends on your oven, but in ours, prebaking the pastry for the full extent of the 10 to 15 minutes suggested in this recipe gave us a perfect crisp crust. In our first test, the pastry shell was set, but it was still white after 10 minutes, and after baking again with the filling, the bottom was soggy. A second try, allowing 15 minutes of prebaking, turned the crust slightly golden and netted an ideal end product.

 wine recommendation A white wine with a bit of smokiness to echo the bacon is what this French classic needs. Pinot Gris from the quiche's home region, Alsace, is just the ticket.

Roll the dough up on your pin and unroll it over the ring, then lightly press the dough in place. To make sturdy sides, push them down about ½ inch all around. Roll your pin over the top to trim off excess dough, then push it up ⅓ inch all around the sides to make a rim.

Using the tines of a table fork, laid flat, press a design on the rim. Prick the bottom of the dough all over with a fork. Cover with plastic wrap and chill at least 30 minutes before baking.

· to form a shell on an upside-down pan Butter the outside of the pan and set it upside down on a baking sheet. Roll out the dough, drape loosely over the pan, and press gently onto pan all around. To make the wall thicker, push dough up on the sides with your thumbs. Press a decorative edging around the sides with the tines of a fork held flat.

· to form a large free-form rectangular tart shell Roll the chilled dough into a 16-by-20-inch rectangle ⅛ inch thick. Roll it up on your pin and unroll onto a lightly buttered rimless baking sheet. Trim the sides perfectly straight, then slice a strip of dough 1 inch wide from each edge of the rectangle. Moisten the outside border of the rectangle with cold water and lay the strips on top to form a raised rim. Press the strips with the tines of a fork to seal and decorate, and prick the bottom all over with the tines of the fork. Wrap and chill.

prebaking a shell—"blind baking" You will always have a crisper crust for tarts baked with a filling when you prebake the shell first.

Slide rack into the lower-middle level, and preheat the oven to 450°F. For a quiche ring, false-bottomed pan, or free-form shell, butter the shiny side of a piece of foil several inches larger than your shell. Press it lightly, buttered side down, against the chilled tart shell on the bottom and sides. To prevent bottom from rising and sides from collapsing, pour in dry beans, rice, or aluminum "pie weights," being sure you also bank them against the sides.

Bake 10 to 15 minutes, until the bottom pastry is set but still soft. Remove foil and beans, prick the bottom again with a fork, and return to oven. For a partial cooking, bake 2 minutes or so more, until pastry just begins to color and to separate from the sides if in a ring. For a fully cooked shell, bake 4 or more minutes, until lightly browned.

hot pepper wings with cilantro sour cream

from *Tom Douglas' Seattle Kitchen*

MAKES 6 SERVINGS

What started out as one of our favorite employee meals is now one of the most popular Palace Kitchen appetizers. At Palace we grill these chicken wings over an apple-wood fire, but you can either grill or broil them. These spicy tidbits seem to cry out for a cold beer, maybe a hearty Hefe-Weizen from Redhook Brewery right here in Seattle.

What really makes these wings is their time in the marinade. You need to marinate them at least a day ahead, and two days is even better than one, so plan accordingly.

2	cups soy sauce
1	cup Dijon mustard
1	cup water
¾	cup Tabasco sauce
¼	cup chopped garlic
2	tablespoons chopped fresh flat-leaf parsley
2	teaspoons chopped fresh thyme
2	teaspoons chopped fresh sage
2	teaspoons chopped fresh rosemary
18	chicken wings

Cilantro Sour Cream (recipe follows)

1 Whisk the soy sauce, mustard, water, Tabasco, garlic, and herbs together in a large bowl. Reserve ½ cup of the marinade to be used for basting and sauce. Add the chicken wings to the remaining marinade, coat them well, cover with plastic wrap, and refrigerate overnight. Turn the wings occasionally to make sure they are well marinated.

FOOD&WINE test-kitchen tips

- These wings are finger food for sure, and we found they were easier to eat when we cut off the wing tips before marinating.

- If you broil the wings and you're a fan of crisp food like we are, start them off meaty side down. Then turn and finish the cooking with the meaty side up so that the skin gets really crunchy.

- Piled on a platter, the wings make great casual party food, too.

2 Fire up your grill or preheat your broiler. Remove the chicken wings from the marinade, then discard this marinade. If grilling, grill the wings over medium-low coals, turning often, until cooked through, about 15 minutes. You want the wings to cook slowly, cooking thoroughly before the glaze burns. If broiling, place the wings in a broiling pan and broil 4 inches from the heat source, 10 minutes per side. If your broiler has a low setting, use that, otherwise, watch carefully so the glaze doesn't burn. While grilling or broiling, heat the reserved marinade in a saucepan and use some of it to baste the wings a few times while cooking. Cut into one of the wings to make sure no pink remains near the bone and serve.

on the plate Spoon the cilantro sour cream on 6 appetizer plates. Pile 3 wings on each plate and drizzle with a teaspoon of the warm reserved marinade. Don't use more than a drizzle, though—it's really strong. Serve whatever is left of the reserved marinade on the side for hearty heat lovers.

a step ahead You can make the marinade a few days ahead. It will keep, covered in the refrigerator, for up to a week.

in the glass An ice-cold beer

cilantro sour cream You can also use this flavorful sour cream in burritos or on tacos. It is also delicious on our Palace Olive Poppers (page 16). The chicken wings are quite salty and hot, so we don't add salt or pepper here. For other dishes add salt and pepper to taste.

MAKES $\frac{1}{2}$ CUP

$\frac{1}{2}$ **cup sour cream**
2 **tablespoons heavy cream**
2 **teaspoons chopped cilantro**
Kosher salt and freshly ground black pepper to taste (optional)

In a small bowl, mix together the sour cream, heavy cream, and chopped cilantro. If not using with Hot Pepper Wings or Palace Olive Poppers, taste for salt and pepper.

fish
& shellfish

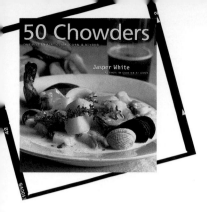

south coast portuguese fish chowder

from *50 Chowders*

MAKES ABOUT 14 CUPS; SERVES 8 AS A MAIN COURSE

This chowder has a relationship to New Bedford and the area New Englanders call South Coast, which includes that part of southeastern Massachusetts west of Cape Cod and a small piece of eastern Rhode Island. The area is ethnically diverse, with a large Portuguese population, but everyone, even those who aren't Portuguese, loves good food. I served this chowder recently to a group at Sakonnet Vineyards in Little Compton, Rhode Island. As soon as word got out that there was chouriço (a dry, spicy, garlicky Portuguese sausage) in the chowder, the crowd demolished it. Almost everyone in this region loves chouriço, which the locals pronounce "shore-eese." All over New England where the Portuguese have settled, chouriço is included in clambakes, clam boils, and other traditional Yankee fare.

With its translucent reddish broth and colorful pieces of bell pepper, tomato, chouriço, potato, fish, and cilantro, this Portuguese-style chowder is very enticing. It has a splendid aroma and a savory spicy flavor, making it an interesting and exciting alternative to milder creamy chowders.

cook's notes Chouriço has a thick casing, so be sure to remove it before you slice it. Make a small lengthwise slit in the sausage and the casing will peel off easily. The chouriço adds a balanced spiciness to this recipe, but it is not overwhelming. If you want to make the chowder even spicier, sprinkle in 1/4 to 1/2 teaspoon crushed red pepper flakes when you add the onions and bell pepper.

I use canned Italian plum tomatoes packed in juice for this chowder because of their robust flavor. The tomatoes are not added until after the potatoes are fully cooked because otherwise, their acidity causes a reaction that prevents the potatoes from releasing their starch.

Silver hake, a cousin of cod, is smaller and has a slightly more pronounced flavor. It is the hands-down favorite of the Portuguese community but, unlike chouriço, hake has never really caught on in the rest of the region. When it is available, it is quite reasonably priced, and it is excellent panfried as well as braised in fish stews and chowder. A note of caution: do not substitute red hake, which fishermen call mud hake. It is flavorful, but the texture is very soft and it doesn't make good chowder. Cod, haddock, and bass are the best substitutes.

I like to serve this chowder with garlic bread or a crusty loaf of Portuguese or Italian bread.

For equipment, you will need a 4- to 6-quart heavy pot with a lid, a wooden spoon, a slotted spoon, and a ladle.

2	tablespoons olive oil
2	dried bay leaves
3	cloves garlic, finely chopped (1 tablespoon)
2	medium onions (14 ounces), cut into ³/₄-inch dice
1	green bell pepper (6 ounces), cut into ¹/₂-inch dice
¹/₄	teaspoon ground allspice
2	pounds Yukon Gold, Maine, PEI, or other all-purpose potatoes, peeled and sliced ¹/₃ inch thick
4	cups Strong Fish Stock (page 49), traditional fish stock, chicken stock, or water (as a last resort)
2	cups canned whole tomatoes in juice (from a 28-ounce can), cut into ¹/₂-inch dice (measured with their juice)
6	ounces spicy chouriço or andouille sausage, casing removed and sliced ¹/₄ inch thick
	Kosher or sea salt and freshly ground black pepper
2	pounds skinless silver hake, cod, haddock, or bass fillets, pinbones removed
10	sprigs fresh cilantro, leaves and tender stems finely chopped (¹/₄ cup)

for garnish

2	tablespoons coarsely chopped fresh Italian parsley

▼

fish & shellfish

FOOD&WINE test-kitchen tips

- If you're making this ahead of time and refrigerating it, wait to add the cilantro until you reheat the chowder.

wine recommendation A Vinho Verde from northern Portugal will have the right acidic kick to partner this hearty soup. Look for a bottle displaying the name of a particular grape, such as Loureiro of Trajadura, for a wine with even more flavor.

1 Heat a 4- to 6-quart heavy pot over medium heat and add the olive oil and bay leaves. As soon as the bay leaves turn brown, add the garlic and cook, stirring constantly with a wooden spoon, for 30 seconds or until it is golden. Add the onions, bell pepper, and allspice and sauté, stirring occasionally, for about 8 minutes, until the onions and peppers are softened but not browned.

2 Add the potatoes and stock; if the stock doesn't cover the potatoes, add just enough water to cover them. Turn up the heat, bring to a boil, cover, and cook the potatoes vigorously for about 10 minutes, until they are soft on the outside but still firm in the center.

3 Reduce the heat to medium, add the tomatoes and sausage, and simmer for 5 minutes. Season the mixture assertively with salt and pepper (you want to almost overseason the chowder at this point, to avoid having to stir it much once the fish is added).

4 Add the whole fillets and cook for 5 minutes, then remove from the heat, gently stir in the cilantro, and allow the chowder to sit for 10 minutes. (The fish will finish cooking during this time.) If you are not serving the chowder within the hour, let it cool a bit, then refrigerate; cover the chowder *after* it has chilled completely. Otherwise, let it sit for up to an hour at room temperature, allowing the flavors to meld.

5 When ready to serve, reheat the chowder over low heat; don't let it boil. Use a slotted spoon to mound the chunks of hake, the chouriço, tomatoes, peppers, and potatoes in the center of large soup plates or shallow bowls, and ladle the savory tomato broth over. Sprinkle with the chopped parsley.

strong fish stock   Julia Child included this recipe in the book from her television series *In Julia's Kitchen with Master Chefs*, which also features my recipe for New England Fish Chowder. As the name implies, this stock has a concentrated fish flavor and is therefore a superb choice for any of my fish chowder recipes. Its intense taste limits its use in shellfish chowders, which are better made with less assertive traditional fish stock. This recipe uses a technique called "sweating" to extract maximum flavor from every ingredient. Although sweating adds a step, this stock is still effortless to make and takes only five minutes longer to cook than traditional fish stock.

▼

I begin by sautéing a very thinly sliced mirepoix (onions, celery, and carrots) with herbs and peppercorns. I then layer fish heads and frames (bones) on top of these vegetables, add a little white wine, and cover the pot. As the heads and bones "sweat" (and steam), the proteins are drawn out. If you peek, you will actually see little white droplets of flavorful proteins coagulating on the surface of the bones. After the sweating is completed (about 15 minutes), I cover the bones with water and simmer them briefly. I let the mixture steep for 10 minutes before straining it, producing a stock that is full-flavored and gelatinous. The fish heads are what endow this stock with its marvelous jellied consistency, which in turn gives a luscious mouth feel to the chowder broth.

cook's notes Strong Fish Stock can be used in any fish chowder, using 1 or 2 heads from haddock or cod mixed with any combination of flounder, sole, bass and/or halibut frames (bones).

You can employ the "sweating" method with any fish you use to make a chowder—simply substitute the same amount of heads and bones. Keep in mind, however, that while the heads and bones of salmon, bluefish, and other species of oily fish make a stock that is right for their own chowders, its flavor is too pronounced to be suitable in other chowders or soups.

For equipment, you will need a 7- to 8-quart heavy stockpot with a tight-fitting lid, a wooden spoon, a ladle, and a fine-mesh strainer.

MAKES ABOUT 2 QUARTS

2   tablespoons unsalted butter
2   medium onions, very thinly sliced
4   stalks celery, very thinly sliced
2   medium carrots, very thinly sliced
2   dried bay leaves
¼   cup roughly chopped fresh flat-leaf parsley leaves and stems
6 to 8 sprigs fresh thyme
2   tablespoons black peppercorns
1   large (6 inches long or more) or 2 small (4 inches long or less) fish heads from cod or haddock, split lengthwise, gills removed, and rinsed clean of any blood
2½ to 3 pounds fish frames (bones) from sole, flounder, bass, and/or halibut, cut into 2-inch pieces and rinsed clean of any blood
¼   cup dry white wine
About 2 quarts very hot or boiling water
Kosher or sea salt

1   Melt the butter in a heavy 7- to 8-quart stockpot over medium heat. Add the onions, celery, carrots, bay leaves, parsley, thyme, and peppercorns and cook, stirring frequently with a wooden spoon, until the vegetables become very soft without browning, about 8 minutes.

2   Place the fish head on the vegetables and stack the fish frames evenly on top. Pour in the wine, cover the pot tightly, and let the bones sweat for 10 to 15 minutes, or until they have turned completely white.

3   Add enough very hot or boiling water to just barely cover the bones. Give the mixture a gentle stir and allow the brew to come to a simmer. Simmer for 10 minutes, uncovered, carefully skimming off any white foam that comes to the surface, trying not to take any herbs, spices, or vegetables with it. (Using a ladle and a circular motion, push the foam from the center to the outside of the pot, where it is easy to remove.)

4   Remove the pot from the stove, stir the stock again, and allow it to steep for 10 minutes. Strain through a fine-mesh strainer and season lightly with salt. If you are not going to be using the stock within the hour, chill it as quickly as possible. Cover the stock *after* it is thoroughly chilled (it will have a light jellied consistency) and keep refrigerated for up to 3 days, or freeze for up to 2 months.

nova scotia lobster chowder

from *50 Chowders*

MAKES ABOUT 12 CUPS; SERVES 6 TO 8 AS A MAIN COURSE

C h o w d e r i s s o identified with New England that many people are unaware of the rich tradition of chowder making in Atlantic Canada. Some historians point to Newfoundland and Nova Scotia, where French and English fishermen have crossed paths since the mid-1600s, as the place where chowder may have originated. In this land of friendly people, breathtaking scenery, and some of the world's finest seafood, chowder making is an old custom (as is rum drinking).

The Canadian government, not surprisingly, regulates lobster fishing, but when the season is on, there is a profusion of lobsters in Nova Scotia, and lobster (or scallops) is added as an embellishment to traditional local fish chowders. Haddock is the fish of choice here. This recipe was inspired by my friend David Chernin, a chowder maker from beautiful Cape Breton Island, Nova Scotia. David uses only lobster knuckles and claws in his chowder because he says they hold up better, but since I don't want to leave you with leftover lobster tails, my recipe calls for whole lobsters.

In this harmonious marriage of the flavors of haddock and lobster, chunks of white fish and brilliant red lobster meat are set against a light pink broth that is lovely to look at and even better to eat. Common crackers, split, buttered, and toasted, can be arranged around the rims of the soup plates or served in a basket on the side.

cook's notes This recipe begins with partially cooking the lobsters; the slightly undercooked meat will finish cooking in the chowder. Shucking the meat from the claws, knuckles, and tails of partially cooked lobster is almost the same process as from fully cooked. Only the claws may be more difficult to remove, but don't worry if the meat tears—it will be diced anyway. If you'd rather not cook whole lobsters, use 8 to 10 ounces of cooked lobster meat. (For more on lobster preparation, see my previous book, *Lobster at Home.*)

The lobster carcasses, tomalley, and shells are used to make a stock that will eventually be combined with fish stock for this chowder. If making two stocks seems unreasonable to you, you can substitute water for the fish stock.

For equipment, you will need an 8-quart stockpot (to par-cook the lobsters), a pair of long tongs, a medium Chinese cleaver or large chef's knife, a 3- to 4-quart pot (to make the stock), a fine-mesh strainer, a 4- to 6-quart heavy pot with a lid (to make the chowder), a slotted spoon, a wooden spoon, and a ladle.

2   live hard-shell lobsters (1¼ pounds each)

Kosher or sea salt

1   teaspoon black peppercorns

for chowder

4   ounces meaty salt pork, rind removed (reserve it for the lobster stock) and cut
    into ⅓-inch dice

1   large onion (10 to 12 ounces), cut into ¾-inch dice (trimmings reserved for the
    lobster stock)

2   medium stalks celery (4 ounces), cut into ⅓-inch dice (trimmings reserved
    for stock)

6 to 8 sprigs fresh thyme, leaves removed (reserve the stems for the lobster stock)
    and chopped (1 tablespoon)

2   tablespoons unsalted butter

2   dried bay leaves

2   teaspoons Hungarian paprika

2   pounds Yukon Gold, Maine, PEI, or other all-purpose potatoes, peeled and
    sliced ⅓ inch thick

2   cups lobster stock (from step 3, next page)

2   cups Strong Fish Stock (page 49), traditional fish stock, chicken stock,
    or water (as a last resort)

Kosher or sea salt and freshly ground black pepper

2   pounds skinless haddock or cod fillets, 1 inch thick or more, pinbones removed

1½ cups heavy cream (or up to 2 cups if desired)

for garnish

2   tablespoons chopped fresh Italian parsley

2   tablespoons minced fresh chives ▼

fish & shellfish

FOOD&WINE test-kitchen tips

- What a satisfying main-dish meal! But we love this as a dinner-party first course, too, and as noted
  in the recipe, you can make it well ahead of time. The recipe will serve 12 as an appetizer.

 wine recommendation There is no better companion to a rich lobster dish than tart, refresh-
ing Champagne. For the ultimate match, as well as a beautiful sight around the table, try a rosé
Champagne from a house such as Ruinart or Louis Roederer.

1 To par-cook the lobsters, fill an 8-quart stockpot with 4 quarts of water, add ⅓ cup salt, cover, and bring to a boil over high heat. One at a time, holding each lobster by the carapace, quickly drop it into the boiling water. Keeping the heat on high, cook for exactly 4½ minutes from the time you put the lobsters into the pot. Using a pair of long tongs, remove the lobsters and let cool to room temperature.

2 When they are cool enough to handle, twist off the claws, with the knuckles attached. Twist off the tails. Remove all the meat and cut into large dice. Be sure to remove the cartilage from the claws and the intestinal tract that runs along the top of the tails. (You should have about 10 ounces—almost 2 cups—of diced lobster meat.) Reserve the shells if you are making the lobster stock. Cover the lobster meat with plastic wrap and refrigerate until later.

3 To make the lobster stock, use a cleaver or large chef's knife to split the lobster carcasses lengthwise in half. Remove the sac from inside the front of each lobster's head. Place the lobster carcasses, along with any tomalley in the carcasses, and the shells from the claws and tail in a 3- to 4-quart pot. Cover with about 4 cups of water, bring to a boil, and skim off the foam from the top. Reduce the heat until the stock is at a brisk simmer, add the peppercorns (along with the rind from the salt pork, any trimmings from the onion or celery, and stems from the thyme) and cook, uncovered, for 1 hour. Strain through a fine-mesh strainer; you should have about 2 cups of strong lobster stock. (The stock can be made a day ahead.)

4 Heat a 4- to 6-quart heavy pot over low heat and add the diced salt pork. Once it has rendered a few tablespoons of fat, increase the heat to medium and cook until the pork is crisp and golden brown. Use a slotted spoon to transfer the cracklings to a small ovenproof dish, leaving the fat in the pot, and reserve until later.

5 Add the butter, onion, celery, thyme, and bay leaves to the pot and sauté, stirring occasionally with a wooden spoon, for about 6 minutes. Add the paprika and cook for 2 minutes longer, or until the onions are softened.

6 Add the potatoes, the reserved lobster stock, and the fish stock. If the stock doesn't cover the potatoes, add just enough water to cover them. Turn up the heat and bring to a boil, cover, and cook the potatoes vigorously for about 10 minutes, until they are soft on the outside but still firm in the center. If the stock hasn't thickened lightly, smash a few of the potato slices against the side of the pot and cook for a minute or two longer to release their starch. Reduce the heat to low and season the mixture assertively with salt and pepper (you want to almost overseason the chowder at this point, to avoid having to stir it much once the fish is added).

7 Add the whole fish fillets and cook for 5 minutes, then remove from the heat and allow the chowder to sit for 10 minutes. (The fish will finish cooking during this time.) Gently stir in the cream and the reserved lobster meat and adjust the seasoning with salt and pepper if needed. If you are not serving the chowder within the hour, let it cool a bit, then refrigerate; cover the chowder *after* it has chilled completely. Otherwise, let it sit at room temperature for up to an hour, allowing the flavors to meld.

8 When ready to serve, reheat the chowder over low heat; don't let it boil. Warm the cracklings in a low oven (200°F) for a few minutes.

9 Use a slotted spoon to mound the chunks of haddock and lobster, the onions, and potatoes in the center of large soup plates or shallow bowls, and ladle the creamy broth around. Scatter the cracklings over the individual servings and finish with a sprinkling of chopped parsley and minced chives.

fish & shellfish

lightly curried mussel chowder

from *50 Chowders*

MAKES ABOUT 9 CUPS; SERVES 8 AS A FIRST COURSE OR 5 OR 6 AS A MAIN COURSE

Mussels are not a typical chowder ingredient, but they should be. They are easy to cook, their texture holds up well, the broth they produce has a lovely enticing fragrance, and they are not expensive. Often, in fact, they're free for the gathering. In addition, mussels have an appealing flavor that goes well with many kinds of seasonings. What else could you ask for? Although you rarely see or hear of a recipe for, or even a mention of, mussel chowder, I'm sure that since necessity often determines the ingredients used in chowder making, mussel chowders do happen, or have happened at some time in the past. They just haven't had their fifteen minutes of fame yet.

This chowder is unrelated to the classic Parisian mussel soup called billi bi, but the use of saffron in billi bi inspired me to investigate how other bold flavors would intermingle with mussels. Adding curry powder to chowder dates back to the clipper ship days in New England, when spices were at the height of their popularity. In the mid-1800s, curry was very trendy and it was called for in several chowder recipes (early fusion cooking). I add a touch of fresh ginger, a few sweet potatoes, and cilantro to this chowder, all of which go superbly with curry. These ingredients may sound peculiar to veteran chowder makers, but the result is still very much a chowder.

cook's notes This recipe calls for 5 pounds of cultivated mussels, which will yield a quart of broth and about a pound of mussel meat. If you use wild mussels, the yield will be a little less, so you may want to start with 6 pounds.

Although in many recipes, salt pork and bacon can be used interchangeably, the smoky flavor of the bacon doesn't work very well with curry. Stay with the salt pork if you can.

FOOD&WINE test-kitchen tips

- To debeard a mussel, firmly pull the hairy bit that protrudes from the shell. If the beard is tenacious, wiggle it back and forth to loosen it as you pull.

- To steam the mussels, the chef's instructions are to bring a cup of water to a boil in a large stockpot, add the mussels, and cover. Stir after 3 minutes, cover, and steam for 3 more minutes or until most of the mussels have opened.

wine recommendation The exotic flavors of this dish call out for a wine with some intrigue of its own. Choose a wine based on the fruity and floral Muscat grape, such as a dry but seductive Muscat d'Alsace.

I like to serve this chowder as the start to a light meal, but it makes a fine main course as well. Accompany with toasted common crackers or Pilot crackers.

For equipment, you will need an 8-quart pot with a tight-fitting lid (for steaming open the mussels), a fine-mesh strainer, a 4- to 6-quart heavy pot with a lid (for the chowder), a slotted spoon, a wooden spoon, and a ladle.

5	pounds medium PEI mussels or other cultivated mussels (or 6 pounds wild)
4	ounces meaty salt pork, rind removed and cut into $\frac{1}{3}$-inch dice
2	tablespoons unsalted butter
1	teaspoon finely chopped fresh ginger (pinky-tip–sized piece)
2	cloves garlic, finely chopped (2 teaspoons)
1	small red bell pepper (4 to 6 ounces), cut into $\frac{1}{2}$-inch dice
1	medium onion (7 to 8 ounces) cut into $\frac{1}{2}$-inch dice
1	tablespoon Madras curry powder
$\frac{1}{4}$	teaspoon cayenne pepper
1	pound Yukon Gold, Maine, PEI, or other all-purpose potatoes, peeled and cut into $\frac{1}{2}$-inch dice
1	pound small or medium sweet potatoes, peeled and cut into $\frac{1}{2}$-inch dice
$1\frac{1}{2}$	cups heavy cream (or up to 2 cups if desired)
	Kosher or sea salt and freshly ground black pepper

for garnish

2	tablespoons chopped fresh cilantro
3	scallions, thinly sliced

1 Clean and debeard the mussels. Steam them open. Strain the broth; you should have 4 cups of broth (and 1 pound of mussel meat). Cover the shelled mussels and keep refrigerated until ready to use.

2 Heat a 4- to 6-quart heavy pot over low heat and add the diced salt pork. Once it has rendered a few tablespoons of fat, increase the heat to medium and cook until the salt pork is a crisp golden brown. Using a slotted spoon, transfer the cracklings to a small ovenproof dish, leaving the fat in the pot, and reserve until later.

▼

3 Add the butter, ginger, garlic, bell pepper, onion, curry powder, and cayenne pepper to the pot and sauté, stirring occasionally with a wooden spoon, for about 10 minutes, until the pepper and onion are softened but not browned.

4 Add the white potatoes and the reserved mussel broth, turn up the heat, and bring to a boil. Cover and cook the potatoes vigorously for 5 minutes. Add the sweet potatoes. The broth should just barely cover the potatoes; if it doesn't, add enough water to cover. Lower the heat to medium, cover, and cook for 6 to 8 minutes longer, until the white and sweet potatoes are soft on the outside but still firm in the center. If the broth hasn't thickened lightly, smash a few potatoes and sweet potatoes against the side of the pot and cook a minute or two longer to release their starch.

5 Remove the pot from the heat and stir in the mussels and cream. Mussels are not as salty as clams, but you will still need to exercise a light hand as you season the chowder with salt. Add black pepper to taste. If you are not serving the chowder within the hour, let it cool a bit, then refrigerate; cover the chowder *after* it has chilled completely. Otherwise, let it sit at room temperature for up to an hour, allowing the flavors to meld.

6 When ready to serve, reheat the chowder over low heat; don't let it boil. Warm the cracklings in a low oven (200°F) for a few minutes.

7 Ladle the chowder into cups or bowls, making sure that the mussels, bell pepper, onion, and potatoes are evenly divided. Scatter the cracklings over the individual servings and sprinkle with the chopped cilantro and scallions.

creole shrimp and oyster gumbo

from *My Mother's Southern Entertaining*

AT LEAST 8 SERVINGS

Although this is not a classic gumbo by virtue of its having no roux or filé powder, to Mother's way of thinking it (like her chicken gumbo) qualifies simply on the basis of okra used as a thickening agent. In any case, this stew plays the leading role at her annual gumbo dinner, and guests always rave about it. Remember not to overcook the shrimp and oysters.

- ⅓ cup butter
- 2 tablespoons vegetable oil
- 1 large onion, finely chopped
- 1 celery rib, finely chopped
- ½ green bell pepper, seeded and finely chopped
- ½ pound fresh okra (or 10-ounce package frozen okra, defrosted), stem ends trimmed and chopped
- 1 garlic clove, minced
- 2 tablespoons all-purpose flour
- 4 cups chicken stock or broth
- 4 ripe tomatoes, chopped, or 2 cups chopped canned tomatoes, drained
- ½ teaspoon dried thyme
- 1 bay leaf
- 2 teaspoons salt
- 2 teaspoons black pepper
- 1½ pounds medium-size fresh shrimp, shelled and deveined
- 1½ dozen oysters, shucked and liquor reserved
- 2 teaspoons Worcestershire sauce
- Tabasco sauce to taste
- 2 cups or more cooked rice

▼

In a large, heavy casserole, heat the butter and vegetable oil together over moderate heat, then add the onion, celery, bell pepper, okra, and garlic and cook for 5 minutes, stirring. Sprinkle the flour on top and cook for 3 minutes, stirring. Slowly add the broth, stirring, then the tomatoes, thyme, bay leaf, salt, and pepper. Bring to a boil, reduce the heat to low, cover, and simmer for 45 minutes.

Add the shrimp, return the heat to a simmer, and cook for 5 minutes. Add the oysters plus the reserved liquor, return to a simmer, and cook till the oysters curl, about 3 minutes. Add the Worcestershire and Tabasco, stir well, check and correct the seasonings, and serve the gumbo over small amounts of rice in soup bowls.

fish biriyani

from *Savoring the Spice Coast of India*

SERVES 6

Although not as popular as meat *biriyani,* the fish version is another treasure of the Mappila community. This stunning fish and rice casserole was shown to me by Haseena Sadick of Kochi. As *biriyani* can be a time-consuming project, she cooked the fish in its slightly sour tomato masala ahead of time.

marinade

¼ teaspoon cayenne

⅛ teaspoon turmeric

¼ teaspoon fennel seeds, finely ground with a mortar and pestle

⅛ teaspoon salt

1½ pounds fish fillets (haddock or cod), skin on

2 tablespoons vegetable oil

masala

4 tablespoons vegetable oil

2 cups sliced onions

1½ teaspoons minced garlic

1½ teaspoons minced ginger

1½ teaspoons minced green chili

1 cup chopped tomato

Ground masala

- 2 teaspoons coriander
- ½ teaspoon cumin
- ¼ teaspoon cayenne
- ¼ teaspoon turmeric
- ⅛ teaspoon black pepper

½ teaspoon Garam Masala (page 64)

¾ teaspoon salt

2 tablespoons plain yogurt

2 teaspoons lime juice

¼ cup chopped fresh cilantro

¼ cup chopped fresh mint

▼

rice

2   cups basmati rice

2   tablespoons vegetable oil

1   (2-inch) piece cinnamon

3   whole cloves

2   cardamom pods, crushed

1   teaspoon salt

garnish

2   tablespoons vegetable oil

1   tablespoon Ghee (page 64)

1   cup sliced onion

¼   cup raw cashews (optional)

¼   cup golden raisins (optional)

1   To prepare the marinade, combine the cayenne, turmeric, fennel, and salt. Cut the fish into large pieces that won't break apart (about 2 x 2 inches). Rub the fish pieces with the spice mixture. Marinate 10 to 15 minutes. (This step helps draw the liquid out of the fish so it holds together during cooking.)

2   Heat 2 tablespoons oil in a nonstick frying pan and fry the fish pieces until they change color but do not become crisp (about 2 minutes on each side). Set aside.

3   Using the same pan, wiped clean, heat 4 tablespoons oil over medium-high heat. Sauté the onions until the edges are nicely browned. Add the garlic, ginger, and green chili and fry for 1 minute. Stir in the tomato, ground masala, garam masala, salt, and ½ cup water. Fry for 2 to 3 minutes or until the tomato begins to soften. Add the yogurt, lime juice, cilantro, and mint and stir until well blended.

FOOD&WINE test-kitchen tips

- To crush the cardamom pods for the rice, lay the flat of a large knife blade over them and give it a whack with your fist. The pods should just be split into a few pieces, not crushed to powder.

 wine recommendation The myriad exotic spices in this dish will be well served by a wine that sits back and lets the Indian flavors shine. The mild taste of a Pinot Blanc from France's Alsace region will do the trick.

4 Carefully add the fish pieces to the pan, spooning the sauce over them. Reduce the heat to low, cover, and simmer for 10 minutes. Swirl the pan from time to time to circulate the sauce, but do not stir or the fish will break apart. Taste for salt. The sauce should look thick and taste a little sour.

5 Place the rice in a large bowl and rinse with changes of cold water until the water no longer appears cloudy. Drain thoroughly in a strainer.

6 To make the garnish, heat 2 tablespoons oil and the ghee in a frying pan. Fry 1 cup onion slowly over medium heat, stirring constantly, until the onion turns reddish brown and crisp (10 to 15 minutes); remove it to a plate. In the remaining oil, fry the cashews until golden brown. Remove and repeat with the raisins, until they become plump and golden brown. Set aside.

7 To prepare the rice, bring 3½ cups water to a boil in a saucepan. Cover and keep over a very low flame.

8 In a large pot with tight-fitting lid, heat the 2 tablespoons oil. Add the cinnamon, cloves, and cardamom, and sauté for 1 minute, or until the spices give off their aroma. Add the drained rice and stir over medium heat until the rice begins to jump slightly in the pan. Add the boiling water and salt and stir. Reduce the heat to low, cover tightly, and cook for 20 minutes until tender.

9 Preheat the oven to 350°F.

10 When the rice is done, fluff it and spread half of it in a heavy casserole or Dutch oven (with a tight-fitting lid). Sprinkle one third of the fried onion over the rice, then add all the fish pieces and half their sauce. Add the rest of the rice, another third of the fried onion, and the remaining sauce. Seal the top with foil, then place the lid over the foil. Bake for 15 minutes.

11 Carefully transfer the rice and fish to a platter, being careful not to break up the fish pieces. Sprinkle with the fried onion, cashews, and raisins. Serve immediately.

PREPARATION TIME: 1½ HOURS

BAKING TIME: 15 MINUTES

RECIPE MAY BE PREPARED IN ADVANCE THROUGH STEP 6

▼

garam masala This recipe comes from the Muslim community in Kerala, and is a variation on the spice mix by the same name used in North India. I do not advise substituting store-bought garam masala in the recipes in this book because it will change the flavor of the dishes.

YIELD: $1/4$ CUP

4	whole pieces star anise
2	teaspoons fennel seeds
2	teaspoons ground cinnamon
2	teaspoons ground clove
2	teaspoons ground cardamom
1	teaspoon ground nutmeg

1 Place the star anise in a coffee grinder and grind to a fine powder. Measure out 2 teaspoonfuls, reserving the rest for another use.

2 Grind the fennel seeds in the coffee grinder to form a fine powder.

3 Combine all the ingredients and store in an airtight jar away from the light. It will keep for 6 months.

ghee This form of clarified butter has a nutty taste and a long shelf life. It is used as a frying medium throughout India and has a richer flavor than oil. In the south it is as indispensable a companion to rice and dhal as butter is to bread. I avoid store-bought ghee because making it is simple and tastier. Ghee will keep for months, and is great to have on hand as a substitute for oil or butter in non-Indian cooking too. Try using it for sautéing vegetables or smearing on warm bread.

YIELD: ABOUT $1/2$ CUP

$1/2$	pound (1 stick) unsalted butter

1 In a heavy, preferably light-colored skillet melt the butter over medium-low heat. The melted butter will sputter gently as the moisture boils out of it, and the bubbles will change from large to fine and foamy.

2 Once the foam appears, push it aside every few seconds to see if the milk solids have settled to the bottom of the pan. When this sediment appears golden brown, remove it from the heat. Do not let it turn dark brown.

3 Cool the ghee for a minute or two, then pour the liquid into a container with a tight-fitting lid, leaving most of the solids behind. Cool it completely, cover, and store at room temperature for 1 month or in the refrigerator for 3 months.

4 Ghee turns to a solid as it cools, so bring it to room temperature before using, or melt it by placing the jar in which it is stored in hot water.

PREPARATION TIME: 15 MINUTES

fish & shellfish

fish with cilantro
and coconut

from *Savoring the Spice Coast of India*

SERVES 6

Many of the Jews who settled in Kochi came from Iraq, and this is a curry from that community. It includes plenty of Kerala's coconut and is flavored with fresh cilantro and dried cumin—both commonly used ingredients in Iraqi Jewish cooking.

¾ cup grated unsweetened coconut

½ cup loosely packed fresh cilantro leaves, plus 2 tablespoons coarsely chopped leaves for garnish

Ground masala

- 2 teaspoons cumin
- ¼ teaspoon cayenne
- ¼ teaspoon turmeric

3 tablespoons vegetable oil

1½ cups thinly sliced onions

2 teaspoons minced garlic

2 fresh green chilies (serrano or Thai), split lengthwise

1 teaspoon salt

1½ pounds skinned fish fillets (cod or haddock), cut into 2-inch pieces

1 In a blender or food processor, blend the coconut, ½ cup cilantro, ground masala, and ¾ cup water (or more) together to form a paste like thick pesto. Set aside.

2 Heat the oil in a 12-inch nonstick frying pan over medium-high heat. Add the onions and fry until the edges begin to brown. Add the garlic and green chilies and fry another minute. Stir in the coconut paste, ¾ cup water, and salt and bring to a boil. Reduce the heat and simmer 8 to 10 minutes, until the mixture thickens and turns a little darker. If it dries out, add more water.

FOOD&WINE test-kitchen tips

- We substituted jalapeño peppers here, since neither serrano nor Thai were available. They worked just fine, but do include the ribs and seeds since that's where the heat is.

 wine recommendation When serving dishes containing chilies, avoid high-alcohol wines, which will only fuel the flame. Instead, seek out a wine with a relatively low alcohol content, such as a German Riesling. A fragrant Mosel Riesling will work exceptionally well here.

3 Stir in another ½ cup water. Place the fish pieces in the pan and spoon the sauce over them. When the mixture returns to a boil, reduce the heat to low and simmer, partly covered, for 8 to 12 minutes (depending on the thickness of the fish) until the fish is flaky and just opaque in the thickest part. Do not turn the pieces, but occasionally swirl the pan to circulate the sauce. Remove from the heat and taste for salt.

4 Carefully transfer the fish pieces to a low serving bowl. Pour the sauce over the fish and garnish with the chopped cilantro.

PREPARATION TIME: 35 MINUTES

RECIPE MAY BE PREPARED IN ADVANCE THROUGH STEP 2

fish & shellfish

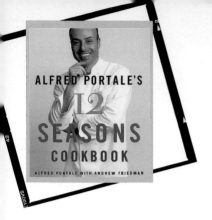

poached atlantic salmon à la nage

from *Alfred Portale's 12 Seasons Cookbook*

MAKES 4 SERVINGS

A *nage* is a finished court bouillon of sorts, because the poaching liquid becomes the broth in which the ingredients being cooked are served. While I love this technique, I've always found that the classic *nage* leaves vegetables tasting slightly pickled. So, here I've tinkered with the recipe to adjust the acidity. I've also balanced the aromatics, adding some green peppercorns for a unique accent. After preparing the *nage,* the vegetables—carrot rounds, thinly sliced celery, and sliced pearl onions—are spooned over the pink fish. The pale, delicate colors create a presentation that is perfect for early springtime.

court bouillon

1½ cups dry white wine

1 cup water

8 baby carrots, peeled and thinly sliced into rounds (about ¾ cup)

8 pearl or small boiling onions, peeled and thinly sliced into rounds (about ¾ cup)

1 rib celery, thinly sliced on the bias (about ½ cup)

3 strips lemon zest, each about ½ inch wide and 3 inches long

1 tablespoon green peppercorns in brine, drained, optional

½ teaspoon coriander seed

1 bay leaf

1 sprig fresh thyme

Coarse salt and freshly ground white pepper to taste

In a large soup pot, combine the wine, water, carrots, onions, celery, zest, peppercorns (if using), coriander seed, bay leaf, and thyme. Season with salt and pepper. Bring to a boil over high heat and cook for about 6 minutes, or until the vegetables begin to soften. Remove from heat and cover to keep warm.

salmon and assembly

4 7-ounce salmon fillets, each about 1 inch thick

Coarse salt and freshly ground white pepper to taste

6 tablespoons extra-virgin olive oil

2 tablespoons finely minced fresh chives

Season the salmon fillets with salt and pepper. Arrange them in a 10-inch sauté pan or a saucepan large enough to hold the fillets in a single layer without touching. Pour the hot court bouillon over the fillets and bring it to a simmer over medium heat. Cook for 3 to 4 minutes. The salmon will still be a little rare. Set the salmon aside in the broth to cool to room temperature for about 10 minutes; the salmon will continue to cook a little as it cools. Refrigerate it in the bouillon for at least 1 hour, until chilled.

Lift the salmon from the court bouillon and transfer the fillets to serving plates. Strain the bouillon through a fine-mesh sieve into a bowl. Remove the thyme and bay leaf. Scatter the vegetables over the salmon. Measure ½ cup of the bouillon and pour it into a small bowl. Whisk in the olive oil and season with salt and pepper. Taste and adjust the sauce with a little more oil or broth as necessary to balance the acidity. Spoon a little sauce over each fillet and garnish with the chives.

thinking ahead   This dish can be prepared as many as 6 hours in advance.

variations   Other fish with a high oil content, such as mackerel, will work in this context. The herbs can be made more interesting with the addition of tarragon, chervil, or—if making the dish with salmon—dill.

fish & shellfish

FOOD&WINE test-kitchen tips

- Small onions can be a nuisance to peel. Try this chefs' trick: Bring a pan of water to a boil, remove from the heat, drop in the onions, and let them sit for a couple of minutes before draining. The skins will come off much more easily after this treatment.

 wine recommendation   Salmon is one of the few fish that has enough flavor to stand up to a big white Burgundy. For good value in this pricey area, look for a wine from one of the less-known towns, such as Rully or St-Aubin.

My Mother's Southern Entertaining

James Villas with Martha Pearl Villas

shrimp and grits

from *My Mother's Southern Entertaining*

Mother first tasted shrimp and grits (or, as they're often called in the Carolina Low Country, "breakfast grits") when we were staying at the old Francis Marion hotel in Charleston, South Carolina, many years ago, and she was so taken with the luscious dish that it soon became the highlight of our Resurrection breakfast. Although she's since been impressed with versions at both the Pinckney Cafe in Charleston and Atherton Mill in Charlotte that have tomatoes in the sauce, she still thinks there's nothing like this age-old classic made with the smallest shrimp possible and a little bacon grease. As far as I'm concerned, shrimp and grits is one of the most distinctive hallmarks of authentic Southern cookery—and not just for breakfast.

for the grits

5   cups water

1   teaspoon salt

1   cup regular hominy grits

2   tablespoons butter

for the shrimp

2   pounds small shrimp, peeled and deveined

2   tablespoons butter

2   tablespoons bacon grease

2   small onions, finely chopped

½   small green bell pepper, seeded and finely chopped

¼   cup all-purpose flour

Salt and black pepper to taste

FOOD&WINE test-kitchen tips

- There's time to make the shrimp while the grits cook, but if this double maneuver seems too stressful, you can prepare the shrimp and their gravy first. Then make the grits, reheat the gravy, and add the shrimp for the last 2 minutes of cooking.

 wine recommendation This delicate dish calls for a wine that's high in acidity but is unoaked, such as a Chablis. If brunch is the venue, consider a sparkling wine, such as an Italian Prosecco or even a Brut Champagne.

To cook the grits, combine the water and salt in a large, heavy saucepan, bring to a brisk boil, and slowly sift the grits through the fingers of one hand into the water while stirring with the other. Reduce the heat to a gentle simmer and continue cooking till the grits are thick, about 30 minutes, stirring frequently to prevent sticking. Add the butter, stir till well blended, cover, and keep warm in a bowl till ready to serve.

To prepare the shrimp, place them in a large saucepan with enough water to just cover. Bring to a boil, remove the pan from the heat, let stand for 1 minute, and drain, reserving the cooking liquid in a bowl.

In a large, heavy skillet, heat the butter and bacon grease together over moderate heat, then add the onions and green pepper and stir for 8 minutes. Sprinkle the flour on top and continue to stir till the mixture begins to brown, about 2 minutes. Gradually add about 2 cups of the reserved shrimp cooking liquid and whisk briskly till the gravy is smooth. Add the shrimp, season with salt and pepper, and stir for 2 minutes, adding a little more cooking liquid if the gravy seems too thick.

Serve the shrimp and gravy over large spoonfuls of grits.

clam linguine with pancetta, chiles, and garlic

from *Tom Douglas' Seattle Kitchen*

MAKES 4 SERVINGS

I add roasted jalapeños to this classic Italian dish to give it a lift of spice and flavor. It's the perfect dish to order late at night at the bar at Etta's with a glass of Pinot Grigio—it's also a great first course for a big Italian feast. I always put Parmesan on these spicy clams, despite the Italian thing about no cheese with fish. Use grated cheese, if you like, or make Parmesan curls with a potato peeler.

If you don't have a sauté pan big enough to cook 2 pounds of clams, you can split the clams up into 2 pans.

2	jalapeño chiles, cut in half and seeded
¼	cup olive oil, plus more for brushing
	Kosher salt and freshly ground black pepper
3	ounces pancetta, diced (½ cup)
1	teaspoon minced garlic
¼	teaspoon red pepper flakes, or to taste
2	pounds clams, scrubbed and rinsed
¼	cup dry white wine
1	pound fresh linguine or dried linguine
¼	cup (½ stick) unsalted butter
4	teaspoons chopped fresh flat-leaf parsley
3	teaspoons fresh lemon juice
2	teaspoons grated lemon zest
½	cup fresh flat-leaf parsley
¼	cup shaved (see How to Shave Cheese, next page) Parmesan cheese
4	lemon wedges

1 Preheat the oven to 400°F and start a pot of salted water boiling to cook the pasta later. Brush the jalapeño halves with oil and sprinkle with salt and pepper. Place them on a baking sheet and roast in the oven for 10 minutes. When cool enough to handle, dice finely.

2 Put a large sauté pan over medium-high heat. Heat the ¼ cup olive oil, add the pancetta, and cook, stirring, until browned, about 2 minutes. Add the jalapeño, garlic, and pepper flakes and cook, stirring, another minute. Turn the heat to high. Add the clams and wine and cover. Cook until the clams open, about 3 minutes. Meanwhile, cook the pasta in the boiling water until *al dente*. Add the butter, chopped parsley, lemon juice, and zest to the clams in the pan and toss until the butter melts into the sauce. Drain the pasta. In a large serving bowl, toss the pasta with the clam sauce and whole parsley leaves. Season to taste with salt and pepper.

on the plate Divide the pasta among 4 shallow bowls or plates and top with the shaved Parmesan. Make sure the clams mostly end up on top of the pasta, facing up. (Move them around with tongs if you need to.) Discard any unopened clams. Garnish with lemon wedges.

in the glass Try a Pinot Grigio from the Veneto, in northern Italy.

how to shave cheese Sometimes long shavings of cheese instead of grated cheese make for a more sophisticated look. An ordinary swivel vegetable peeler is all you need to produce these shavings. Just pull the peeler along a chunk of hard cheese, like Parmesan or an aged goat cheese, that you are holding in your hand.

FOOD&WINE test-kitchen tips

- In our testing, we found the best clams to use for this dish are small littlenecks. They open right on cue at the 3 minutes given in the recipe and reveal a perfect bite-size morsel.

- Clams must be alive when cooked. If any are gapping open, pinch the shells together with your fingers. Unless the clam clamps shut, throw it away.

quick-fried shrimp with sweet toasty garlic
camarones al mojo de ajo

from *Mexico One Plate at a Time*

SERVES 6 GENEROUSLY

¾   **cup peeled garlic cloves (about 2 large heads)**

1 cup good-quality oil, preferably extra-virgin olive oil

Salt

Juice of 1 lime

2   **canned chipotle chiles** *en adobo,* **seeded and cut into thin strips**

2   **limes, cut into wedges**

2   **pounds (about 48) medium-large shrimp, peeled (leaving the last joint and tail intact if you wish)**

3   **tablespoons chopped fresh cilantro or flat-leaf parsley (optional)**

1 preparing the *mojo de ajo* Either chop the garlic with a sharp knife into ⅛-inch bits or drop the cloves through the feed tube of a food processor with the motor running and process until the pieces are roughly ⅛ inch in size. You should have about ½ cup chopped garlic. Scoop into a small (1-quart) saucepan, measure in the oil (you need it all for even cooking) and ½ teaspoon salt and set over medium-low heat. Stir occasionally as the mixture comes *barely* to a simmer (there should be just a hint of movement on the surface of the oil). Adjust the heat to the very lowest possible setting to keep the mixture at that very gentle simmer (bubbles will rise in the pot like sparkling mineral water) and cook, stirring occasionally, until the garlic is a *soft,* pale golden (the color of light brown sugar), about 30 minutes. The slower the cooking, the sweeter the garlic.

▼

FOOD&WINE test-kitchen tips

- To hasten the garlic peeling, use the method described in the Test-Kitchen Tips on page 198. You can also drop the cloves into boiling water for 1 to 2 minutes and then cool them under cold running water; the skins will slip right off. If you like gadgets, try one of those garlic peelers that looks like a piece of rubber hose; they work well.

 wine recommendation Shrimp and Extra Brut Champagne make a wonderful pair; so use this dish as an excuse to uncork some bubbly. If you're in a downscale mood, a beer will also work just fine.

Add the lime juice to the pan and simmer until most of the juice has evaporated or been absorbed into the garlic, about 5 minutes. Stir in the chiles, then taste the *mojo de ajo* and add a little more salt if you think it needs it. Keep the pan over low heat, so the garlic will be warm when the shrimp are ready. Scoop the lime wedges into a serving bowl and set on the table.

2 the shrimp Devein the shrimp if you wish: One by one, lay the shrimp on your work surface, make a shallow incision down the back and pull or scrape out the dark (usually) intestinal tract.

Set a large (12-inch) heavy skillet (preferably nonstick) over medium-high heat and spoon in 1½ tablespoons of the oil (but not any garlic) from the *mojo.* Add *half* of the shrimp to the skillet, sprinkle generously with salt and stir gently and continuously until the shrimp are just cooked through, 3 to 4 minutes. Stir in *half* the cilantro or parsley, if you're using it. Scoop the shrimp onto a deep serving platter. Repeat with another 1½ tablespoons of the garlicky oil and the remaining shrimp.

When all of the shrimp are cooked, use a slotted spoon to scoop out the warm bits of garlic and chiles from the *mojo* pan, and scatter them over the shrimp. (You may have as much as ⅓ cup of the oil left over, for which you'll be grateful—it's wonderful for sautéing practically anything.) If you're a garlic lover, you're about to have the treat of your life, served with the lime wedges to add sparkle.

working ahead The *mojo de ajo* keeps for a couple of weeks in the refrigerator (the oil will become solid but will liquify again at room temperature), so I never recommend making a small amount. *Mojo* in the refrigerator represents great potential for a quick wonderful meal. Warm cold *mojo* slowly before using. For the best texture, cook the shrimp immediately before serving. Or cook them an hour or so ahead, douse them with the garlic *mojo* and serve it all at room temperature.

squid with ginger-garlic sauce

muoc tuoi (from Vietnam)

from *Hot Sour Salty Sweet*

SERVES 4 TO 6 AS AN APPETIZER OR AS PART OF A RICE MEAL

All along the coast of southern Vietnam, squid boats, small round coracles, sit out on the beach in the sun. Come evening, they're loaded into larger boats and carried offshore. There they're put into the water, each one manned by a fisherman with a bright light. The squid swim up, attracted by the light, and the fishermen use a net to haul them in.

These days cleaned flash-frozen squid is widely available; there's no more cleaning and peeling to be done (though instructions for cleaning squid are given below, just in case). We like this simple dish. It takes us back to a beach outside Da Nang, where we sat one afternoon long ago, on our first trip to Vietnam, eating freshly caught, freshly cooked squid at a small beachside stand. We dipped it, mouthful by mouthful, into a garlicky ginger sauce and washed it down with local beer.

squid

2   pounds cleaned squid or 3 pounds small or medium whole squid

2 to 3 tablespoons fresh lime juice

½   cup coriander leaves (optional)

garnish and accompaniments

Leaf lettuce or Vietnamese Herb and Salad Plate (recipe follows)

Ginger-Garlic Sauce (recipe follows)

1   lime, cut into wedges

Salt and freshly ground black pepper

▼

fish & shellfish

FOOD&WINE test-kitchen tips

- If you can't find a serrano or bird chile for the sauce, substitute a jalapeño as we did. You need to use the seeds and ribs, along with the flesh, to give the needed kick of heat.

 wine recommendation Once slightly obscure, the Albariño grape from Spain has been making fans out of foodies the world over. Its bracing acidity brings out the best in a wide variety of fish and shellfish. Albariños from the Rías Baixas region of Spain have the most character, making them the ideal choice for this high-spirited dish.

Wash the squid thoroughly. If using whole squid: To clean, hold the body of the squid in one hand and gently pull the head and tentacles off (taking care not to break the ink sac). The intestines will automatically come away with the head. Separate the tentacles from the rest, wash thoroughly, and set aside. Peel off the outer red-brown skin from the body. Turn the squid body inside out; remove the cartilage and wash again thoroughly until no longer gritty. Turn right side out.

Slice the squid bodies into ¼-inch-wide rings or into 1½- to 2-inch slices. Leave the tentacles whole or cut in half, as you like.

Fill a large pot with water and bring to a boil. Toss in the squid and cook until tender, 4 to 6 minutes. Drain well, place in a bowl, and pour over the lime juice. Toss to coat. Add the coriander leaves if you wish, and toss.

Transfer the squid to a shallow serving bowl or place on a bed of lettuce on a small platter. Serve with the salad and herb plate if you wish, and with condiment dishes of the ginger-garlic sauce, wedges of lime, and salt and pepper. Use the lettuce or salad greens and herbs to pick up the squid, then drizzle on a little sauce or squeeze on lime juice and season to taste, mouthful by mouthful.

ginger-garlic sauce

MAKES ABOUT ⅓ CUP SAUCE

2	tablespoons minced ginger
2	cloves garlic, minced
1	bird or serrano chile, finely chopped
1	teaspoon sugar
3	tablespoons Vietnamese or Thai fish sauce
3	tablespoons fresh lime juice
1 to 2 tablespoons water	

If you have a mortar and pestle, crush and blend together the ginger, garlic, chile, and sugar. If you don't, simply combine the ingredients in a small bowl. Add the fish sauce, lime juice, and water to taste and blend well.

Leftovers will keep in a well-sealed glass container in the refrigerator for 3 days.

vietnamese herb and salad plate *xalach dia* *Xalach dia* is an essential part of the Vietnamese table, especially in the south, a wonderful tradition that brings freshness and variety to every meal. The salad vegetables are used to wrap, to accompany, to enhance, or to alter the other dishes, or they are eaten simply on their own. The salad platter gives each person a chance to vary tastes and textures, mouthful by mouthful, as the various herbs and salad vegetables complement the cooked foods with fresh flavors. What's more, the salad platter brings color and beauty to the table.

Halfway around the world, in Iran, Armenia, and the Eastern Mediterranean, there's a very similar salad plate tradition, and its role in the meal is almost identical. In all cases, it makes each person a lively participant in how the meal comes together.

If the list of options looks daunting, just begin by putting out a bowl of salad greens, without dressing, and a bowl of fresh herbs, coriander sprigs, for example, or Asian basil leaves. Encourage your guests to use the greens and herbs as a freshening mouthful between bites of cooked food, as well as to wrap combinations of different foods.

some or all of
Asian or sweet basil leaves
Mint leaves
Coriander sprigs
Leaf lettuce (one or more kinds), separated into leaves
Small scallions, trimmed
Small lime wedges
Bird chiles, whole or minced
Cucumber slices or chunks
Bean sprouts, raw or briefly parboiled and drained

Set out the ingredients of your choice on one or more plates or shallow bowls to accompany any meal.

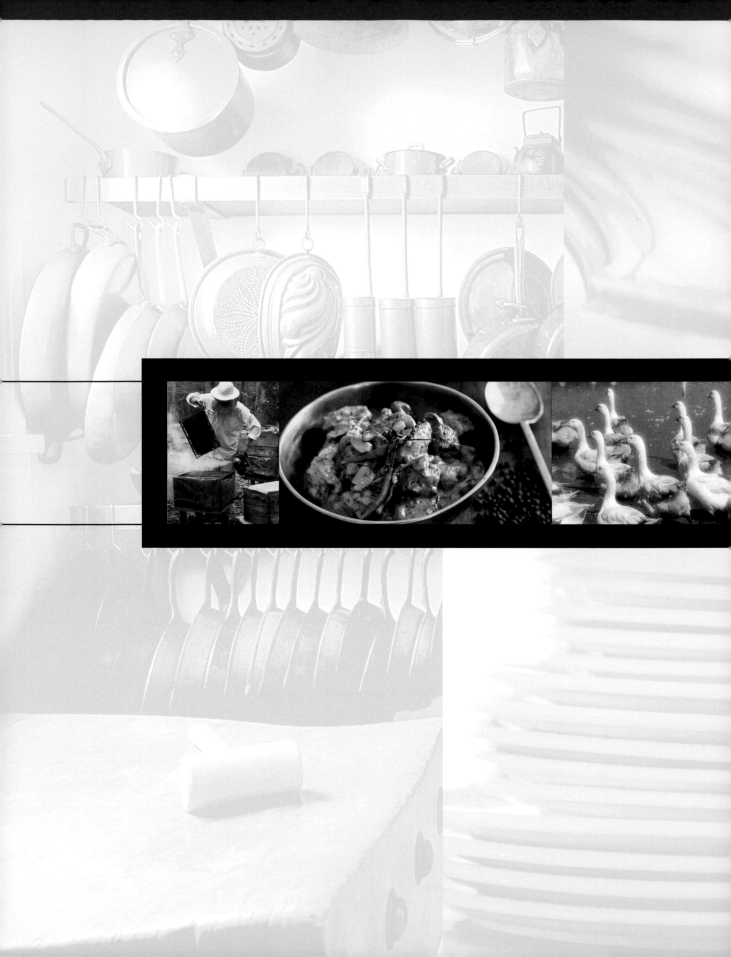

chicken & other birds

Julia's Kitchen Wisdom

ESSENTIAL TECHNIQUES AND RECIPES
FROM A LIFETIME OF COOKING

JULIA CHILD

chicken salad

from *Julia's Kitchen Wisdom*

SERVES 6 TO 8

6   cups cooked chicken, cut up into good-sized pieces

Salt and freshly ground white pepper

1 to 2 tablespoons olive oil

2 to 3 tablespoons fresh lemon juice

1   cup diced tender celery stalks

½   cup diced red onion

1   cup chopped walnuts

½   cup chopped parsley

1   teaspoon finely cut fresh tarragon leaves (or ¼ teaspoon dried tarragon)

⅔   cup or so mayonnaise (recipe follows)

Fresh salad greens, washed and dried

for decoration

All or a choice of sliced or chopped hard-boiled eggs, parsley sprigs,
      strips of red pimiento

Toss the chicken with salt, pepper, olive oil, lemon juice, celery, onion, and walnuts. Cover and refrigerate at least 20 minutes or overnight. Drain out any accumulated liquid; toss with the parsley and tarragon. Taste analytically and correct seasonings. Fold in just enough mayonnaise to enrobe ingredients. Shred the greens, arrange on a platter, and mound the salad on top. Spread a thin coat of mayonnaise over the chicken and decorate with the eggs, parsley, and pimiento strips.

variations

- **turkey salad** Follow the same general system as for chicken.
- **lobster, crab, or shrimp salad** Follow the same general system, and use some of the shells for decoration.

FOOD&WINE test-kitchen tips

- Here's a chefs' trick for drying curly parsley quickly: Squeeze the washed bunch dry with your hands. You can practically wring it out; the water will run off, and the tightly curled leaves will spring right back into shape. Don't try this with Italian parsley, though; you'll crush its flat leaves, and the water will still cling.

 wine recommendation This old favorite calls for a wine that has enough acidity to refresh the palate after each mayonnaise-rich bite but not such a strong flavor that it overpowers the chicken. Choose an Orvieto or Soave Classico from northern Italy.

processor mayonnaise Break 1 whole egg into the container of a food processor, add 2 egg yolks, and process 30 to 45 seconds, or until thick and lemon-colored. With the machine running, add 1 tablespoon fresh lemon juice and/or wine vinegar, 1 teaspoon Dijon-type mustard, ½ teaspoon salt, and several grinds of white pepper. Still with the machine running, and by very small dribbles at first, start adding up to 2 cups of olive oil and/or vegetable oil. After about ½ cup has gone in, add the oil a little faster, until you have a thick mayonnaise. Taste carefully, processing in lemon or vinegar and seasonings as needed.

storage Refrigerate in a covered container; the sauce will keep for about a week. Note that a chilled sauce can sometimes turn or thin out when stirred up—best to transfer it by spoonfuls into a warmed mixing bowl, whisking as you add each to the bowl.

troubleshooting If the sauce separates or thins out, let it sit for several minutes, until the oil has risen over the clotted residue. Spoon as much of the oil as you quite easily can into a separate bowl. Dip a tablespoon of the residue into a clean bowl. By hand or with a portable mixer, whisk it vigorously with ½ tablespoon of Dijon-type mustard until creamed and thickened. Then by half teaspoons at first, whisk in additional residue, letting the sauce cream and thicken after each addition. Finally, continue with the oil, adding it by dribbles. (Note that using the same techniques you can also accomplish this in the electric blender.)

chicken & other birds

Anne Willan From My Château Kitchen

salad of honey roast chicken wings and bacon

from *From My Château Kitchen*

SERVES 4

The first time I read this recipe, I shuddered but I have to admit that the sweet-salt combination of honey and bacon with chicken is a winner. Use the same glaze for other chicken pieces, too, to make a fine first course or lunch for four.

½ lb/250 g mixed salad greens

1 tablespoon vegetable oil

3 to 4 slices of bacon, diced

8 to 10 chicken wings (about 1 lb/500 g)

¼ cup/60 ml red wine vinegar

1 heaping tablespoon honey

for the vinaigrette dressing

2 tablespoons sherry vinegar

½ teaspoon Dijon-style mustard

Salt and pepper

1 tablespoon port (optional)

½ cup/125 ml olive oil

Heat the oven to 425°F/220°C. Wash and dry the salad greens and pile them in a bowl. For the dressing, whisk the vinegar, mustard, salt, and pepper in a small bowl until mixed. If you like a touch of sweetness to balance the salty bacon, add the port. Gradually whisk in the olive oil, starting drop by drop so the dressing emulsifies and thickens slightly, then adding it more steadily in a slow stream. Taste, adjust the seasoning, and set the dressing aside while you cook the chicken wings.

FOOD&WINE test-kitchen tips

• The honey in this recipe makes the wings prone to burn, as mentioned in the recipe. Put them on the middle rack of the oven so that they don't brown too much on either top or bottom.

 wine recommendation Vouvray from the Loire Valley of France is one of the most versatile of wines with food. Look for the words demi-sec (half-dry) on the label to get a wine with just enough sweetness to complement the honey in this recipe.

If it has not already been done, chop off the tips of the chicken wings (they make a fine addition to a stockpot), leaving you with the 2 meatier portions of the wing still joined together. Heat the oil in a large skillet or frying pan with a heatproof handle and fry the bacon until crisp, stirring occasionally. Transfer the bacon with a slotted spoon to drain on paper towels. Add the chicken wings to the pan and brown them on all sides over medium heat, taking 5 to 7 minutes. Remove the wings and set them aside. Discard all the fat from the pan, return it to the heat, and add the vinegar. Stir in the honey until dissolved. Return the wings to the pan and toss them to coat well with the honey mixture.

Transfer the pan of wings to the oven and roast until they are very tender and caramelized by the honey to a rich brown, 25 to 30 minutes. You'll need to stir them often and watch closely toward the end of cooking as they scorch easily.

To serve, add the dressing to the salad greens, toss them, and taste to see if more seasoning is needed. Pile the greens on 4 plates and arrange the hot chicken wings around the edge of each. Sprinkle the crisp bacon on top and serve at once.

parmesan chicken wings

from *My Mother's Southern Entertaining*

6 TO 8 SERVINGS

Mother's favorite part of any chicken has always been the wings ("the sweetest meat," she exclaims), which is why she has so many chicken wing recipes. This latest one, created for old friends who'd finally moved from their large Colonial house to a more sensible condo, is utterly delectable and perfect for a housewarming—or picnic, cookout, or elaborate cocktail buffet.

3   pounds chicken wings

1   cup finely grated Parmesan cheese

2   tablespoons finely chopped fresh parsley leaves

1   teaspoon dried tarragon

1   teaspoon dried marjoram

1   teaspoon mild Hungarian paprika

Salt and black pepper to taste

Pinch of cayenne pepper

½   cup (1 stick) butter, melted

Preheat the oven to 375°F. Grease a large, heavy baking sheet and set aside.

Disjoint the chicken wings and cut off and discard the tips. On a large plate, combine the cheese, parsley, tarragon, marjoram, paprika, salt and black pepper, and cayenne and stir till well blended. Dip each chicken piece into the melted butter, dredge lightly in the cheese mixture, tapping off any excess, place on the prepared baking sheet, and bake till golden brown and crispy, about 1 hour. Serve the wings hot or at room temperature.

FOOD&WINE test-kitchen tips

- We found that 2½ teaspoons of salt and just a few grindings of black pepper was right for this recipe.

 wine recommendation The dominant flavor here is Parmesan, a cheese that will be flattered by many wines, as long as they have fairly full body and flavor, including some fruitiness. Try a Nero d'Avola from Sicily.

chipotle chilaquiles (tortilla "casserole")

chilaquiles al chipotle

from *Mexico One Plate at a Time*

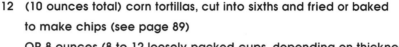

SERVES 4 AS A CASUAL MAIN DISH

12   (10 ounces total) corn tortillas, cut into sixths and fried or baked
    to make chips (see page 89)
    OR 8 ounces (8 to 12 loosely packed cups, depending on thickness) thick,
    homemade-style tortilla chips (such as ones you buy at a Mexican grocery)

One 28-ounce can good-quality whole tomatoes in juice, drained
    OR 1½ pounds (3 medium-large round or 9 to 12 plum) ripe tomatoes

2 to 3 canned chipotle chiles *en adobo*
    OR 2 to 3 dried chipotle chiles, stemmed

1½   tablespoons vegetable or olive oil

1   large white onion, sliced ¼ inch thick

3   garlic cloves, peeled and finely chopped

2½   cups chicken broth, vegetable broth or water, plus a little extra if needed

Salt

About ⅓ cup homemade *crema* (page 91), *crème fraîche* or store-bought sour
    cream thinned with a little milk

1½   cups coarsely shredded cooked chicken, preferably grilled,
    roasted or rotisserie chicken (optional)

¼   cup grated Mexican *queso añejo* or other dry grating cheese,
    such as Romano or Parmesan

2   cups sliced red Swiss chard leaves or lamb's-quarters *(quelites)* (optional)

3   tablespoons roughly chopped fresh *epazote*
    OR ½ cup chopped fresh cilantro

1 the chips Make the chips or measure out the store-bought chips.

2 the brothy sauce If using canned tomatoes, place them in a blender jar. If using
fresh tomatoes, spread them onto a baking sheet and place 4 inches below a very hot broiler. Roast until splotchy-black and thoroughly soft, about 6 minutes per side. Cool. Peel (col-
lecting the juices) and, for round tomatoes, cut out the hard cores. Transfer to a blender,
juices and all.

▼

If using canned chipotles, add them to the blender, seeds and all. If using dried chipotles, toast them in a dry skillet over medium heat for about a minute, turning frequently, until very aromatic. Place in a small bowl, cover with hot tap water and let rehydrate for 30 minutes. Drain and add to the blender.

Blend the tomatoes and chiles to a slightly coarse puree, one that still retains a little texture. You should have about 2¼ cups puree.

Set a medium (4- to 5-quart) pot or Dutch oven or a large (12-inch) deep skillet over medium heat—you'll need a lid for whichever vessel you choose. Measure in the oil, add *half* of the onion and cook, stirring regularly, until golden, about 7 minutes. Add the garlic and stir for another minute, then raise the heat to medium-high. Add the tomato puree and stir nearly constantly for 4 to 5 minutes, until the mixture thickens somewhat. Stir in the broth or water and season with salt, usually about ½ teaspoon if you are using salted chips. (Cover the pot and turn off the heat if not continuing with Step 3 right away.)

3 cooking and serving the *chilaquiles* Set out the remaining onion, the *crema* (or its stand-in), chicken (if using) and cheese. Put the pot over medium-high heat until the brothy sauce boils. Stir in the chard or lamb's-quarters (if using), the *epazote* (if using cilantro, set it aside to add later) and the tortilla chips, coating all the chips well. Let return to a rolling boil, cover and turn off the heat. Let stand for 5 minutes (no longer).

Uncover the pot and check that the chips have softened nicely—they should be a *little* chewy, definitely not mushy. (If they're too chewy, stir in a few tablespoons more broth, cover and set over medium heat for a couple minutes more.) Sprinkle with the cilantro, if that's the herb you're using.

Spoon onto warm plates. Drizzle with the *crema* (or its stand-in), strew with the sliced onion and optional chicken and dust generously with the cheese.

FOOD&WINE test-kitchen tips

- Do not think for a moment that this recipe has anything to do with the goopy, misnamed tamale casserole of old. This is, in fact, an authentic and rather light dish, close to a soup. Plan to serve it in shallow bowls.

- If you make your own tortilla chips with unsalted corn tortillas, you'll need to add salt to the recipe. We found that about 2½ teaspoons was right.

 wine recommendation The exuberant and lusty white wines of the Rhône Valley will be a knockout here. The best ones are based on Roussane and Marsanne grapes, both great foils for Latin flavors.

working ahead The brothy sauce (Step 2) can be completed up to 3 or 4 days ahead; store in the refrigerator, covered. *Chilaquiles* lose texture once they're made, so complete the simple tasks of cooking and serving them when everyone's ready to eat. Homemade chips for *chilaquiles* are fine made a day or two in advance.

fried or baked tortilla chips If you're going to use these chips for *chilaquiles,* you should buy medium-thick tortillas, ones that weigh 10 ounces per dozen. Choosing these will yield the right weight/volume for making Chipotle *Chilaquiles.* For snacking chips, choose the thinner, drier tortillas that are made from more coarsely ground corn—especially for frying light, crisp and greaseless. Baked chips can be nearly as good as fried ones (especially right out of the oven), and they are leaner. We counted: Baked chips take about 80 spritzes of oil (a total of 1 tablespoon oil spritzed over 12 tortillas).

MAKES ENOUGH FOR 6 TO 8 AS A SNACK, OR THE RIGHT AMOUNT
TO USE IN MAKING CHIPOTLE *CHILAQUILES*

12   corn tortillas
Vegetable oil to a depth of at least 1 inch (1½ inches is even better) for frying
      OR vegetable oil in a spray bottle
Salt

1 the tortillas For the crispest, most greaseless chips, the tortillas you start with should not be at all warm or moist—in fact cold, dryish, slightly stale tortillas are best. Separate the tortillas (make sure none are stuck together) and cut each into 6 wedges (it's most efficient to cut stacks of 4 or 5 tortillas). Spread out the wedges on your cutting board to air-dry for a few minutes.

▼

chicken & other birds

89

2 · option 1: frying the tortillas In a heavy pot, preferably at least 8 inches across and 3 to 5 inches deep, heat 1 to 1½ inches of oil over medium to medium-high. For greatest consistency, attach a deep-fry thermometer and adjust the heat to keep the oil at 375°F. Lacking a thermometer, the most accurate way to judge temperature is with your nose—at about 325°F, the oil will begin to give off that characteristic hot oil smell—and with your eyes—you'll notice a shimmering surface on the oil (but no smoking) when it's about 375°F. You should also use good old trial-and-error: Lay a tortilla triangle in the oil, and if it sizzles happily, the temperature's about right; if it languishes with only a trickle of bubbles, the oil's too cool; or, if it gets zapped unmercifully, you've got smoking-hot oil that is dangerous and will give the chips a bad taste.

Working with a small handful (about 12 pieces) at a time, fry the chips, stirring them around nearly constantly, until they've darkened just a shade and the bubbling has slowed way down, 45 seconds to a minute. Use tongs or a skimmer to remove them from the oil and drain on paper towels. Sprinkle with salt.

· option 2: baking the tortillas Heat the oven to 375°F. Spread the triangles into a more-or-less single layer on two baking sheets. Using a spray bottle of oil, evenly mist them on both sides. Bake, stirring them around once or twice, until they're crisp and slightly golden, 10 to 15 minutes. Sprinkle with salt.

working ahead Allowed to cool completely and stored in an air-tight container, chips for snacking are okay for several days after they're made. But just-made chips are heads-and-shoulders above chips made even, say, 2 hours before. For *chilaquiles,* they can be made a week or so ahead.

mexican-style thick cream *crema mexicana* This is the luscious stuff that burns a simple dish into your memory. A little edgy, a little nutty and really voluptuous. Did they ever call Marilyn Monroe *crema*?

MAKES ABOUT 1 CUP

1 **cup heavy whipping cream**
¼ **cup good-quality commercial sour cream with active cultures**
   OR 2 tablespoons buttermilk with active cultures

In a small saucepan, heat the cream just long enough to take the chill off—to bring it to body temperature. If you have ready access to a low-range instant-read thermometer, it should be about 100°F. Off the heat, whisk in the sour cream (or buttermilk) and pour into a glass jar. Set the lid on the jar (but don't tighten it), then place the jar in a warmish place (it shouldn't be over 90°F). After 12 hours, the cream should be noticeably thicker. Refrigerate (you can tighten the lid now) for at least 4 hours or, better yet, overnight to complete the thickening. *Crema* will last for at least a week in the refrigerator.

THE JAPANESE KITCHEN
HIROKO SHIMBO

Foreword by Ming Tsai

pan-fried flavored chicken
tori no usugiriyaki

from *The Japanese Kitchen*

YIELDS 3 TO 4 SERVINGS

This is a very quick, delicious dish of thin-sliced chicken, briefly marinated and then pan-fried. Served here with parboiled spinach and plain cooked rice, the chicken also makes a good salad topping.

1	pound boned and skinned chicken thighs or breasts
3	tablespoons white sesame seeds, toasted (see opposite)
¼	cup minced *naganegi* long onion, or scallions
2	garlic cloves, minced
3	tablespoons *shoyu* (soy sauce)
1	tablespoon honey

Fresh-ground black pepper

2	tablespoons sesame oil

4 to 6 tablespoons vegetable oil

10	ounces spinach or soybean or mung-bean sprouts, cooked in boiling water for 1 minute, and drained

Cut the chicken thigh or breast diagonally into ½-inch-wide slices. In a *suribachi* or other mortar, roughly crush the sesame seeds.

In a bowl, combine the sesame seeds, long onion or scallion, garlic, *shoyu*, honey, black pepper, and sesame oil. Add the chicken, and marinate it for 20 minutes.

FOOD&WINE test-kitchen tips

- The recipe suggests that you cook the chicken 2 to 3 minutes per side, which we found to be exactly right. We cooked slices of breast about 2 minutes on each side and meat from the thigh the whole 3 minutes.

 wine recommendation The sweet and savory Asian flavors of this dish practically beg for sake. For a smooth, high-quality rendition, look for the words Ginjo or Daiginjo on the label.

Heat a skillet until hot, and add 2 tablespoons of the vegetable oil. When the oil is hot, reduce the heat to medium-low, add several slices of chicken, and cook them until they are golden on both sides and cooked through, 2 to 3 minutes. Cook the rest of the chicken in the same way, adding oil to the skillet as necessary. Keep the chicken warm while you cook the spinach or sprouts.

Rinse the skillet with hot water, wipe it with a paper towel, and place the skillet over medium heat. Add 1 tablespoon vegetable oil. When the oil is hot, add the spinach or sprouts, and cook for 1 minute, stirring.

Serve the chicken with the spinach or sprouts, accompanied by plain cooked white or brown rice.

to toast sesame seeds Heat a skillet over low to medium heat. When it is hot, add the seeds and cook them, shaking the skillet occasionally, until the seeds are heated through and plump-looking, about 1 to 2 minutes.

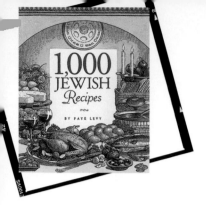

old-fashioned roasted chicken

from *1,000 Jewish Recipes*

MAKES **4** SERVINGS

When I was growing up, this was the way my mother most often prepared chicken for our Friday night dinner. I still love the natural taste of chicken prepared this way.

If you like, fill the chicken with stuffing. After you stuff the bird, if you have extra stuffing, spoon it into a small greased baking dish. Bake it for the last 40 to 45 minutes of the chicken's roasting time. Remember that stuffed chickens take longer to roast, so allow another 20 minutes, and insert a skewer into the stuffing to be sure it is hot.

> One 3½- to 4-pound chicken
> ¼ teaspoon salt (optional)
> ¼ teaspoon freshly ground pepper
> ½ teaspoon paprika
> 2 to 3 teaspoons vegetable oil (optional)
> ½ cup chicken stock or broth

1 Preheat oven to 375°F. Trim excess fat around chicken cavity; remove giblets. Mix salt if using, pepper, paprika, and oil, if using, in a bowl. Rub chicken all over with spice mixture. Set chicken in a roasting pan.

2 Roast chicken 30 minutes. Add stock to pan. Roast another 45 minutes to 1 hour, basting chicken occasionally with pan juices. To check whether chicken is done, insert a skewer into thickest part of thigh; juices that run from chicken should be clear. If juices are pink, continue roasting chicken a few more minutes and check again.

3 Transfer chicken to a carving board or platter. Carve chicken and serve hot. If you like, serve with pan juices.

FOOD&WINE test-kitchen tips

- One of the reasons kosher chickens taste so good is that salting is part of the koshering process. If you use a standard chicken, be sure to salt it generously.

 wine recommendation The uncomplicated flavor of this dish allows for a great many wine pairings. Take advantage of the opportunity to try something you haven't had before, perhaps a Riesling from Austria or a Viognier from southern France.

the no-hassle roast chicken dinner

from *How to Cook Without a Book*

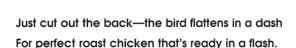

SERVES 4

Just cut out the back—the bird flattens in a dash
For perfect roast chicken that's ready in a flash.

W h o l e   r o a s t   c h i c k e n would be perfect supper food if it didn't take so long. Preparing even a small chicken and roasting it in a hot oven takes an hour and fifteen minutes.

However, I have discovered that butterflying, or cutting out the back and flattening a chicken, shaves nearly half an hour off the roasting time, making it a weeknight dinner possibility. Not only does removing the back save time, it also flattens out the chicken, allowing it to cook more evenly, ensuring that the breast does not overcook and dry out. If I've got forty-five minutes (forty of which is roasting time for the bird and free time for me), butterflied roast chicken with vegetables is one of the simplest meals I can get on the table.

A butterflied chicken is also easier to season. Sprinkling the skin of a whole chicken with salt and pepper does nothing for the meat, and seasoning it under its skin is difficult. But with its back cut out, the skin of a butterflied chicken is as easy to lift as a backless hospital gown, making it possible to distribute the seasonings easily directly on the meat.

First, start by preheating the oven to 450 degrees. After that, rinse the chicken, cut out its back, flatten it with your palm or fist (I don't bother with a meat pounder anymore), and pat it dry. Transfer the butterflied chicken to a foil-lined roasting pan large enough to hold the chicken (and vegetables in a single layer if you are roasting them alongside the bird) and shallow enough to ensure that the chicken browns well. When roasting both chicken and vegetables, my pan of choice is a heavy-grade 18- by 12-inch pan with a 1-inch lip, but I have successfully roasted chicken and vegetables on a large jelly roll pan of similar dimensions.

With the chicken on the roasting pan, pull back the skin from each leg and thigh, sprinkling them with salt, pepper, and an herb if you like. To loosen the breast skin, cut under the skin along the breastbone, seasoning the breast as you have the legs and thighs. If preparing roast chicken for a special dinner or if you have a little more time, rub the meat with a garlic/herb paste. After pulling the skin back in place, drizzle the chicken with a little olive oil or rub it with softened butter. If you use butter, however, the chicken skin has to be thoroughly dry.

Since the average home oven takes ten to twelve minutes to reach 450 degrees, you don't have to wait until it's fully preheated. As soon as the chicken and vegetables are prepared, put the pan in the oven. After that, you're done until dinner.

▼

If you want to make a pan sauce to go with the chicken, do not line the roasting pan with foil. After removing the chicken and vegetables, place the roasting pan on two burners set on medium heat and pour ¼ cup each dry vermouth or white wine and chicken broth into the pan, stirring carefully to loosen the brown bits. You can roast two butterflied chickens in the 18- by 12-inch pan, but you'll need a second shallow pan if roasting vegetables too. Before pre-heating the oven, adjust the racks to the upper and lower-middle positions, then roast the chickens on the top rack and the vegetables on the lower rack.

One final benefit of a butterflied chicken—it's a breeze to carve. Just one cut down the breast with kitchen shears or a chef's knife, and all that's left is a quick snip of the skin holding each leg to each breast.

vegetables that roast well Although many vegetables roast well, the following are a few that complement the chicken and roast in about the same amount of time. (Tomatoes are the only exception.) If using an 18- by 12-inch pan, you should be able to fit two of the following vegetables in the pan with the chicken.

- 4 yellow onions. Remove loose outer skins but it is not necessary to peel them. Halve the onions, then toss them with a generous drizzling of olive oil and season with salt and pepper.
- 4 red bliss potatoes or small russet potatoes. Scrub, halve, toss with a generous drizzling of olive oil, and season with salt and pepper.
- 8 new potatoes. Scrub, halve, toss with a generous drizzling of olive oil, and season with salt and pepper.
- 8 Italian plum tomatoes. Halve lengthwise, toss with a generous drizzling of olive oil, and season with salt and pepper. (Tomatoes are the only vegetable added to the pan part-way through cooking.)
- 4 ears of corn. Shuck, brush with softened butter, and wrap in foil.
- 1 pound of cauliflower. Cut into large florets, toss with a generous drizzling of olive oil, and season with salt and pepper.

FOOD&WINE test-kitchen tips

- The easiest way to remove the backbone is with kitchen shears.

 wine recommendation A broad range of possibilities will work here, but if you make the lemon, rosemary, and garlic variation, try a highly perfumed Pinot Gris from Alsace, which will match the equally aromatic rosemary.

no–hassle roast chicken If your chicken is larger than the suggested size, make sure to increase roasting time.

SERVES 4

> 1   chicken (3 to 3½ pounds), rinsed, patted dry, and butterflied (see page 95)
> Salt and ground black pepper
> 2   tablespoons olive oil or softened butter

1 Adjust the oven rack to the lower-middle position and heat the oven to 450 degrees. After butterflying the chicken, place it on a foil-lined 18- by 12-inch or similar-sized shallow roasting pan. Season under the skin with salt and pepper. Pat the skin back in place and drizzle with oil or rub with butter.

2 Roast until the chicken is golden brown and its juices run clear, about 40 minutes. Let stand 5 minutes, then cut it into two breast/wing pieces and two leg/thigh pieces. Serve.

roast chicken with lemon, rosemary, and garlic

rosemary-garlic rub

> 1   teaspoon fine-grated lemon zest
> 2   garlic cloves, minced
> 1½ teaspoons minced fresh rosemary leaves
> ½   teaspoon salt
> ¼   teaspoon pepper
> ½   lemon

1 Mix the first five ingredients in a small bowl.

2 Follow the No-Hassle Roast Chicken recipe, rubbing the herb paste under the loosened skin. Roast the chicken for 30 minutes. Squeeze the lemon over the chicken. Return to the oven and continue to roast until juices run clear, 5 to 10 minutes longer.

Roasted tomatoes and potatoes partner well with this chicken. Arrange prepared potatoes, cut side down, in a single layer on the pan and roast alongside the chicken. After 20 minutes, add the prepared tomatoes, cut side up. Continue to roast until chicken is done, squeezing lemon juice on at the appropriate time, for 20 minutes longer.

chicken & other birds

97

grilled chicken gai yang

from Cracking the Coconut

MAKES 6 SERVINGS

This chicken tastes best if marinated overnight or for at least 3 to 4 hours. Cooking time is about 1 hour. After grilling, you can keep the chicken warm and moist for up to 30 minutes by wrapping it in aluminum foil, and placing it in a 150°F oven. You can also grill it ahead, cool it completely, and refrigerate. Reheat in a 500°F oven, uncovered, for 5 minutes, then lower the heat to 300°F and cook for another 10 minutes, or until hot.

for the marinade

2   tablespoons Big Four Paste (recipe follows)

One 1-inch chunk fresh ginger, minced

8   cloves garlic, minced

1   teaspoon cumin seeds, dry-roasted (see page 100) and ground

1   teaspoon caraway seeds, dry-roasted (see page 100) and ground

One 2-inch chunk fresh turmeric, peeled and minced,
     or 1 teaspoon turmeric powder

3   tablespoons vegetable oil

One 3-pound chicken, fat trimmed, halved lengthwise, rinsed thoroughly, and patted dry
Vegetable oil spray

For the marinade, in a medium mixing bowl, combine the Big Four Paste, ginger, garlic, cumin, caraway, and turmeric. Whisk in the oil until well blended.

Place a chicken half, skin side down, on a chopping board. Pound with a mallet or heavy frying pan to crack the bones and flatten slightly. Flip it over and repeat the process. Repeat with the other half.

FOOD&WINE test-kitchen tips

- Without an outdoor grill in our test kitchen, we found that you can make this chicken very nicely in a covered grill pan over medium-high heat. Allow about half an hour rather than an hour after the original searing.

- For authenticity, you can certainly chop the finished chicken into bite-size pieces as suggested, but we simply cut it into 8 pieces. In a Western menu, it serves 4.

wine recommendation When serving a dish flavored with ginger, look for a wine that has a strong aromatic profile of its own. Two distinctive possibilities are Scheurebe from Germany, and Viognier, the traditional white grape of the northern Rhône Valley.

Transfer the marinade to a large Ziploc bag, add the chicken halves, seal the bag, and toss the chicken pieces until coated with the marinade. Let sit at room temperature for at least 30 minutes or up to 1 hour. Or refrigerate and marinate for at least 3 hours, or overnight; remove the chicken from the refrigerator at least an hour before cooking to allow it to reach room temperature.

Prepare the grill. (Set a gas grill to medium-high.) When the coals are white-hot, spray the chicken generously with vegetable oil spray and put it skin side down on the hot grill. Sear for 1 to 2 minutes, or until the skin is golden. Flip it over and spray the top with vegetable oil spray. After 1 to 2 minutes, cover the coals with ashes or remove the chicken from the grill and lightly spray the coals with water to cool them. Return the chicken to the grill to continue cooking. (If you are using a gas grill, lower the heat to medium.) Cover the grill and grill-roast the chicken for about 1 hour, checking frequently and turning occasionally to prevent burning. When the chicken is completely cooked, the juices will run clear if you prick the thigh joint and an instant-read thermometer inserted in the thigh will read 160°F. Transfer to a platter, tent with foil to keep hot, and let rest for 10 minutes until ready to serve. Chop into bite-sized pieces and serve.

the big four paste *glurh, ka-tiem, prikk thai, rugg pakk chee* The Big Four Paste, which can be made ahead and refrigerated for a month, is extremely versatile. For pungency, this ancient recipe relies on white peppercorns, which are gentler and more subtle than chiles. First you smell the wonderful aroma from the roasted peppercorns, then, as you eat, you experience a gentle rush of warmth that lingers. For a less pungent paste, decrease the peppercorns to 2 teaspoons and the coriander seeds to 1 teaspoon. If you are concerned about salt, you can leave it out, though I wouldn't advise it. Here, salt helps preserve the paste as well as bring out its flavor.

MAKES ¾ CUP

1 tablespoon coriander seeds
2 tablespoons Thai white peppercorns
1 teaspoon sea salt
12 to 15 cloves garlic, minced (½ cup)
1 cup minced cilantro stems and roots

▼

to prepare with a mortar and pestle Heat a 7-inch skillet over medium-high heat. Add the coriander seeds and dry-roast, sliding the skillet back and forth over the burner, until the seeds are fragrant, about 3 minutes. Transfer the seeds to a small bowl to cool and repeat with the peppercorns. When cool, grind the coriander seeds and peppercorns separately in an electric spice or coffee grinder and transfer to separate bowls.

  Place a mortar on top of a damp towel on the kitchen counter, preferably waist-high. Add the sea salt and garlic to the mortar and pound them together by holding the pestle securely in the center of your palm and pounding straight up and down into the center of the mortar. Use a spoon or spatula to scrape the ingredients from the sides into the center of the mortar as needed, and pound until a paste forms. Add the cilantro roots and stems and pound to a smooth paste. Add the ground coriander and peppercorn powders and pound and blend until the paste is smooth. Transfer the paste to a jar, seal, and refrigerate.

to prepare with a food processor Roast and grind the coriander seeds and peppercorns as above. Fit the food processor with the steel blade. Add the sea salt, garlic, and cilantro roots and stems and pulse until finely minced, scraping down the side of the bowl frequently. Add the ground spices and process to a paste. Transfer to a jar, seal, and refrigerate.

cook's note The paste made in the food processor will be coarser than paste made using the mortar and pestle.

dry-roasting *pow* Dry-roasting is the process of roasting dried spices, chiles, and raw or cooked rice in a shallow pan or skillet without oil or liquid. Dry-roasting cooks the surface of these ingredients and turns them golden brown, producing a smoky and very slightly burnt flavor.

  To dry-roast, use a 7- or 8-inch shallow saucepan or skillet. Add a tablespoon or two of the spices called for in the recipe, or, if roasting chiles, rice, coconut, seeds, or nuts, enough to make a single layer in the pan, leaving plenty of room for the ingredients to be shaken around. Cook over high heat, sliding the pan constantly back and forth over the burner, for 1 minute, then lower the heat to medium. Roast for several more minutes, or until you can smell the aroma of the ingredients and they turn brown. Remove from the heat and transfer to a plate to cool completely. Store in a tightly sealed jar at room temperature.

melicia's chicken and dumplings

from *Staff Meals from Chanterelle*

SERVES 8

No matter how finely tuned or worldly our adult palates may become, each of us has favorite dishes from our childhoods that never fail to please. When Melicia was growing up, her grandmother and mother made this homey dish often. And Melicia carried on the tradition: When she joined the kitchen at Chanterelle, it was one of her first contributions to our staff meal. The light, fluffy dumplings are gently steamed on top of the simmering stew, allowing them to absorb all of the stew's wonderful aroma and flavors as they puff up, creating the epitome of comfort food.

for the stew

2   chickens (3 to 3½ pounds each)
2   tablespoons canola or other vegetable oil
2   small onions, diced
2   large cloves garlic, minced
1   cup dry white wine
8   cups chicken stock, canned low-sodium chicken broth, or water
1   teaspoon dried thyme leaves
3   bay leaves
10   grinds of black pepper
Small pinch of cayenne pepper
4   medium carrots, peeled and cut into ½-inch rounds
3   large white turnips, peeled and diced
Coarse (kosher) salt, to taste

for the dumplings

2   cups all-purpose flour
4   teaspoons baking powder
1½ teaspoons salt
1   teaspoon snipped fresh chives
1   teaspoon chopped fresh flat-leaf parsley leaves
1   cup milk
Walnut-size piece of *beurre manié* (see page 103), chilled

▼

chicken & other birds

1 Rinse the chickens, inside and out, under cold running water, removing any excess fat. Cut each chicken into ten pieces and pat dry with paper towels.

2 Heat the oil in a large Dutch oven or large, wide, flameproof casserole over medium-high heat. When it just begins to smoke, add only enough chicken pieces to fit into the pot without touching and sauté until well browned on all sides, about 4 minutes per side. Using tongs, transfer the chicken to a platter and set aside while you sauté the remaining pieces.

3 When all the chicken pieces have been removed from the pot, add the onions and garlic and reduce the heat to medium low. Sauté, stirring occasionally, until the onions are softened but not browned, about 5 minutes.

4 Return the chicken to the pot, along with any accumulated juices, and add the wine. Increase the heat to medium high and bring to a boil. Cook, uncovered, until the wine is reduced by half, about 5 minutes, then add the chicken stock, thyme, bay leaves, black pepper, and cayenne. Bring to a boil, then reduce the heat to low and cook at barely a simmer, partially covered, until the chicken is almost done, about 1 hour, uncovering occasionally to skim any foam.

5 Add the carrots and turnips and continue simmering until the chicken is very tender and almost (but not quite) falling off the bone and the vegetables are tender, about 15 minutes.

6 Meanwhile, prepare the batter for the dumplings. Combine the flour, baking powder, salt, chives, and parsley in a medium-size bowl and whisk thoroughly to mix. Pour in the milk and stir to make a thick batter. Set aside.

7 Using a slotted spoon, gently transfer the chicken pieces to a bowl or platter and set them aside. Remove and discard the bay leaves. Taste the broth and add salt as necessary, then add the chilled *beurre manié* and whisk until it is completely incorporated and the liquid is somewhat thickened. Return the chicken to the pot and bring to a simmer.

FOOD&WINE *test-kitchen tips*

- You can cut this recipe in half without a problem.

wine recommendation Comforting dishes call for simple wines. A Mâcon-Villages from Burgundy will be the perfect complement to this dish.

8 Drop the dumpling batter by the tablespoonful directly onto the simmering stew. You should have sixteen dumplings. The dumplings will expand quite a bit, so don't crowd them too much; leave about an inch between them. Cover tightly and simmer over low heat for exactly 15 minutes. Don't be tempted to peek; after 15 minutes the dumplings will be perfect.

9 Remove from the heat and serve directly from the pot, or transfer the chicken and vegetables to a platter, surrounding them with the dumplings and spooning the sauce over everything.

beurre manié *Beurre manié* (kneaded butter) is a mixture of equal parts softened unsalted butter and all-purpose flour that is thoroughly worked together to form a paste. It is used as a thickener for a variety of sauces and stews and, in particular, to slightly thicken the simmering gravies of braised meat dishes if they appear to be a bit too thin. It should be whisked quickly into the liquid, which then should be allowed to simmer until the flour loses its raw, starchy taste, at least 15 minutes more.

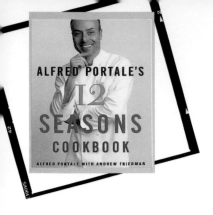

ALFRED PORTALE'S 12 SEASONS COOKBOOK

ALFRED PORTALE WITH ANDREW FRIEDMAN

grilled chicken marinated in cumin, lemon, and garlic

from *Alfred Portale's 12 Seasons Cookbook*

MAKES 4 SERVINGS

This Middle Eastern chicken recipe employs one of my favorite techniques for a marinade—making a paste of puréed vegetables. In this case, onion and garlic are combined in a food processor and the mixture is liquefied with oil. Toasted and ground coriander seeds, cumin, and cinnamon are added, creating a highly seasoned paste that is used to coat the chicken pieces. To ensure an intense penetration of flavors, the chicken is marinated overnight.

The following day, the excess marinade is scraped off, and the chicken is seasoned and grilled over charcoal. The result is a wonderful dialogue between the fresh acidity of the lemon, the smokiness of the grill, and the fragrant spices—a sublime contrast that welcomes the company of any number of grilled vegetables. (See Variations.)

This dish also provides delicious leftovers and will travel well for a picnic.

thinking ahead Ideally, the chicken should be marinated overnight.

1½ tablespoons cracked white peppercorns

2 teaspoons coarsely ground cumin

1 teaspoon coarsely cracked coriander seeds

½ teaspoon ground cinnamon

1 cup chopped onion

¼ cup fresh lemon juice

¼ cup canola oil

4 tablespoons chopped fresh flat-leaf parsley

2 tablespoons grated lemon zest

12 cloves garlic, peeled, mashed to a paste, and sprinkled with coarse salt

2 3-pound free-range chickens, quartered

Coarse salt to taste

In a sauté pan, combine the peppercorns, cumin, coriander seeds, and cinnamon; toast the spices, shaking the pan gently, over medium heat for about 1 minute, until fragrant. Take care not to burn them. Transfer them to a food processor or spice grinder and pulse to blend.

In a stainless-steel mixing bowl, combine the onion, lemon juice, canola oil, parsley, lemon zest, and garlic. Season the chicken with the ground spices, then add the chicken pieces to the bowl with the marinade. Mix well. Put the chicken in a dish, cover, and refrigerate for at least 8 hours.

Build a charcoal fire in a grill and let the coals burn until covered with white ash. Spread them out in the grill. Lightly oil the grill grate.

Lift the chicken from the dish and scrape off the excess marinade. Season the chicken with salt, and grill it, turning the pieces several times, for 20 to 25 minutes, or until the chicken is cooked through and the thigh juices run clear when pricked with a small, sharp knife.

what to drink Serve this dish with a high-quality microbrew, preferably an amber lager.

variations Serve the chicken with grilled eggplant or squash, and/or with spinach, fava beans, or couscous.

FOOD&WINE test-kitchen tips

- You can make this recipe indoors, too. We broiled it for 25 to 30 minutes, turning it once.
- The chef suggests a stainless-steel bowl for mixing the marinade. The point is to avoid a metal such as aluminum that would react with the lemon juice to produce an off flavor. Glass is also fine.

peppery chicken curry

from *Savoring the Spice Coast of India*

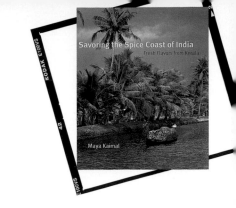

SERVES 6

A Christian friend, Celine Sani, served this dish to our family over twenty years ago, and my father could never forget it. The curry has a nice balance of sweet coconut milk and pungent peppercorns, but it's the cashews that are the surprise. Serve with any vegetable stir-fry and plain rice.

Ground masala

- 2 teaspoons coriander
- 2 teaspoons cumin
- ½ teaspoon turmeric

1¼ teaspoons black peppercorns, coarsely ground with a mortar and pestle

1 teaspoon salt

2 pounds boneless skinless chicken thighs, trimmed and cut into 1-inch cubes

4 tablespoons vegetable oil

2 cups sliced onion

1½ teaspoons minced garlic

1½ teaspoons minced ginger

1 teaspoon minced fresh green chili (serrano or Thai)

¾ cup canned coconut milk

1 tablespoon Ghee (page 64) or butter

½ cup halved or broken raw cashews

1 teaspoon fresh lemon juice

1 Mix together the ground masala, black pepper, and ¼ teaspoon of the salt. Rub the chicken pieces with this mixture and refrigerate for 1 hour.

▼

FOOD&WINE *test-kitchen tips*

- Be sure to use unsweetened coconut milk, not the kind for piña coladas.

 wine recommendation One of the hottest wines of the moment, Grüner Veltliner from Austria has its own bit of pepperiness and will be perfect for this difficult-to-match dish. Check the label for the word Smaragd, which indicates the fullest bodied of the Veltliners.

2 In a wide deep nonstick pan heat the oil over medium-high heat and sauté onions until they are medium brown. Add the garlic, ginger, and green chili and fry for 1 minute. Put in the marinated chicken and remaining ¾ teaspoon salt and fry, stirring frequently until the chicken pieces lose their pink color. Stir in ¼ cup of the coconut milk and ¼ cup water, cover, and simmer for about 30 minutes over low heat.

3 Heat the ghee or butter in a frying pan. Sauté the cashews until golden brown, stirring constantly over medium heat. Set aside.

4 When the chicken is cooked add the remaining ½ cup coconut milk. Bring to a simmer and remove from the heat. Stir in the lemon juice and taste for salt. Garnish with cashews and serve.

MARINATING TIME: 1 HOUR

PREPARATION TIME: 1 HOUR

RECIPE MAY BE PREPARED IN ADVANCE THROUGH STEP 3

roasted cornish hens with apricot–pine nut mole

pollitos en mole de chabacano y piñon

from *Mexico One Plate at a Time*

SERVES 4, WITH WELCOME LEFTOVERS OF SAUCE (WITH THE HENS, YOU'LL SERVE LESS THAN HALF OF THE 7 CUPS *MOLE* YOU MAKE)

5	ounces (3 medium) tomatillos, husked and rinsed
½	cup (about 2½ ounces) sesame seeds
½	cup rich-tasting pork lard or vegetable oil, plus a little more if necessary
12	medium (6 ounces total) dried ancho chiles, stemmed and seeded
4	garlic cloves, peeled
⅔	cup (about 3 ounces) pine nuts
⅔	cup (about 4 ounces) dried apricots, coarsely chopped
7	cups chicken broth, plus a little more if needed, store-bought or homemade
½	teaspoon cinnamon, preferably freshly ground Mexican *canela*
¼	teaspoon black pepper, preferably freshly ground

A scant ⅛ teaspoon cloves, preferably freshly ground

1	ounce (about one-third of a 3.3-ounce tablet) Mexican chocolate, roughly chopped
1	slice firm white bread, darkly toasted and broken into several pieces

Salt

4 to 5 tablespoons sugar

4 Cornish game hens (each about 1¼ pounds)

A little vegetable oil for the hens

Sprigs of watercress or fresh flat-leaf parsley for garnish

1 getting started To ensure success and to make this rather complex preparation as simple as possible, first set out all the ingredients, completing basic preparations as described: Husk and rinse the tomatillos, stem and seed the dried chiles, peel the garlic, grind the spices if you're using whole, toast the bread, chop the chocolate.

Spread the tomatillos on a baking sheet and roast them 4 inches below a very hot broiler until darkly roasted, even blackened in spots, about 5 minutes. Flip them over and roast on the other side for 4 or 5 minutes, until splotchy-black, blistered and soft.

Set out two large bowls and scrape the tomatillos, juice and all, into one of them. Set out a pair of tongs and a slotted spoon.

▼

2 initial toasting and frying In an ungreased small skillet over medium heat, toast the sesame seeds, stirring constantly, until golden, about 5 minutes. Scrape *two-thirds* of them in with the tomatillos; set the rest aside for garnish.

Measure the lard or oil into a large (8- to 9-quart) pot (preferably a Dutch oven or Mexican *cazuela*) and set over medium heat. Turn on an exhaust fan or open a window or door. Tear the chiles into flat pieces, and, when the lard or oil is hot, fry the chiles, three or four pieces at a time, flipping them nearly continually with the tongs, until their interior side has changed to a lighter color, about 20 to 30 seconds total frying time. Don't toast so darkly that they begin to smoke—that would make the *mole* bitter. As they're done, remove them to the empty bowl, being careful to drain as much fat as possible back into the pot. Cover the toasted chiles with hot tap water and place a small plate on them to keep them submerged. Let stand for about 30 minutes.

Meanwhile, remove any stray chile seeds left in the fat. With the pot still over medium heat, fry the garlic, stirring regularly, until browned and soft, about 5 minutes. With the slotted spoon, remove to the tomatillo bowl, draining as much fat as possible back into the pot. Add the pine nuts to the pot and stir until they're lightly toasted, 1 to 2 minutes. Remove with the slotted spoon, letting as much fat as possible drain back into the pot, and add to the tomatillo bowl. Add the apricots as well.

3 blending and straining Use tongs to transfer the rehydrated chiles to a blender, leaving the soaking liquid behind. Taste the soaking liquid, and, if it is not bitter, measure 2½ cups into the blender. If it is, throw it away and measure in 2½ cups water. Blend the chiles to a smooth puree, adding a little extra water if necessary to keep the mixture moving through the blades. Press the chile mixture through a medium-mesh strainer back into the empty chile-soaking bowl.

FOOD&WINE test-kitchen tips

- As noted in this recipe, the sauce quantity is over double what's needed for the hens. You can cut the quantity in half, of course. But we loved the complex melded flavor of the sauce so much that we were glad to have extra and found it was excellent on chicken, pork, and shrimp.

 wine recommendation Sauces made from fresh and dried fruits call for a wine that is just the slightest bit sweet, or off-dry. Try a flavor-packed Kabinett Riesling from Germany's Rheingau region.

Without washing the blender jar, scrape the tomatillo mixture into it. Add *1 cup* of the broth along with the cinnamon, pepper, cloves, chocolate and bread. Blend to a smooth puree, adding a little extra broth if necessary to keep the mixture moving. Press through the strainer back into the tomatillo bowl.

4 searing and simmering Check the fat in the pot: If there's more than a light coating over the bottom, pour off the excess; if the pot's pretty dry, film the bottom with a little more lard or oil. Set over medium-high heat. When quite hot, scrape in the chile puree and stir nearly constantly until the mixture has darkened considerably and thickened to the consistency of tomato paste, 10 to 15 minutes. Add the tomatillo puree and continue stirring until once again the mixture has thickened to the consistency of tomato paste, another 5 to 10 minutes.

Add the remaining *6 cups* broth to the pot and stir to combine thoroughly. Partially cover, reduce the heat to medium-low and simmer gently, stirring occasionally, for 45 minutes. Check the consistency: The *mole* should be thick enough to coat a spoon, but not too thickly. If it's too thin, simmer it briskly over medium to medium-high heat until a little thicker; if too thick, stir in a little water.

Taste and season with salt, usually about 1 teaspoon, and the sugar (if you're new to seasoning *mole,* keep in mind that it's a delicate balance of salty, sweet and spicy; it's best to start with the minimum quantities I've suggested, then refine the seasoning just before serving). Keep warm, over very low heat, partially covered, while you roast the hens.

5 roasting and serving the cornish hens Heat the oven to 450°F. Rinse the hens and pat dry. Tie the legs together and twist the last joint of the wings up over the breast and then down behind the "shoulders," tucking them in firmly to keep them in place. Lightly oil a large roasting pan and place the birds in it, breast side up and legs facing out. Brush or spray the hens with a little oil and sprinkle them generously with salt. Roast for about 35 minutes, until the juices run clear when the thighs are pierced with a knife.

Ladle a generous amount of *mole* onto each of four warm dinner plates. Set the hens into the sauce, sprinkle liberally with the reserved sesame seeds and decorate with watercress or parsley. Your very special dinner is ready.

working ahead *Mole* can be successfully made ahead—even getting better after 2 or 3 days in the refrigerator; cover well. Just before serving, roast the hens and warm the *mole.*

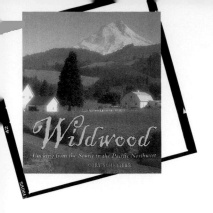

duck breast with mushroom spaetzle and red wine– braised cabbage

from *Wildwood*

SERVES 4 AS AN ENTRÉE

Spaetzle is a classic Austrian noodle. The batter is passed through a perforated pan into boiling water to produce the noodles, which are then cooked in hot butter until golden brown and crispy. By introducing vegetable purées or ground spices into the mix, you can transform this somewhat uneventful white noodle into an innovative starch. This recipe adds dried mushrooms to the spaetzle dough and is a great duck accompaniment.

mushroom spaetzle

½	cup milk
2	tablespoons ground dried mushrooms (use a spice mill)
1	cup flour
1	large egg, beaten
2	tablespoons minced mixed fresh thyme, flat-leaf parsley, and chives
1	teaspoon salt
½	teaspoon ground white pepper

2	whole cloves
1	teaspoon fennel seeds
1	teaspoon juniper berries
4	tablespoons unsalted butter
1	small red onion, halved vertically and cut into crescents
1	small head red cabbage, cored and thinly sliced
2½	teaspoons salt
2½	teaspoons freshly ground black pepper
½	cup Merlot
½	cup apple cider
4	boneless duck breasts, trimmed of excess fat

To make the spaetzle dough: In a small saucepan, heat the milk over low heat just until it simmers. Remove from heat, stir in the ground mushrooms, and let stand for 15 minutes. In a large bowl, combine the milk mixture, flour, egg, herbs, salt, and pepper. Mix the batter until smooth, cover, and refrigerate for 1 hour.

To cook the spaetzle: Bring a large pot of salted water to a rolling boil. Place a colander or perforated pan over (not touching) the boiling water. Pour the batter into the colander or pan. Using a rubber spatula or your hand, quickly press the batter though the holes into the boiling water. Once all of the batter has been forced though the holes, remove the colander or pan. Stir the spaetzle and cook for 1 minute. Drain well and toss with a little olive oil; set aside.

To make the cabbage: In a spice mill, grind the cloves, fennel, and juniper; set aside.

In a 4-quart pot, melt 2 tablespoons of the butter over medium heat. Add the onion and sauté for 3 minutes, or until translucent. Mix in the cabbage, 1 teaspoon of the salt, and 1 teaspoon of the pepper and cook until the cabbage begins to wilt. Stir in the wine, cider, and spices. Cover and cook, stirring frequently, for 25 to 30 minutes, or until the cabbage is soft to the bite.

To prepare the duck: Heat 2 heavy sauté pans or skillets over high heat. Season the duck with 1 teaspoon of the salt and 1 teaspoon of the pepper and add to the pan, skin-side down. Cook for 4 to 5 minutes, using the rendered fat to baste the meat. Reduce heat and cook the duck for 10 to 12 minutes, or until the skin is crisp. Turn over the breasts and cook for 1 minute. Remove from heat, cover, and let stand for 5 minutes.

To finish the spaetzle: Using a 10-inch nonstick skillet, melt the remaining 2 tablespoons butter over medium-high heat. Add the spaetzle, season with the remaining ½ teaspoon each salt and pepper, and cook until brown and crispy.

To serve, portion the braised cabbage and spaetzle onto each plate. Thinly slice each duck breast and place on top.

FOOD&WINE test-kitchen tips

- Spaetzle is wonderful, but if you don't want to take the time to make it, the duck and cabbage also go beautifully with buttered egg noodles.

wine recommendation The bold flavors here call for a big red, such as the Syrah-based wine from the northern Rhône Valley. For a special treat, try a bottle from one of the best towns, such as Côte-Rôtie or Hermitage.

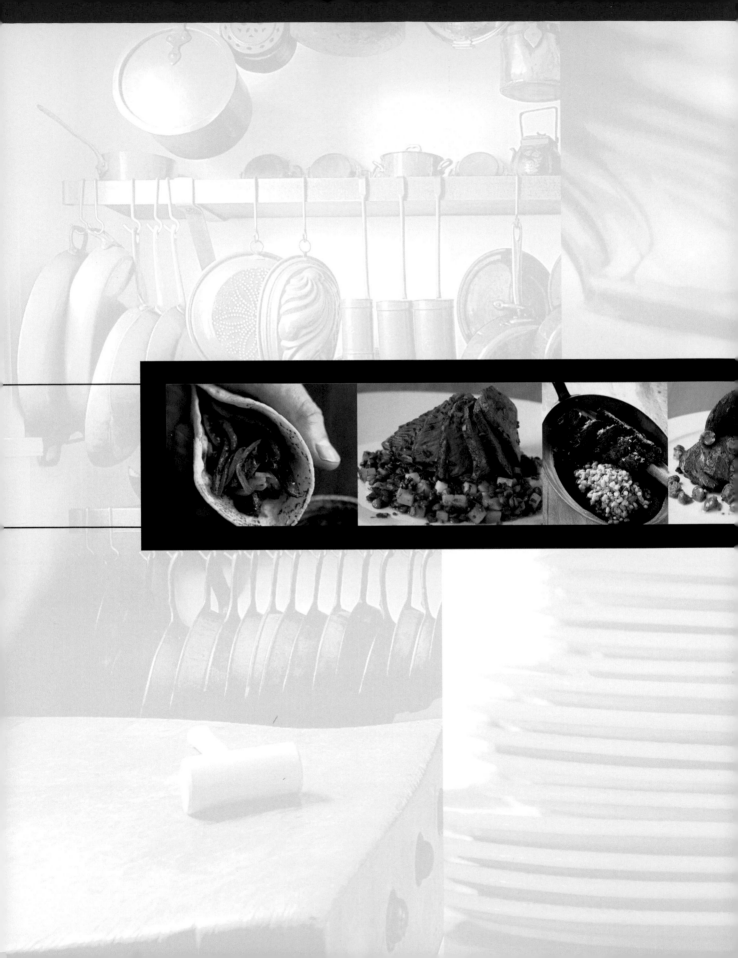

pork, veal, beef & lamb

stir-fried pork and tomato
hong san du (from Yunnan)

from *Hot Sour Salty Sweet*

SERVES 2 TO 4 AS PART OF A RICE MEAL

Chunks of tart green tomato, softened in the hot wok, give this Yunnanese stir-fry a fresh distinctive taste though it also works well with ripe red tomatoes. There is some heat from the chiles (this will vary with the chiles you have available) and a smooth succulence from the chopped pork and the dash of sesame oil that rounds out the dish. Make this just before you wish to serve it; it will take you less than ten minutes. Leftovers (if you're lucky) are delicious the next day.

⅓	pound pork (such as trimmed shoulder or butt)
2 to 3	long medium-hot green chiles (such as Cubanelles, Anaheim, or Hungarian wax)
2	tablespoons peanut or vegetable oil
½	pound tomatoes, preferably mixed red and green, cut into ¾-inch dice (about 2 cups)
¾	teaspoon salt, or to taste
1	teaspoon roasted sesame oil
1	teaspoon cornstarch, dissolved in 2 tablespoons water

Use a cleaver to thinly slice the pork, then cut crosswise to coarsely mince. Set aside.

Trim the stems from the chiles, then make one cut lengthwise in each to expose the seeds; strip them out and discard. Roll-cut the chiles crosswise on the diagonal into approximately ¾-inch chunks: Lay each one on the cutting board and slice, rotating the chile a quarter turn between slices. You should have about 1 cup.

FOOD&WINE test-kitchen tips

- We can't always find the peppers called for in this recipe and therefore tried jalapeños. The dish was delicious. If you make this substitution, be sure to taste the chiles before adding them to the pan. If they're fiery (a rarity with the jalapeños available these days), cut back on the quantity.

 wine recommendation The acidity in tomatoes can pose a real challenge to the wine enthusiast. A red wine that is fruity but not tannic will be your best bet. Try the charming Rosso di Montalcino, whose earthiness will also be right at home with the pork.

Place all the ingredients near your stovetop. Have a serving plate ready.

Heat a wok or large heavy skillet over high heat until hot, then add the oil. When the oil is hot, add the pork and stir-fry, separating the meat to expose all surfaces to the heat, until it has all changed color, about 2 minutes. Add the chiles and tomatoes and stir-fry for about 3 minutes, until the chiles are beginning to soften and the tomatoes are getting tender. Add the salt and stir-fry for another minute or so, until the chiles are softened and the tomatoes are soft but still have some shape, then add the sesame oil. Stir briefly, then stir the cornstarch mixture well and add it to the wok. Stir-fry for about 30 seconds, until the sauce thickens, then turn out onto the serving plate and serve hot.

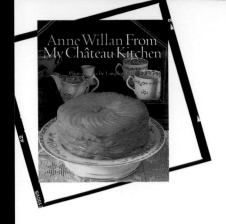

pork chops with
mustard and bacon

from *From My Château Kitchen*

SERVES 4

Even older than the Burgundian taste for spices is the love of mustard, a favorite of the Romans. The great dukes of Burgundy liked to speed parting guests with the gift of a barrel of mustard. Legend has it that the name derives from 1382, when Duke Philip the Bold of Burgundy granted the city of Dijon a coat of arms bearing the motto "*Moulte Me Tarde* (Much Awaits Me)," a trademark adopted by today's mustard makers. A more likely derivation is equally picturesque: *moulte ardre* means "much burning." No matter what the origins, the name refers to a type of mustard, not to the place where it is made. Dijon mustard must contain only black mustard seeds (the strongest and most expensive), which are stripped of their skin before grinding. Mustard from Meaux, just east of Paris, is more coarsely ground and includes the skins, giving a rougher texture, darker color, and less intense taste. As for the mustard from Bordeaux, smooth, mild, and often flavored with herbs, Burgundians dismiss it as effeminate.

It is no accident that the traditional centers of French mustard production are famous for their wines (Meaux borders Champagne). Good French mustard needs wine vinegar or verjuice (the juice of sour grapes), and often wine itself to develop characteristic flavors that vary from region to region. Recipes of the top Dijon manufacturers—Maille, Grey Poupon, and the like—are secret and all are subject to appellation controlée quality standards. Most Dijon mustard has a clean, sharp taste, designed to be a condiment though it is also perfect for cooking. Do not, however, overheat mustard as this destroys the enzymes that contribute much to its taste—mustard in a sauce should always be added toward the end of cooking or it will turn bitter.

FOOD&WINE test-kitchen tips

- A bouquet garni is defined by Anne Willan in her glossary as ". . . a sprig of thyme, a bay leaf, and several sprigs of parsley, tied together with string." If you don't have a sprig of thyme, a quarter teaspoon of dried leaves will do fine. In this case, tie the herbs in cheesecloth or put them in a small tea ball and suspend it from the edge of the pan.

 wine recommendation This dish, with its pork, mustard, and bacon, calls for a medium-bodied red wine. And the richness of the cream begs for high acidity to refresh the palate between bites. Look for a Cru Beaujolais, a wine from one of the best villages in the Beaujolais area: Brouilly, Chénas, Chiroubles, Côte de Brouilly, Fleurie, Juliénas, Morgon, Moulin-à-Vent, Régnié, or St-Amour.

This modest little dish is a mainstay of many a Burgundian bistro where it is served with boiled or panfried potatoes. The few ingredients complement each other just right. Choose thick pork chops so they serve four people generously.

4   thick pork chops
2 to 3 tablespoons flour
Salt and pepper
1   tablespoon vegetable oil
A 4-oz/125-g piece of lean bacon, diced
¾   cup/175 ml dry white wine
1   cup/250 ml veal or chicken stock, more if needed
A bouquet garni
½   cup/125 ml crème fraîche or heavy cream
1   tablespoon Dijon-style mustard, or to taste
1   tablespoon chopped parsley

Heat the oven to 350°F/175°C. Put the flour in a shallow bowl and season it with salt and pepper. Coat the pork chops with the flour, patting to remove any excess, and set them aside. Heat the oil in a sauté pan or deep frying pan with an ovenproof handle and fry the bacon until browned. Remove the bacon and set it aside. Add the chops to the pan and brown them well, 2 to 3 minutes on each side. Pour in the wine and simmer with the chops for 2 minutes. Add the stock and the bouquet garni, and replace the bacon. Cover the pan, transfer it to the oven, and cook until the chops are very tender when pierced with a two-pronged fork, 1 to 1¼ hours. Turn them from time to time, and add more stock if at any time the pan seems dry.

Transfer the chops to a warm serving dish or individual plates and keep them warm. Add the cream to the pan and bring the sauce to a boil, stirring to dissolve the pan juices. After 3 to 5 minutes, take the pan from the heat, discard the bouquet garni, and whisk in the mustard, parsley, salt, and pepper. Taste and adjust the seasoning, adding more mustard to your taste; don't let the sauce come back to a boil once you've added the mustard. Spoon the sauce over the chops and serve them right away.

My Mother's
Southern Entertaining

James Villas with Martha Pearl Villas

barbecued country-style pork ribs

from *My Mother's Southern Entertaining*

8 SERVINGS

Cut from the shoulder end of the loin, country-style pork ribs have not only the highest meat-to-bone ratio but the least fat of all ribs. While most people just plop the ribs on a grill and brush them with a commercial barbecue sauce (a method that almost guarantees toughness), Mother first simmers hers slowly till fork-tender, then finishes them off in the oven with a tangy homemade sauce. And trust me, never will you taste better ribs. Just be careful not to burn the sauce by baking the ribs too long.

8	meaty country-style pork ribs
¼	cup vegetable oil
1	medium-size onion, finely chopped
1	celery rib, finely chopped
1	garlic clove, minced
1½	cups water
1	cup catsup
½	cup cider vinegar
3	tablespoons Worcestershire sauce
1	tablespoon chili powder
1	tablespoon firmly packed dark brown sugar
1	teaspoon dry mustard
1	teaspoon salt
1	teaspoon black pepper

Arrange the ribs in a large pot, add enough water to cover, and bring to a boil, skimming the top if there's any froth. Reduce the heat to low, cover, and simmer the ribs till fork-tender, about 2 hours.

FOOD&WINE test-kitchen tips

- It's wisely suggested here that you save the liquid from simmering the ribs to moisten them as needed and to keep leftovers from drying out. The broth is definitely too good to throw away. We'd keep it all in any case—to use for risotto, in sauces, as the base for a quick soup, or anytime a light stock is needed. If you don't have an immediate use for it, stick it in the freezer.

 wine recommendation Classic barbecued ribs call for the all-American wine, Zinfandel, a varietal found virtually only in California. The fruity, full-flavored wine will stand up to the tangy sauce.

Meanwhile, heat the oil in a large, heavy, stainless steel or enameled saucepan over moderate heat, then add the onion, celery, and garlic and stir for about 5 minutes. Add the remaining ingredients and stir till well blended. Bring the sauce to a simmer and cook, uncovered, for 20 minutes, stirring from time to time to prevent sticking.

Preheat the oven to 350°F.

With a slotted spoon, transfer the ribs from the water to a large, shallow baking dish, pour the sauce over the ribs, and bake till slightly browned, about 20 minutes. Turn the ribs over and bake till the other sides are slightly browned, 15 to 20 minutes, basting several times with the sauce.

Serve the ribs and sauce on a large, deep platter.

martha pearl advises Whenever preboiling beef shortribs, pork ribs, or chicken before baking with other ingredients, I always save the flavorful simmering liquid in case a little is needed to keep the baked dish from drying out and burning. The liquid is also essential to pour over leftovers I plan to store in the refrigerator.

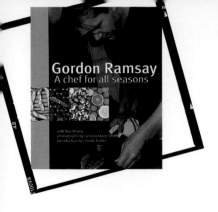

veal chops with a cream of winter vegetables

from *Gordon Ramsay A Chef for All Seasons*

SERVES 4 AS A MAIN DISH

Veal is not overly popular, which is a shame because it has such a great flavor and is so versatile. You can serve it simply roasted or cooked with a sauce—a cream sauce as in a *blanquette de veau* or a punchy tomato-based sauce such as in *osso bucco.* This is a nice recipe for a mid-week dinner—meat and vegetables all in one, celeriac and onions served with blanched baby spinach.

4	veal loin chops, about 7 ounces each
¼	cup olive oil
1	teaspoon chopped fresh rosemary
8 to 12 baby onions	
5	ounces celeriac
3	tablespoons butter
7	ounces baby leaf spinach (about 2 cups)
1	tablespoon Dijon mustard
1	cup heavy cream
Sea salt and freshly ground black pepper	

1 Trim the chops, then place flat on a board. Using a rolling pin, beat the loin lightly to flatten slightly. Brush both sides of each chop with a little olive oil and sprinkle with rosemary. Leave to marinate for about 2 hours.

2 Meanwhile, blanch the onions in boiling water for 30 seconds. Drain and rinse in cold water. The skins should slip off easily. Heat 1 tablespoon of oil in a small pan and sauté the onions for 5 to 7 minutes until golden brown. Remove with a slotted spoon and set aside.

FOOD&WINE test-kitchen tips

- The author suggests this as an ideal mid-week meal. Now, isn't that just like a chef? We loved this scrumptious dish when we made it in the test kitchen and would consider it dinner-party special in our own home kitchens. You can make the Cream of Winter Vegetables ahead of time and also cook the spinach. Then all you need to do just before serving is reheat them and sauté the chops for 6 to 8 minutes.

 wine recommendation Either a white or a red wine will pair well with this luxurious dish. For a white, try a high-quality white Burgundy, such as Meursault. If you are in the mood for red, look for a Barbera d'Alba from Italy's Piedmont region.

3 Peel the celeriac and cut into dice (you should have about 1 cup). Heat the remaining oil and 2 tablespoons of the butter in the same pan and sauté the celeriac for about 5 minutes, turning once or twice. Season nicely and return the onions to the pan. Set aside.

4 Blanch the spinach in boiling water for 1 minute, then drain and refresh under cold running water. Drain well again and press out as much water as possible. (In my kitchen, I squeeze the leaves in a clean dish towel.)

5 Stir the mustard and cream into the celeriac and onions, and bring slowly to a boil. Check the seasoning. Keep warm.

6 Now for the veal. Heat a heavy-based non-stick frying pan and, when hot, put in the veal chops. Season as they cook, allowing 3 to 4 minutes on each side. Baste once or twice with any pan juices or any leftover marinade.

7 Reheat the spinach with the remaining butter. Divide the celeriac and onions among four warmed plates, sit the chops on top, and spoon the spinach around. Serve hot.

meatballs with rice and herbs in lemon broth

soutzoukakia lemonata

from *The Foods of the Greek Islands*

MAKES ABOUT 26 MEATBALLS; 4 TO 6 SERVINGS

Meatballs similar to these are cooked all over Greece, but only on Cyprus are you likely to find cilantro mixed with the other herbs. This recipe is my own version, based on an exceptional one of my friend Despina Drakaki, from Paros.

1   pound lean ground beef, veal, lamb or pork, or a combination

½   cup medium-grain rice, such as Arborio

3 to 4 scallions (white and most of the green parts), finely chopped

1   cup finely chopped fresh flat-leaf parsley

½   cup finely chopped fresh dill

½   cup chopped fresh cilantro

⅓   cup chopped fresh mint

1   large egg, lightly beaten

⅓   cup olive oil

Salt and freshly ground black pepper

1   large onion, chopped

1   cup dry white wine

2½ to 3½ cups chicken stock or beef stock

3 to 4 tablespoons freshly squeezed lemon juice

Sprigs of fresh flat-leaf parsley, dill, mint and/or cilantro

In a large bowl, combine the meat, rice, scallions, parsley, dill, cilantro, mint, egg, 2 tablespoons of the oil, salt and pepper to taste. Knead well, cover and refrigerate for at least 1 hour.

Shape 2-tablespoon-sized portions of the meat mixture into balls. Place on a plate, cover and refrigerate.

In a large, deep skillet with a lid or a Dutch oven, heat the remaining 3 tablespoons oil and sauté the onion over medium-high heat for 2 to 3 minutes, or until soft. Add the wine and simmer for 1 minute. Add 2 cups of the stock and salt to taste. Add the meatballs to the skillet; they should be completely covered. Bring to a boil, reduce the heat to low, cover and simmer for 15 minutes.

Add ½ cup of the stock and 3 tablespoons lemon juice and cook for 10 minutes more, or until the meatballs are cooked through and the liquid is reduced to 1 cup. If the meatballs are not cooked, add more stock and cook briefly. Taste and adjust the seasonings with lemon juice, salt and/or pepper. Serve in soup bowls, garnished with herb sprigs.

variation   If you like, thicken the sauce with an egg-lemon sauce: Add only half the lemon juice to the broth. When the meatballs are cooked, remove with a slotted spoon and keep warm. In a small bowl, beat 1 large egg with 3 tablespoons water. Gradually whisk in the remaining lemon juice and the sauce from the pan. Return the sauce to the pan and gently reheat over very low heat, stirring constantly. Pour over the meatballs and serve.

pork, veal, beef & lamb

FOOD&WINE test-kitchen tips

- This kept beautifully in the test-kitchen refrigerator for a week. You can freeze it, too.

 wine recommendation   Agiorgitiko, the full-bodied, slightly spicy red wine from Greece, is the perfect match for this dish. If your wine store hasn't caught on to the fad for Greek wines, look for a Chianti Classico from Italy.

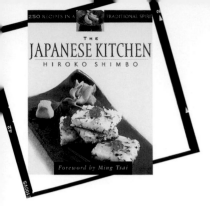

mom's pot-cooked "roast beef"

"rosuto-bifu!"

from *The Japanese Kitchen*

YIELDS 4 TO 6 SERVINGS

Until I reached late elementary school age we did not have an oven at home, so my mother cooked beef roast in her way, in a pot. She proudly called it *rosuto-bifu,* "roast beef," although it had little relationship to real roast beef. Even after my mother obtained an oven, she continued cooking her beef in this way, until one day my sister came back from her Western cooking class with an authentic roast beef recipe. My mother was surely impressed with this new preparation.

Once in a while, however, I still enjoy my mother's version of *rosuto-bifu.* She served the sliced beef with wasabi, grated daikon, and a delicious sauce made from the liquid left in the cooking pot.

Salt

Fresh-ground black pepper

1½ pounds beef top round

3   garlic cloves, crushed

3   tablespoons vegetable oil

1   tablespoon sugar

½   cup *sake* (rice wine)

¼   cup *mirin* (sweet cooking wine)

⅓   cup *shoyu* (soy sauce)

Top leaves from 2 bunches watercress

1   tablespoon wasabi

1   cup grated daikon

FOOD&WINE test-kitchen tips

- Ask your butcher for a two-inch-thick piece of top round.

- If you can't find the daikon, you can skip it without qualm. We couldn't get any when we tested this and didn't feel any lack. There are plenty of flavors going on with the outstanding combination of meat, sauce, watercress, and wasabi.

 wine recommendation A wine made from the spicy Grenache grape will be an excellent match for the spiciness of the dish. For a treat, look to a Châteauneuf-du-Pape, home to the world's best Grenache-based wines.

Salt and pepper the beef, and rub it with garlic. Let the beef rest for 15 minutes.

Heat a large skillet, and add the vegetable oil. When the oil is hot, add the beef, and cook it until the outside is lightly browned. Sprinkle the sugar over the beef, and turn the beef to caramelize all surfaces. Remove the beef from the skillet, and set it aside.

In a medium pot, combine the *sake* and *mirin.* Bring the mixture to a boil over medium heat. Turn the heat to low, add the beef, and cover the pot with a drop lid (a lightweight lid or piece of foil about 1 inch smaller than the diameter of the pot). Cook the beef for 10 minutes.

Add the *shoyu,* and cook the beef for 5 to 8 minutes longer, turning it for even coloring and flavoring.

Remove the beef from the pot, and let the beef stand, covered, for 10 minutes. The beef will be quite rare.

Strain the remaining cooking liquid through a fine sieve into a small saucepan. Cook the sauce over low heat until it thickens.

Cut the beef into thin slices. Serve it on a large platter, garnished with watercress. Serve the sauce, the wasabi, and the daikon in separate small bowls on the side.

grilled skirt steak tacos with roasted poblano rajas

tacos de arrachera al carbón con rajas

from *Mexico One Plate at a Time*

MAKES 12 TACOS, SERVING 4 AS A LIGHT MEAL

2   medium white onions, sliced into ½-inch rounds
     (keep the rounds intact for easy grilling)

3   garlic cloves, peeled and roughly chopped

3   tablespoons fresh lime juice

¼   teaspoon cumin, preferably freshly ground

Salt

1   pound beef skirt steak, trimmed of surface fat as well as the
     thin white membrane called "silverskin"

3   medium (about 9 ounces total) fresh poblano chiles

Vegetable or olive oil for brushing or spritzing the onions and meat

A small bowlful of lime wedges for serving

12   warm, fresh corn tortillas (see page 130 to reheat store-bought ones)

1 marinating the meat In a food processor or blender, combine one-quarter of the onions, the garlic, lime juice, cumin and ½ teaspoon salt. Process to a smooth puree. Place the skirt steak in a nonaluminum baking dish. Using a spoon, smear the marinade over both sides of the skirt steak. Cover and refrigerate for at least 1 hour or up to 8 hours.

2 making the grilled chile-and-onion *rajas* Turn on the oven to its lowest setting. Heat a gas grill to medium-high or light a charcoal fire and let it burn just until the coals are covered with gray ash and very hot. Either turn the burner(s) in the center of the grill to medium-low or bank the coals to the sides of the grill for indirect cooking. Set the

---

FOOD&WINE test-kitchen tips

- Because Rick Bayless is so very careful to preserve authentic flavor in his recipes, we hesitate to mention this, but when we tested these, there were no fresh poblanos to be found, and we substituted always-available jalapeños. The tacos were superb. The jalapeños on the market the last couple of years seem to be bigger and milder than they used to be, which is the kind you need here if you're making the substitution.

wine recommendation Although grilled steak is often the best backdrop for a truly great wine, the fire in this dish will steal center stage from anything truly elegant. So save that special bottle for another night and go instead for a simple, straightforward red, such as a Côte-du-Rhône from the South of France.

cooking grate in place, cover the grill and let the grate heat up, 5 minutes or so.

Lay the chiles on the hottest part of the grill, and cook, turning occasionally, until the skin is blistered and uniformly blackened all over, about 5 minutes. Be careful not to char the flesh, only the skin. Remove the chiles from the grill and cover with a kitchen towel.

While the chiles are roasting, brush or spray the remaining onion slices with oil and lay the whole rounds of onions on the grill in a cooler spot than you chose for the chiles. When they're starting to soften and are browned on the first side, about 10 minutes, use a spatula to flip them and brown the other side. Transfer to an ovenproof serving dish and separate the rings (if they haven't started separating during grilling).

Rub the blackened skin off the chiles, then pull out the stems and seed pods. Rinse briefly to remove any stray seeds and bits of skin. Slice into 1/4-inch strips and stir into the onions. Taste the mixture and season it with salt, usually about 1/4 teaspoon. Keep warm in the oven.

3 grilling the meat Remove the steak from the marinade and gently shake off the excess. Oil the steak well on both sides and lay it over the hottest part of the grill. Grill, turning once, until richly browned and done to your liking, about 1 1/2 to 2 minutes per side for medium-rare (the way I like skirt steak).

4 serving the tacos Cut the long piece of skirt steak into 3- to 4-inch lengths, then cut each section *across the grain* (that is, in line with the full length of the steak) into thin strips. Mix with the chiles and onions, season with a little salt and set on the table along with the lime wedges and hot tortillas, for your guests to make into soft tacos.

working ahead Thin steaks like skirt taste best with a relatively short tour in the marinade—1 to 8 hours. Leave them longer, and the marinade overpowers the flavor and saps the rosy color of the meat. The poblano-and-onion *rajas* can be made several hours ahead and left at room temperature; rewarm before serving. The steak, of course, must be grilled just before you're ready to eat.

▼

reheating corn tortillas There are several methods for reheating corn tortillas: dry heat (gas flame), moist heat (steamer and microwave) and oily heat (dry-frying).

• **dry heat** This easy method works only if your tortillas have been made that day. Heat the tortillas directly over the flame (or on a griddle or skillet), flipping them until toasty and pliable.

• **moist heat of a steamer** This is easier for larger quantities of corn tortillas, especially if you need to hold them hot for a little while. Pour ½ inch water into the bottom of the steamer, then line the steaming basket with a clean heavy kitchen towel. Lay the tortillas in the basket in stacks of 12 (a small vegetable steamer will accommodate only one stack; a large Asian steamer will hold three or four stacks). Fold the edges of the towel over the tortillas to cover them, set the lid in place, bring the water to a boil and let boil only for 1 minute, then turn off the fire and let stand, covered, for 15 minutes. If you wish to keep the tortillas hot for up to an hour, slip the steamer into a low oven or reheat the water periodically.

• **moist heat of a microwave** This easy method works best with no more than a dozen tortillas. Drizzle a clean kitchen towel with 3 tablespoons water and wring the towel to evenly distribute the moisture. Use the towel to line a microwave-safe casserole dish (8 or 9 inches in diameter is best). Lay in a dozen tortillas, cover with the towel and the lid, then microwave at 50 percent power for 4 minutes. Let stand for 2 to 3 minutes. The tortillas will stay warm for 20 minutes.

• **oily heat** Though it's not much a part of home cooking, street vendors of seared-meat tacos reheat fresh tortillas with the heat of a slightly oily griddle—they're not so much frying the tortillas (which would mean completely submerging the tortillas in oil) as griddle-heating them with a tiny bit of oil.

When just-baked tortillas come off the griddle or when they've been reheated, they're traditionally kept warm in a tightly woven basket *(chiquihuite)* lined with a cloth; some have lids, others don't. In the Yucatan, they use hollowed-out gourds. And in modern households, they use Styrofoam containers—which are so efficient that they now come in many decorated styles. If you're having a party, hold hot tortillas in an insulated chest (like an ice chest) lined with a towel.

131

khmer stir-fried ginger and beef

saiko cha k'nye (from Cambodia)

from *Hot Sour Salty Sweet*

SERVES 4 WITH RICE AND ANOTHER DISH

Sao Pheha introduced me to several easy dishes from the Khmer home-cooking repertoire. This was perhaps the simplest, and also the most surprising. It's a stir-fry in which ginger has the role of featured vegetable, warming and full of flavor. The ginger is cut into julienne twigs and then fried with a little beef. The result is a mound of beef slices and tender ginger, all bathed in plenty of gravy, a great companion for rice.

Be sure to buy firm ginger for this dish (ginger with wrinkled skin will be tough and stringy), and, if there's a choice, young ginger rather than the tan mature ginger. Serve with a sour stew or soup and some simple greens.

Generous ½ pound boneless sirloin, eye of round, or other lean beef
½   pound ginger, preferably young ginger
3   tablespoons vegetable or peanut oil
3 to 4 cloves garlic, smashed and minced
2   tablespoons Thai fish sauce
2   teaspoons sugar

Thinly slice the beef across the grain and set aside. Peel the ginger, then cut it into fine matchstick-length julienne (this is most easily done by cutting thin slices, then stacking these to cut into matchsticks). You'll have about 2 cups.

Heat a wok over medium-high heat. Add the oil and, when it is hot, add the garlic. Cook until golden, 20 to 30 seconds. Add the meat and stir-fry, using your spatula to separate the slices and to expose them all to the heat, until most of the meat has changed color. Add the fish sauce and sugar, toss in the ginger twigs, and stir-fry until just tender, 4 to 5 minutes. Serve hot with rice.

FOOD&WINE test-kitchen tips

- Don't worry when the ginger becomes deep caramel brown. It will be delectable.

 wine recommendation To bring out the best in dishes flavored with ginger, look for a wine that has an aromatic punch of its own. A spicy California Zinfandel will be the perfect partner for this dish.

loin of beef with watercress purée

from *Gordon Ramsay A Chef for All Seasons*

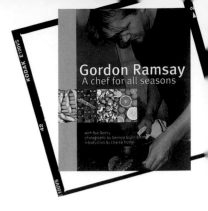

SERVES 4 AS A MAIN DISH

A top loin or strip roast comes from the short loin. It is a nice round shape, cooks well, and—more important—has a great flavor and texture. We buy it in 4½-pound roasts and "set" the shape by rolling it tightly into a *ballotine* and storing it in the fridge for 2 days. It can then be cut into thick steaks and broiled or pan-fried. We serve strip loin steaks with an eye-catching watercress purée that is embarrassingly simple to make. (In the restaurant we wring out the watercress purée in a cloth and serve it as a soft quenelle, but if you prefer a pouring sauce then use the maximum amount of cream.) Sit the steaks on a bed of sautéed mushrooms of your choice. I prefer chanterelles, but you can use cèpes, oyster mushrooms, or cremini.

1¼-pound piece beef top loin

3 tablespoons olive oil

1 tablespoon butter

7 ounces mushrooms (see above), sliced if large

2 fat cloves garlic, minced

2 teaspoons chopped fresh parsley

Sea salt and freshly ground black pepper

sauce

10 ounces watercress leaves (about 3 cups)

4 ounces spinach leaves (about 1 cup)

¼ to 1 cup heavy cream

1 First, make the sauce. Put a pan of salted water on to boil. Push in all the watercress and boil for 5 minutes. Add the spinach and cook for another minute or so until wilted. Drain in a colander. Press with the back of a ladle to extract as much moisture as possible.

2 Put the leaves into a food processor and blend to a fine purée, scraping down the sides occasionally. Pour ¼ cup of the cream through the processor funnel and keep the blades whirling for what seems like an eternity. You will eventually get a sauce with a texture like silk. It will be so smooth, you will not need to pass it through a sieve. If you want a pouring sauce, add the remaining cream. Check the seasoning, and pour into a small saucepan ready for reheating.

▼

3 Cut the beef loin into 4 even steaks and rub each side using 1 tablespoon oil. Heat a heavy, non-stick frying pan until you can feel a good heat rising. Lay in your steaks—they should give a good hiss as they hit the hot pan. Season the tops and cook for about 3 minutes, then flip over and cook the other side for 2 minutes. Slip the butter into the pan at this stage and season the second side. Remove the steaks from the pan and leave to rest while you cook the mushrooms.

4 Sauté the mushrooms with the garlic in the remaining oil. Season and mix with the parsley.

5 Reheat the watercress purée/sauce. Place the steaks on warmed plates (sliced first if you like), trickle any pan juices over, and spoon on the mushrooms. If your watercress purée is firm, shape it into quenelles. If it is a sauce, spoon some over the steaks and pass the rest separately. Serve with whatever accompaniment you like to eat steak with. Fries are great, or why not try slices of really fresh baguette?

FOOD&WINE test-kitchen tips

- The chef seems to prefer the watercress as a purée (as pictured) rather than as a sauce, which he says you can make if you like by adding more cream. We tried it both ways, and for once in our lives, we think less is more, and so we quite agree with him. The intense purée works beautifully as a counterpoint flavor, whereas the sauce gets on every bite of meat and, depending on the strength of the flavor of your beef, can be overwhelming.

wine recommendation Vegetable purées are necessarily concentrated in flavor, and they give many wines an unpleasant vegetal taste. A fruity Cabernet Sauvignon from California or Australia will stand up to the watercress and make an admirable companion to the beef as well.

lime-marinated flank steak

from *Staff Meals from Chanterelle*

SERVES 4

F l a n k   s t e a k is an easy cut of beef to prepare, and the price is right. The grilled or broiled meat slices up nice and tender when cooked just to the right juicy redness. Cut at an angle against the grain, slices come out pleasantly wide and are especially good served hot over a room-temperature salad. If you're in the mood for a simpler, yet satisfying, side dish, plain rice certainly fills the bill. A few sprigs of cilantro make a nice garnish.

3	cloves garlic, finely minced
¼	cup Thai fish sauce *(nam pla)*
¼	cup good-quality soy sauce, such as Kikkoman
	Juice of 5 limes
¼	cup sugar
½	cup water
1	tablespoon hot red pepper flakes
1	beef flank steak (about 2 pounds), trimmed of fat

1 Place all the ingredients except the steak in a bowl and whisk to blend. Place the flank steak in a wide, shallow bowl and pour the marinade over it. Turn the meat, making sure it is completely coated with the marinade. Refrigerate, covered, for at least 4 hours and up to 24. Turn the meat occasionally as it marinates.

FOOD&WINE test-kitchen tips

- In addition to an outdoor grill or the broiler, as suggested in the recipe, you can also use a grill pan over medium-high heat.

- To cut nice wide slices as the chef suggests, hold your knife so that the flat of the blade is almost parallel to the meat, just tilted a tiny bit, and begin slicing about 1½ inches from the end of the steak. Cut at a very slight angle—nearly horizontally across the meat—from that point to the end. Move the blade back a fraction of an inch and cut horizontally again to the end for the second thin, broad slice, and so on.

 wine recommendation The robust cut of meat as well as the assertive flavors in the marinade call for a wine that packs a punch. Primitivo, made in the heel of the Italian boot, is just the ticket.

2 Preheat the grill to very high or preheat the broiler.

3 Remove the flank steak from the marinade and pat dry. Oil the grill rack, place the meat on the rack, and grill, making sure to watch the heat carefully; the sugar and soy sauce tend to cause the meat to blacken quickly. Flank steak is tender when cooked no more than medium rare, about 4 minutes per side.

4 Let the meat rest for 2 minutes, then slice thinly against the grain and serve.

pork, veal, beef & lamb

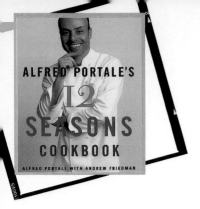

ALFRED PORTALE'S
12
SEASONS
COOKBOOK
ALFRED PORTALE WITH ANDREW FRIEDMAN

grilled marinated rib-eye steak

from *Alfred Portale's 12 Seasons Cookbook*

MAKES 4 SERVINGS

We all have things we don't understand about our parents. I, for example, have no idea what in the world my father thought he was doing when he made the dish that inspired this recipe.

One weekend each July, my entire extended family would descend on our house on Crystal Beach. The central event was an Italian-American feast for which everyone would bring a dish.

My father would light up the charcoal, and while the coals were burning down, he mixed olive oil, red wine vinegar, salt, pepper, garlic salt (as opposed to fresh garlic),and dried oregano. But instead of dressing the salad with this, he marinated the steaks in it for 20 minutes, and then—while they were grilling—he basted them every so often with the remaining marinade.

I now understand that there are cultural precedents in cooking for this technique. Building on this encouraging observation, I've adjusted the recipe, using a great deal of fresh garlic, fresh oregano, black peppercorns, and a high-quality olive oil.

4	12-ounce rib-eye steaks, each about 1¼ inches thick
3	tablespoons coarsely cracked black peppercorns
6	tablespoons extra-virgin olive oil
3	tablespoons aged red wine vinegar
2	tablespoons chopped fresh oregano, or 1 tablespoon dried oregano
1	tablespoon chopped fresh rosemary
3	cloves garlic, peeled and finely minced

Coarse salt to taste

FOOD&WINE test-kitchen tips

- We tested this on a cold February day, definitely not an inspiration to outdoor cooking. So we made the recipe on the stove, in a grill pan over medium-high heat. The times given were still exactly right for medium-rare steak.

 wine recommendation Steak can take on the tannin of a big red, such as a Madiran from the Southwest of France. The garnet-colored wine has a slight spiciness of its own, which will stand up to the strong flavors of the marinade.

Season the steaks on both sides with the peppercorns, pressing them into the meat with your fingertips. Transfer the steaks to a shallow dish.

In a small bowl, combine the olive oil, vinegar, oregano, rosemary, and garlic. Stir well and pour the mixture over the steaks. Turn the steaks to coat both sides, cover, and marinate at room temperature for 30 minutes, or in the refrigerator for up to 2 hours. Remove from the refrigerator about 15 minutes before grilling.

Build a charcoal fire in a grill and let the coals burn until covered with white ash. Spread them out in the grill. Lightly oil the grill grate.

Lift the steaks from the marinade, reserving the marinade. Season both sides of the steaks with salt and grill them for about 4 minutes on each side for rare; 5 minutes on each side for medium-rare. During the first few minutes of grilling, baste the steaks with the marinade. Let the steaks rest for about 5 minutes before carving them into thick slices.

long-bone short ribs with chinook merlot gravy and rosemary white beans

from Tom Douglas' Seattle Kitchen

MAKES 6 SERVINGS

I love the awesome look of big short rib bones lying across the plate—some of our cooks refer to these as Flintstone bones. But you could use the short-cut or English-cut short ribs instead. This is a great rib-sticking (excuse the pun) dish for our long, gray, drizzly winters.

My friends Kay and Clay, who own Chinook Wines in Prosser, Washington, make great Merlot, and it's a tradition in our house to drink and cook with it when we make this dish. Of course, another Merlot will do if you can't get Chinook.

This recipe takes a long time to cook, but can easily be made the day before and reheated before serving. In fact, like most braises, it will taste even better.

1½	cups all-purpose flour
1	tablespoon kosher salt
1	teaspoon freshly ground black pepper
6	long-bone short ribs (about 1½ pounds each) or other short ribs
¼	cup olive oil
2	onions, roughly chopped (about 3½ cups)
2	carrots, roughly chopped (about 1 cup)
1	tablespoon chopped garlic
2	teaspoons chopped fresh thyme
2	bay leaves
1	teaspoon black peppercorns
2	cups Chinook Merlot or other dry red wine
3	cups chicken stock
	Kosher salt and freshly ground black pepper
	Rosemary White Beans (recipe follows)
	Horseradish Gremolata (recipe follows)

1 Preheat the oven to 325°F. On a baking sheet, combine the flour, salt, and pepper. Coat the short ribs evenly with the seasoned flour, shaking off any excess. In a large roasting pan over high heat on the stovetop, heat the oil, then brown the ribs on all sides (in batches if necessary), about 15 minutes. Remove the ribs from the roasting pan and set aside.

2 To the same pan, add the onions and carrots and cook, stirring until softened, about 10 minutes, adding the garlic, thyme, bay leaves, and peppercorns for the last few minutes. Return the short ribs to the roasting pan, bone side up. Pour the Merlot and chicken stock over the ribs. Bring the liquids to a simmer on top of the stove, then cover the pan with aluminum foil (or a lid) and braise in the oven until the meat begins to pull away from the bone, about 2½ hours. Carefully remove the roasting pan from the oven. Reduce the oven temperature to 200°F. Lift out the ribs and place them in a clean pan. Cover this pan and keep the ribs warm in the oven while you finish the sauce.

3 Pour the braising liquids from the roasting pan through a sieve into a deep, tall container (like a large pitcher), pressing on the vegetables to get as much liquid as possible. Discard the vegetables. Allow the liquids to rest about 5 minutes, then skim off all the fat with a ladle and discard. (A tall container makes it easy to remove the fat in one deep layer.) Short ribs are fatty, so there will be quite a bit of fat to remove at this point.

4 Pour the strained and skimmed braising liquid into a large sauté pan and reduce over high heat until thickened, about 15 minutes. You should end up with about 2 cups sauce. You want this to be a sauce, not glue, so don't overreduce it. It should be the consistency of heavy cream, just thick enough to cling to the meat when you ladle it over. Season with salt and plenty of freshly ground black pepper.

on the plate Spoon the white beans and some of their broth into 6 large, shallow bowls. Remove the short ribs from the oven and place a short rib in the center of each bowl. Ladle the sauce over each rib. Garnish with the gremolata. You can also remove the meat from the bone so that it is easier to eat.

a step ahead You can braise the ribs a day ahead and store them, covered, in the refrigerator. Store the sauce separately, covered, in the refrigerator. When you are ready to reheat the short ribs, preheat the oven to 400°F. Place the ribs in a pan with 1 cup hot chicken stock. Cover the pan and place it in the oven for about 25 minutes until the meat is warmed through. Heat the sauce to a simmer in a small saucepan on the stovetop.

in the glass For me, it has to be Chinook Merlot.

▼

pork, veal, beef & lamb

rosemary white beans Serve these beans in wide, shallow soup bowls with our Long-Bone Short Ribs (page 140). Or pair them with other roasted meats, birds, or sausages.

For the best flavor, cook the beans in chicken stock. The beans need to start soaking the day before, so plan accordingly.

MAKES 6 SERVINGS

2	cups dried white beans, picked over and rinsed
¾	cup diced bacon (2 thick strips, about 3 ounces)
1	cup chopped onions
1	teaspoon chopped garlic
4	cups chicken stock
4	cups water
2	tablespoons chopped fresh rosemary
2	tablespoons (¼ stick) unsalted butter

Kosher salt and freshly ground black pepper

1 Generously cover the beans with cold water and allow to soak overnight, refrigerated. The beans will double in volume (at least), so put them in a container that can hold them and at least twice their volume of water.

2 The next day, heat the bacon in a large pot over medium-high heat until the fat is rendered and bacon crisp, 8 to 10 minutes. Add the onions and cook until soft, stirring, 8 to 10 minutes. Add the garlic and cook, stirring, 1 minute longer. Add the chicken stock and water and heat to a simmer. Drain the beans of their soaking liquid and add them to the pot. Cook the beans over medium heat until soft, about 1½ hours.

FOOD&WINE test-kitchen tips

- If fresh rosemary isn't available, put a teaspoon of dried in before (rather than after) cooking the beans.

- Not being able to leave well enough alone, we sprinkled coarse sea salt over the ribs and loved what it did for the texture and the taste of this outstanding dish.

3 By the time the beans are soft, there should be just enough liquid left in the pot to make the beans slightly brothy. If the beans seem to have too much liquid, turn the heat to high and reduce the cooking liquid a bit. Stir in the rosemary and butter and season to taste with salt and pepper.

a step ahead The beans can be cooked a day ahead and stored, covered, refrigerated. Add the butter and rosemary when you are reheating them.

horseradish gremolata

    2   **tablespoons chopped fresh flat-leaf parsley**
    1   **tablespoon peeled and grated fresh horseradish root**
  1½ **teaspoons minced lemon zest**

To make the gremolata, combine the parsley, horseradish, and lemon zest in a small bowl.

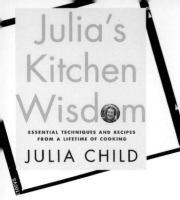

beef bourguignon—
beef in red wine sauce

from *Julia's Kitchen Wisdom*

SERVES 6 TO 8

Optional, but traditional for added flavor: 6 ounces blanched bacon *lardons*
    (see opposite)

2 to 3 tablespoons cooking oil

About 4 pounds trimmed beef chuck, cut into 2-inch cubes

Salt and freshly ground pepper

2   cups sliced onions

1   cup sliced carrots

1   bottle red wine (such as zinfandel or Chianti)

2   cups beef stock (see opposite) or canned beef broth

1   cup chopped tomatoes, fresh or canned

1   medium herb bouquet (see Test-Kitchen Tips, below)

beurre manié for the sauce

3   tablespoons flour blended to a paste with 2 tablespoons butter

for the garnish

24   brown-braised small white onions (page 146) and 3 cups sautéed
    quartered mushrooms (page 146)

FOOD&WINE test-kitchen tips

- This oh-so-flavorful version of a classic stew just gets better with time—literally. We found that it kept for a week in the test-kitchen refrigerator.

- As Julia suggests elsewhere in the book, for the herb bouquet tie together in cheesecloth 6 parsley sprigs, an imported bay leaf, ¾ teaspoon dried thyme, 3 whole clove or allspice berries, and some celery or leek leaves.

wine recommendation Beef in a red-wine sauce naturally calls for a full-flavored wine. Try a Pinot Noir from Oregon or, more traditionally, from the Côtes de Nuits region of Burgundy.

If using *lardons*, sauté them to brown lightly in a little oil; set them aside and reserve the rendered fat. Choose a large frying pan and brown the chunks of meat on all sides in hot oil or in the fat rendered from the *lardons*, season with salt and pepper, and turn them into a heavy casserole. Remove all but a little fat from the frying pan, add the sliced vegetables and brown them, and add to the meat. Deglaze the pan with wine, pouring it into the casserole along with enough stock almost to cover the meat. Stir in the tomatoes and the *lardons* and add the herb bouquet. Bring to the simmer, cover, and simmer slowly, either on the stove or in a preheated 325°F oven, until the meat is tender—eat a little piece to check.

Drain through a colander set over a saucepan and return the meat to the casserole. Press juices out of the residue into the cooking liquid, then degrease and boil down the liquid to 3 cups. Off heat, whisk in the *beurre manié,* then simmer for 2 minutes as the sauce thickens lightly. Correct seasoning and pour over the meat, folding in the onions and mushrooms. (May be completed a day in advance to this point.)

To serve, bring to the simmer, basting meat and vegetables with the sauce for several minutes until thoroughly hot throughout.

COOKING TIME: ABOUT 2½ HOURS

blanched *lardons* Drop 6 to 8 slices of bacon or salt pork into 2 quarts of cold water, bring to the boil, and simmer 6 to 8 minutes. Drain, rinse in cold water, and dry on paper towels. Cut into ¼-inch-thick pieces about 1 inch long.

simple beef stock Arrange a collection of meaty raw and/or cooked beef bones, such as shank, neck, oxtail, and/or knuckle, in a roasting pan, adding (for every 2 to 3 quarts of bones) ½ cup each of roughly chopped onions, celery, and carrots. Baste lightly with vegetable oil and brown for 30 to 40 minutes in a 450ºF oven, turning and basting with oil or accumulated fat several times. Scoop bones and vegetables into a stockpot. Pour fat out of roasting pan and deglaze with 2 cups of water, simmering and scraping up coagulated juices. Pour into pot, adding cold water to cover ingredients by 2 inches. Add more chopped onion, celery, and carrot (½ cup each for every 2 to 3 quarts of bones), a chopped fresh tomato, 2 large cloves of smashed unpeeled garlic, and a medium herb bouquet. Bring to the simmer, skim off scum for several minutes, then salt very lightly. Cover loosely and simmer 2 to 3 hours, adding water if needed. Strain and degrease.

▼

sautéed mushrooms Heat 1½ tablespoons butter and ½ tablespoon oil in a large frying pan, and when butter foam is subsiding, turn in ¾ pound quartered fresh mushrooms. Sauté for several minutes, tossing frequently as the butter is absorbed and then reappears on the surface when the mushrooms begin to brown. Toss in ½ tablespoon chopped shallots, season with salt and pepper, and sauté another 30 seconds.

brown-braised onions To peel, drop 24 small white onions, about 1 inch in diameter, into boiling water for exactly 1 minute. Drain and refresh in cold water. Shave off ends; slip off skins. Pierce a cross ¼ inch deep in root ends, to prevent bursting. Sauté peeled onions in 1 layer in a saucepan with 1 tablespoon each butter and oil until colored. Then add chicken stock or water to come halfway up and 1½ teaspoons sugar. Season lightly with salt, cover, and simmer slowly 25 minutes, or until tender.

sirloin of new season's lamb with lentils

from *Gordon Ramsay A Chef for All Seasons*

SERVES 4 AS A MAIN DISH

This is a good homey dish similar to many served up and down France. We serve the lamb with creamy gratin potato. By par-cooking potatoes in milk before finishing them in ramekins, they cook more evenly. It's a neat little trick.

4	thick lamb sirloin steaks or chops, about 7 ounces each
	3 to 4 tablespoons olive oil
1	sprig fresh thyme
¾	cup *lentilles de Puy*
1	medium carrot
½	small head celeriac
1	medium leek
2	tablespoons coarsely chopped fresh parsley
¼	cup Classic Vinaigrette (page 148)
	Sea salt and freshly ground black pepper

gratin potatoes

1	pound medium, slightly waxy boiling potatoes
1¼	cups milk
1¼	cups heavy cream
1	clove garlic, sliced
1	sprig fresh thyme
1	bay leaf
¾	cup grated Gruyère cheese

1 Remove the central bone from the chops. Trim off fat and neaten to nice "rump" shapes. Place in a bowl or plastic bag with half of the oil and the tips from the thyme sprig. Set aside to marinate in the fridge.

2 Cook the lentils in boiling salted water for about 15 minutes. Drain and season.

3 Cut the carrot, celeriac, and leek into ½-inch squares (we call this a *brunoise*). Heat the remaining oil in a saucepan and sauté the vegetables until lightly browned, 5 to 7 minutes. Mix with the lentils and half the parsley, then bind with 2 tablespoons of the vinaigrette. Set aside.

▼

4 For the gratin potatoes, preheat the oven to 400°. Peel the potatoes and slice thinly (use a mandoline or the slicing blade of a food processor). Bring the milk and cream to a boil with some sea salt, the garlic, and herbs, and simmer for a couple of minutes. Add the sliced potatoes and simmer for about 5 minutes until just tender. Drain in a colander set over a bowl to catch the creamy milk.

5 Mix the potatoes gently with two-thirds of the cheese. Layer neatly into four medium ramekins or cocotte dishes, seasoning in between the layers. Spoon a little of the saved creamy milk on top of each ramekin and sprinkle with the last of the cheese. Place the ramekins on a baking sheet and bake for 8 to 10 minutes until the cheese just turns a golden brown.

6 Meanwhile, heat a heavy-based non-stick frying pan until really hot. Remove the lamb steaks from the bowl or plastic bag, wiping off any thyme tips, and brown for 3 to 5 minutes on each side, seasoning lightly as they cook. The lamb should be served lightly pink—medium rare.

7 Reheat the lentils and spoon into the center of four plates. Place the lamb steaks on top (slice them first, if you like). Deglaze the frying pan with the last of the vinaigrette, stirring for a minute, then spoon these juices over the lamb. Sprinkle with the remaining parsley. Serve the gratin potatoes, still in their individual dishes, on the same plate. Simple and delicious!

classic vinaigrette This has many uses apart from dressing salads.

Whisk together 1 cup extra virgin olive oil and 1 cup peanut oil with 1 teaspoon fine sea salt, ¼ teaspoon ground black pepper, the juice of 1 lemon, ¼ cup white wine vinegar, and ¼ cup sherry vinegar. Store in a large screwtop jar and shake to re-emulsify before use.

MAKES ABOUT 2½ CUPS

FOOD&WINE *test-kitchen tips*

- If you want to slice the lamb as pictured, let it rest for 5 minutes before cutting, so that the juices have a chance to redistribute throughout the meat and don't escape the minute you start slicing.

 wine recommendation Lamb and Bordeaux are a classic couple as magical as Bogey and Bacall. Look for a bottle from Pomerol or St-Emilion, where the wines contain a high percentage of Merlot, a grape whose plummy softness will be a great foil for the earthy lentils.

other
main dishes

luang prabang fusion salad

salat luang prabang (from Laos)

from *Hot Sour Salty Sweet*

SERVES 6 TO 8

This surprising salad is a brilliant fusion of French salad traditions and Lao flavorings. There are two dressings: First, a quickly cooked mixture of ground pork, garlic, and seasonings is poured, hot, over the lettuce and herbs. Then a lime juice and fish sauce dressing is added moments later, just before you toss and serve the salad. When you finish serving the salad, there will be a large, yummy puddle of dressing left on the platter; this is how it's done in Luang Prabang, and it's how it's meant to look, so don't worry.

You can serve Fusion Salad as a salad course, but we prefer it as a main dish, on its own or to accompany rice (the Lao way).

3 to 4 large or extra-large eggs, preferably free-range

2 medium heads leaf or Bibb lettuce, washed and dried

4 scallions, trimmed, smashed flat with the side of a cleaver, cut lengthwise in half or into quarters, and then cut crosswise into 2-inch lengths

1 cup coriander sprigs

1 cup loosely packed, coarsely chopped or torn Chinese celery leaves, or substitute flat-leaf parsley sprigs

lime juice dressing

1 tablespoon minced ginger

2 bird or serrano chiles (optional)

1 to 2 cloves garlic, minced

3 tablespoons Thai fish sauce

2 tablespoons fresh lime juice

FOOD&WINE test-kitchen tips

- We put this in a main-course chapter because the authors say they prefer to serve it as such, but keep in mind that the portions are a bit small by Western standards. In the test kitchen, four of us enjoyed the salad for our lunch, and happily polished off the whole recipe.

 wine recommendation Accompany the exotic flavors of this salad with a wine that will cool the fire and refresh the palate. Choose a tart Riesling from Germany and look for the word *trocken* on the label, indicating the dry style that will be your best bet here.

2	tablespoons peanut or vegetable oil or minced pork fat
8	cloves garlic, minced
½	pound ground pork
1	teaspoon salt
1	tablespoon sugar
¾	cup hot water
½	cup rice or cider vinegar

2 to 3 tablespoons dry-roasted peanuts, coarsely chopped

Put the eggs in a saucepan with cold water to cover. Bring to a boil, then reduce the heat and cook at a gentle rolling boil for 10 minutes. Drain and set aside to cool.

Tear the salad greens into large coarse pieces. Place all the greens, including the scallions and herbs, in a large bowl and set aside.

Peel the hard-cooked eggs and cut crosswise in half. Transfer the yolks to a small bowl and mash; set aside. Slice the whites crosswise and set aside.

In a medium bowl, mix together all the lime juice dressing ingredients; set aside.

When you are ready to proceed, put the ingredients for the cooked dressing near your stovetop. Heat a wok or heavy skillet over high heat. Add the oil or fat and heat for 20 seconds, then add the minced garlic. Stir-fry briefly, until the garlic starts to change color, about 20 seconds, then toss in the pork. Use your spatula to break up the pork into small pieces as you stir-fry. Once all the pork has changed color completely, after 1 to 2 minutes, add the salt and sugar, then add the hot water and bring to a boil. Add the vinegar, add the reserved mashed egg yolks, and stir to blend.

Pour the hot liquid and pork over the prepared greens and toss gently. Add the lime juice dressing and toss. Transfer the salad to a large flat platter (or to individual dinner plates) and mound it attractively. Sprinkle on the chopped roasted peanuts, arrange slices of egg white attractively on top, and serve immediately.

other main dishes

mushroom-studded tortilla soup with chipotle chiles and goat cheese

sopa de tortilla y hongos con chile chipotle y queso de cabra

from *Mexico One Plate at a Time*

SERVES 6 AS A FIRST COURSE, 4 AS A CASUAL MAIN DISH

1½ tablespoons vegetable oil or rich-tasting pork lard, plus a little oil to spray or brush on the tortillas

4 garlic cloves, peeled and left whole

1 small white onion, sliced

One 15-ounce can good-quality whole tomatoes in juice, drained
OR 12 ounces (2 medium-small round or 4 to 6 plum) ripe tomatoes, cored and roughly chopped

6 cups good chicken broth, store-bought or homemade

8 ounces full-flavored mushrooms (I love shiitakes here), stemmed (discard woody stems or finely chop them) and sliced ¼ inch thick (you'll have about 2 generous cups slices)
OR 1½ ounces dried shiitake, chanterelle or porcini mushrooms, soaked in hot water for 30 minutes, then drained and sliced ¼ inch thick

Salt

6 corn tortillas

2 to 3 canned chipotle chiles *en adobo,* removed from the canning sauce

4 ounces goat cheese, cut or broken apart into roughly ½-inch cubes

1 large ripe avocado, peeled, pitted and cut into ½-inch cubes

1 large bunch watercress, leaves only

FOOD&WINE test-kitchen tips

• The chef calls for good-quality canned tomatoes. Our favorite brand is Muir Glen. Their cans are lined, so there's no metallic taste.

 wine recommendation The zingy flavors of Sauvignon Blanc have a natural affinity for tangy goat cheese. With so many intense flavors in this recipe, you should look for a bottle from a region known for its full-flavored, full-bodied wines, such as California or Oregon.

1 the soup In a medium-large (4-quart) saucepan, heat the oil or lard over medium. Add the garlic and onion and cook, stirring regularly, until golden, about 7 minutes. Use a slotted spoon to scoop up the garlic and onion, pressing them against the side of the pan to leave behind as much oil as possible and transfer to a food processor or blender; set the pan aside. Add the tomatoes to the garlic and onion and process to a smooth puree.

Set the saucepan over medium-high heat. When hot, add the puree and stir nearly constantly until it has thickened to the consistency of tomato paste, about 10 minutes. Add the broth and sliced mushrooms and bring to a boil, then partially cover and gently simmer over medium to medium-low heat for 30 minutes. Taste and season with salt, usually ½ teaspoon, depending on the saltiness of your broth.

2 toasting the tortillas Heat the oven to 375°F. Cut the tortillas in half, then cut crosswise into ¼-inch strips. Spread out the tortilla strips in a single layer on a baking sheet and spray or lightly brush with oil and toss to coat evenly. Set in the oven and bake, stirring around every couple of minutes or so, until lightly browned and crispy, about 8 minutes.

3 serving the soup Cut open the chipotle chiles and scrape out their seeds. Cut the chiles into thin strips. In each soup bowl, place a portion of the cheese and cubed avocado, a generous sprinkling of the watercress leaves and a few strips of chipotle. Ladle the broth into the bowls, top each with a little handful of crispy tortilla strips and you're ready to eat.

working ahead Step 1 can be done several days in advance—in fact, the soup gets better with a day or two for the flavors to mingle. Store made-ahead soup in the refrigerator, covered. Complete Steps 2 and 3 shortly before serving.

other main dishes

egg chowder with bacon and new potatoes

from *50 Chowders*

MAKES ABOUT 8 CUPS; SERVES 5 OR 6 AS A MAIN COURSE

Eggs are amazing! They are so versatile and at the same time so complete in themselves. But unless you've gone through hard times, it's easy to take the common, ubiquitous, inexpensive egg for granted. My beloved late grandparents, Josephine and Tim Donahue, who lived in Portlaoise, Ireland, loved soft-boiled eggs and ate them for supper (never at breakfast) about twice a week. Watching them slowly eat an egg, waiting for the tiny drops of butter to melt, then carefully salting and peppering each bite, and relishing it as if they were drinking a forty-year-old Château d'Yquem, is a memory that has stayed with me my entire life. I love eggs too, so when I spotted a New Hampshire recipe for egg chowder in *The New England Yankee Cookbook* (1939), I figured it would be easy to make a rustic farm-house chowder with the combination of eggs, bacon, and potato, which we all know are so good together.

As it turned out, it wasn't so simple. I realized that this classic combination works best when the flavors are somewhat separate (like a plate of eggs and bacon with home fries). But that is not the nature of chowder, where flavors blend to become one. After two attempts, I knew I had to depart from my usual style of chowder making and try something different. New potatoes aren't generally suitable for chowder, because their low starch prevents them from blending with the other ingredients—in this case, though, it was exactly the quality I needed. Keeping the bacon separate was easy. And I let the egg flavor dominate the broth. The result: a surprisingly tasty chowder with colorful slices of red potato, large pieces of golden brown bacon, small cubes of chopped hard-boiled egg, and little specks of green chives.

cook's notes This recipe is too humble for entertaining, and it's too filling to eat as starter, but it makes a nice family dish for lunch or supper.

Serve with toasted common crackers or Pilot crackers.

FOOD&WINE test-kitchen tips

- The recipe suggests reheating the bacon in a low oven. The crisp bacon also reheats nicely in the microwave.

 wine recommendation Oak-aged wines have a smokiness that makes them excellent partners with smoked meat or fish. With this dish, a white Graves from one of the better areas, such as Pessac-Léognan, would be lovely. A less pricey alternative would be a bottle from neighboring Montravel.

For equipment, you will need a 1½- to 2-quart saucepan (for boiling the eggs), a 10- to 12-inch skillet or sauté pan (for the chowder), a wooden spoon, a slotted spoon, and a ladle.

6	large eggs
¼	cup distilled white vinegar
8	ounces thick-sliced bacon
4	tablespoons unsalted butter
1	medium onion (8 ounces), cut into ¾-inch dice
2 to 3	sprigs fresh thyme, leaves removed and chopped (1 teaspoon)
1	teaspoon Coleman's dry English mustard
1½	pounds red or white new potatoes, halved and sliced ⅓ inch thick
3	cups chicken stock
1	cup heavy cream
	Kosher or sea salt and freshly ground black pepper

for garnish

2	tablespoons minced fresh chives

1 Place the eggs in a 1½- to 2-quart saucepan and add the vinegar and enough water to completely cover them. Bring to a boil, then lower the heat and cook the eggs at a steady simmer for 5 minutes. Remove the eggs from the heat and let sit for 10 minutes.

2 Rinse the eggs under cold running water until cool enough to handle, then peel them. Cut 5 eggs into medium dice: quarter them lengthwise, then cut each quarter into 3 or 4 pieces. Cover and leave at room temperature to add to the chowder. Chop the remaining egg into ⅓-inch dice, cover, and refrigerate for garnish; remove from the refrigerator about 15 minutes before you serve the chowder.

3 In a 10- to 12-inch skillet or sauté pan, gently fry the slices of bacon, in batches, over medium-low heat until crisp and golden brown. Drain on paper towels. Pour off all except 1 tablespoon of the fat from the pan, and set the pan aside. Cut the bacon into large pieces about 1 inch wide. Place in an ovenproof dish, cover, and reserve until later.

▼

4 Return the pan to the stove and turn the heat up to medium. Add the butter, onion, and thyme and sauté, stirring occasionally with a wooden spoon, for 6 to 8 minutes, until the onion is softened but not browned. Stir in the dry mustard and cook for 1 minute more.

5 Add the potatoes and stock. The stock should just barely cover the potatoes; if it doesn't, add enough water to cover them. Bring to a simmer over medium heat and simmer for about 10 to 12 minutes, until the potatoes are fully cooked and tender.

6 Remove the pan from the heat, stir in the medium-dice eggs and the cream, and season to taste with salt and black pepper. If you are not serving the chowder within the hour, let it cool a bit, then refrigerate; cover the chowder *after* it has chilled completely. Otherwise, let it sit at room temperature for up to an hour, allowing the egg flavor to blend into the broth.

7 When ready to serve, reheat the chowder over low heat; don't let it boil. Even though they are hard-boiled, the egg yolks will lightly thicken the chowder. Warm the bacon in a low oven (200°F) for a few minutes.

8 Using a slotted spoon, mound the onions, potatoes, and eggs in the center of large soup plates or bowls, then ladle the broth around. Scatter the bacon over the individual servings and sprinkle with the diced egg and chives.

omelet stuffed with stir-fried chicken and bean threads *padd neur gai sai sen*

from *Cracking the Coconut*

CRACKING THE COCONUT
CLASSIC THAI HOME COOKING

Su-Mei Yu

MAKES 2 SERVINGS

King Chulalongkhorn was the first Thai monarch to travel abroad. While visiting Europe in 1897, His Majesty wrote to the Queen frequently, sharing his experiences, including detailed accounts of foreign foods and fascinating new ways of cooking. In one letter, he described an omelet that had been served to him on the ship. After his return, the Royal Kitchen tried to duplicate the dish, but with a Thai touch. Duck eggs were used instead of chicken, and chicken liver was used in the filling. You may omit it, but I encourage you to try it. The combination of textures and flavors is unlike any Western omelet filling.

for the filling

¼   cup vegetable oil

1   tablespoon Big Four Paste (page 99)

½   pound boneless, skinless chicken breast, sliced lengthwise into paper-thin strips

½   pound medium shrimp, peeled, deveined, and cut into small pieces

2   ounces chicken liver, thinly sliced lengthwise

2   fresh bird chiles or 1 serrano chile, minced (with seeds—fewer seeds for moderately spicy, more for hotter)

1   teaspoon sugar

1   tablespoon fish sauce *(namm pla)*

2   whole scallions, thinly sliced on the diagonal

2   ounces bean threads (glass noodles), softened in cold water and cut into 2- to 3-inch lengths

for the omelet

4   large eggs

Sea salt

2   tablespoons vegetable oil

for the garnishes

2   whole scallions, trimmed

10 to 12 thin slices cucumber

10 to 12 sprigs cilantro

▼

Arrange the filling ingredients, in the order they are listed, near the stove. Heat a 12-inch skillet over high heat. Put your hand about 2 inches above the skillet. When you can feel the heat, the skillet is ready for frying. Add the oil and heat it for a minute. Add the Big Four Paste and cook, stirring, until fragrant, about 1 minute. Add the chicken and cook, stirring, until the meat turns white, about 2 minutes. Add the shrimp and cook, stirring, until it turns slightly pink, about 1 minute. Add the liver and cook, stirring, until the shrimp are bright pink and the liver has browned, about 1 minute. Add the chiles, sugar, and fish sauce, mixing well, and reduce the heat to low. Add the scallions and mix well, then add the bean threads and mix well (they will clump slightly). Transfer the filling to a bowl, cover, and keep warm.

Put 2 of the eggs in a small bowl, put the remaining 2 in another small bowl, and beat well. Add a pinch of salt to each bowl and mix well. Clean and dry the skillet, then heat it until very hot. Add 1 tablespoon of the oil and when the oil begins to smoke, add one bowl of the beaten eggs, swirling quickly to make a paper-thin film in the skillet. Lower the heat and shake the pan to loosen the omelet; use a spatula to loosen the edges. When the eggs start to set and the bottom of the omelet is slightly browned, 1 to 2 minutes, immediately slide it onto a big plate, brown side down. Spoon half of the filling into the center. Fold the sides over the filling to make a square. Gently slide the spatula under the folded omelet, put your hand over the top to secure the folds, and invert onto a serving plate. Repeat to make the other omelet. Garnish with the scallions, cucumber slices, and cilantro sprigs and serve hot.

other uses for the big four paste (page 99)

for grilling Coat 1 pound meat, fish, or shellfish with the juice of 1 lemon and 1 tablespoon olive oil; rub generously with 1 teaspoon Big Four Paste. Cover and refrigerate for an hour. Grill, leaving steaks and other meats and fish whole or threading chunks on skewers.

for roast chicken or turkey For chicken, rub a 3-pound bird with 2 tablespoons olive oil and the juice of 1 lemon, then massage 1 tablespoon Big Four Paste all over the bird, under its skin, and in the cavity. Place in a plastic bag, seal tightly, and refrigerate overnight. For a 16-pound turkey, use 1 cup olive oil, the juice of 2 lemons, and ¾ cup Big Four Paste.

for stir-fries Use 1 tablespoon Big Four Paste for each ¼ to ½ pound meat, fish, or shellfish and 2 to 3 cups sliced vegetables. Or use the same amount for stir-frying 2 cups noodles, adding ¼ to ½ pound each sliced meat, fish, and shellfish and 1 cup sliced vegetables. Add the Big Four Paste at the beginning of stir-frying, after you've added the oil to a hot skillet.

for meatballs for soup, curry, or noodles Add 1 tablespoon Big Four Paste per each pound ground meat mixture and shape into meatballs. Add to the boiling broth. Meatballs can also be grilled.

for meat loaf Add 1 tablespoon Big Four Paste for each pound of ground meat, mixing it in with the other ingredients.

other main dishes

sage tagliarini

from *Tom Douglas' Seattle Kitchen*

MAKES 4 TO 6 SERVINGS

A big dish of noodles with butter and Parmesan is one of my daughter Loretta's favorite things in the world (which is why we have My Kid's Favorite Oodles of Noodles on the menu every day at Dahlia). Here we have added the classic Italian touch of crispy, fried sage leaves.

For this we use the finest Parmigiano-Reggiano, and we often take a little chunk of it and shave it with a vegetable peeler directly over the pasta for nice-looking curls.

1	pound tagliarini, fresh or dried, or linguine or spaghetti
½	cup (1 stick) unsalted butter
3	sprigs fresh sage (about 3 tablespoons leaves)
	Kosher salt and freshly ground black pepper
¼	cup freshly shaved Parmigiano-Reggiano or other dry cheese (about 1 ounce)

Bring a large pot of salted water to a boil. Cook the pasta until *al dente.* Meanwhile, melt the butter in a sauté pan over medium-high heat. When the butter is melted, add the sage leaves and fry them for a few minutes until they start to get crisp. Drain the pasta and toss it with the sage, butter, and salt and pepper to taste in a large bowl.

on the plate Divide the pasta among the plates. Shave the cheese over each serving.

in the glass A Barbera d'Alba from Piedmont, in northern Italy

---

FOOD&WINE test-kitchen tips

- To show this light sauce to best advantage, serve it with delicate fresh pasta, ideally your own. The suggested tagliarini is egg pasta cut into very thin strips. It can be difficult to get ready-made. We found the recipe was wonderful with good-quality store-bought fresh pasta, such as fettuccine, or a skinnier egg pasta if available.

pastina with milk and eggs

from *Simply Tuscan*

SERVES 4 TO 6

6	cups milk
10	ounces (4 fistfulls) pastina (tiny pasta, sometimes in the shape of stars or seeds)
3	eggs, beaten
3	ounces grated Parmigiano cheese
	Salt and freshly ground pepper

Bring the milk to a boil in a large, heavy saucepan over high heat. Add the pastina and cook until it is slightly softer than *al dente*, and the milk is as thick as cream. Remove the pan from the heat and stir in the eggs, cheese, and salt and pepper to taste.

FOOD&WINE test-kitchen tips

- Pastina is sometimes hard to find. We tested this with orzo and loved the dish. It's Italian macaroni and cheese—yummy and virtually instant. The orzo cooked and the milk thickened in about 12 minutes.

 wine recommendation This straightforward dish will be well paired with a relatively simple wine. A Pinot Blanc from Alsace will be just the ticket, especially since its clear fruit flavors will also contrast nicely with the richness of the pasta.

SIMPLY TUSCAN

PINO LUONGO

tagliatelle soufflé

from Simply Tuscan

SERVES 8 TO 10

for the béchamel

6 tablespoons butter

⅓ cup flour

4 cups hot milk

½ teaspoon grated nutmeg

Salt and freshly ground pepper to taste

for the soufflé

¾ cup freshly grated Parmesan cheese

1 cup freshly grated Emmenthaler cheese

4 egg yolks

13 ounces dry tagliatelle (flat, narrow egg noodles—if you use fresh,
you'll need 1 pound)

6 tablespoons butter, room temperature

6 egg whites

make the béchamel In a saucepan over medium-low heat, melt the butter. Add the
flour and stir constantly until the roux turns golden brown, about 3 minutes. Add the milk, a
little at a time, stirring constantly to prevent lumps. Cook until the sauce thickens, about 5
minutes. Remove from the heat, stir in the nutmeg, and season with salt and pepper.

FOOD&WINE test-kitchen tips

- So that this interesting dish will be full of flavor, be sure to use enough salt in the pasta-boiling water
  (a good handful) and in the béchamel. Otherwise both the pasta and the béchamel are bland,
  bland, bland, even with the amount of cheese in this recipe. We found that 1¼ teaspoons was right
  for the béchamel.

 wine recommendation The airiness of this dish calls for a wine that is just as light. Look for a
Muscadet from the Loire region of France. Sèvre-et-Maine is the best part of the Muscadet area,
and so a wine with this name on the label will typically have a bit more character than others—
and will also be more expensive.

make the soufflé Stir the grated cheeses into the béchamel while it's still hot, but off the heat. When the sauce is no longer hot, but still warm, mix in the egg yolks, one at a time. In a large pot of boiling salted water, blanch the tagliatelle for just a couple of minutes—they will cook more in the oven. Drain the pasta, but reserve 5 tablespoons of the water in which they were cooked. In a large mixing bowl, toss the tagliatelle with 4 tablespoons of the butter and the reserved pasta water. Add the béchamel to the pasta, stirring all the while to mix everything thoroughly. Let the mixture cool to room temperature, mixing once in a while to prevent settling, separation, and sticking.

While the pasta is cooling, preheat the oven to 375ºF. Use the remaining 2 tablespoons of butter to grease a 3-quart soufflé dish. In a bowl, whip the egg whites to stiff peaks. When the pasta has cooled down, stir the beaten egg whites carefully into the soufflé mixture. Add the soufflé mixture to the soufflé dish, evening the surface with a spatula. Bake in the preheated oven for 30 minutes. Reduce the heat to 350º and cook for 10 minutes more. Do not open the oven while the soufflé is cooking—if you do, it is likely to fall. When the soufflé has "puffed" up about 1 to 2 inches over the top of the dish, remove it from the oven gently and bring it to the table immediately to serve.

toasted penne with herbs, goat cheese, and golden bread crumbs

from *Tom Douglas' Seattle Kitchen*

MAKES 6 SERVINGS

I got the idea for toasting dry pasta in a hot oven, before boiling, on a trip to Italy years ago. This technique is quite easy and gives the pasta a slightly different color and texture than untoasted pasta.

1	tablespoon extra virgin olive oil
⅔	cup fine dry bread crumbs
	Kosher salt and freshly ground black pepper
⅓	cup finely chopped fresh flat-leaf parsley
1	tablespoon grated lemon zest
1	pound penne
2	tablespoons (¼ stick) unsalted butter
¼	cup minced shallots
1	teaspoon minced garlic
¼	teaspoon red pepper flakes
2	cups heavy cream
1	teaspoon chopped fresh rosemary
1	teaspoon chopped fresh thyme
1	teaspoon chopped fresh sage
3	tablespoons freshly grated Parmesan cheese
5	ounces soft, fresh goat cheese

1 To make the toasted bread crumbs, heat a medium-size sauté pan over medium-high heat with the olive oil. Add the bread crumbs and stir until the crumbs begin to brown and get crunchy. Season with salt and pepper. Allow to cool. Once the bread crumbs are cool, combine with the parsley and lemon zest. Set aside.

2 Bring a large pot of salted water to a boil and preheat the oven to 400°F. Place the penne on a baking sheet and bake until the pasta just begins to brown, 5 to 6 minutes. Watch carefully, because it goes from yellow to brown very fast. Allow the pasta to cool off for a few minutes, then dump it into the pot of boiling water and cook until it is just *al dente*, 10 to 12 minutes. Drain.

3 Meanwhile, make the sauce. Heat the butter in a large wide-bottomed saucepan or a deep straight-sided sauté pan over medium heat and cook the shallots, stirring, about 3 minutes. Add the garlic and the pepper flakes and cook, stirring, for another minute. Add the heavy cream and simmer until it reduces by a third, about 5 minutes. Add the herbs, penne, and Parmesan and remove the pan from the heat. Crumble the goat cheese into the pasta and toss, seasoning to taste with salt and pepper.

on the plate Divide the penne and sauce among 6 shallow bowls and sprinkle with the toasted bread crumbs.

in the glass Try a Sangiovese from Umbria, a richer style than Tuscany, or a Sangiovese from Washington State.

FOOD&WINE test-kitchen tips

- If you have trouble finding all four fresh herbs, you can make some substitutions. The parsley absolutely must be fresh, but for any of the other herbs, the dried form can stand in. Use about a quarter of the quantity specified and add it before you simmer the cream, rather than after, so it has time to reconstitute and to infuse the cream with its flavor.

gnocchi with tomato sauce and mozzarella

strangulapreti alla sorrentina

from *Holiday Food*

SERVES 4 TO 8

Who knows the true story behind these gnocchi's colorful name? Suffice it to say they are so irresistible even a priest could be tempted to gorge himself (the literal translation of *strangulapreti* is "priest stranglers.") The circumstances of a priest's demise aside, these are my family gnocchi and they are particularly tender.

gnocchi dough

3   pounds russet potatoes

2   cups all-purpose flour

1   extra-large egg

Pinch of kosher salt

½ cup olive oil

condiment

1   teaspoon hot red pepper flakes

4   cups Basic Tomato Sauce (page 171)

Approximately 1 teaspoon kosher salt, or to taste

¼   cup fresh basil leaves, lightly packed

½   pound fresh mozzarella di bufala, cut into ¼-inch cubes

Boil the whole potatoes until they are soft, about 45 minutes. While still warm, peel the potatoes and pass them through a food mill onto a clean pasta board.

Bring 6 quarts of water to a boil and set up an ice bath with 4 cups ice and 3 quarts water next to the stove.

▼

Make a well in the center of the potatoes and sprinkle with the flour. Place the egg and salt in the center of the well and, using a fork, stir the egg into the flour and potatoes. Bring the dough together, kneading gently until a ball is formed and continue to knead gently another 4 minutes until the dough is dry to the touch. Cut a tennis ball–size hunk of dough off the main ball and roll it into a dowel about ¾ inch thick. Cut across the dowel to form pellets about 1 inch long. Flick each pellet down the tines of a fork to form the traditional gnocchi shape. Repeat with the remaining dough. Drop a third of the gnocchi into the boiling water. When they are floating aggressively (after 3 to 4 minutes of cooking), remove the gnocchi to the ice bath. Repeat with the 2 remaining batches of gnocchi and allow all gnocchi to cool in the ice bath. Drain the cooled gnocchi well, stir in the olive oil, cover, and refrigerate until ready to cook. The gnocchi will keep up to 36 hours in the fridge.

When you are ready to serve the gnocchi, bring 6 quarts of water to a boil and add 2 tablespoons salt. In a 14- to 16-inch fry pan, combine the pepper flakes, tomato sauce, and 1 teaspoon salt. Bring to a boil, reduce heat, and simmer 15 minutes, or until the sauce is as thick as a good porridge. (At this point the sauce could be refrigerated for up to 2 days.)

Drop the gnocchi into the boiling water and cook until floating aggressively, 4 to 5 minutes. Carefully transfer the gnocchi to the pan with the sauce, using a slotted spoon. Turn the heat to medium and toss gently for about 30 seconds. Tear the basil leaves into a few pieces and add to the sauce along with the mozzarella cubes. Toss together for 30 seconds longer, pour into a heated bowl, and serve immediately.

FOOD&WINE test-kitchen tips

- We tested this recipe using a food mill and also with a ricer, both of which worked perfectly. Lacking either, you can puree the potatoes with a standard potato masher, though they won't be quite so light.

 wine recommendation The tartness of tomato sauce calls for a wine with a sprightly acidity of its own—and definitely no oak. Try a refreshing Greco di Tufo, which also has a nutty taste that will mesh nicely with the earthy potato flavor of the gnocchi.

basic tomato sauce

¼   cup extra-virgin olive oil

1   large onion, cut into ¼-inch dice

4   garlic cloves, thinly sliced

3   tablespoons chopped fresh thyme leaves, or 1 tablespoon dried

½   medium carrot, finely shredded

2   28-ounce cans peeled whole tomatoes, crushed by hand and juices reserved

Kosher salt to taste

In a 3-quart saucepan, heat the olive oil over medium heat. Add the onion and garlic and cook until soft and light golden brown, 8 to 10 minutes. Add the thyme and carrot and cook 5 minutes more, until the carrot is quite soft. Add the tomatoes and juice and bring to a boil, stirring often. Lower the heat and simmer for 30 minutes until as thick as hot cereal. Season with salt. This sauce holds 1 week in the refrigerator or up to 6 months in the freezer.

other main dishes

Gordon Ramsay
A chef for all seasons

pumpkin and pancetta risotto

from Gordon Ramsay A Chef for all Seasons

SERVES 4 AS A FIRST COURSE OR 2 AS A MAIN DISH

It is a poor autumn kitchen indeed that does not have a plump pumpkin available. There are so many ways to take advantage of its creamy, sweet golden flesh, from soups and stews through to pasta fillings and pies. A risotto with a lightly browned diced pumpkin *brunoise,* some smoky, crisp pancetta, and tangy Parmesan makes a good light meal.

$\frac{1}{3}$ cup chopped pancetta

2 to 2$\frac{1}{2}$ cups Light Chicken Stock (recipe follows)

2   large shallots, chopped

1   pound pumpkin flesh, cut into $\frac{1}{2}$-inch cubes (about 4 cups)

3   tablespoons olive oil

Scant 1 cup risotto rice (Carnaroli, Arborio, or Vialone Nano)

$\frac{1}{2}$ cup dry white wine

2   tablespoons mascarpone

$\frac{1}{4}$ cup freshly grated Parmesan cheese

Sea salt and freshly ground black pepper

1 Heat a dry non-stick frying pan and, when hot, fry the pancetta until browned and crisp. Drain and set aside. Heat the stock to a gentle simmer in a saucepan.

2 In a large saucepan, gently sauté the shallots and pumpkin in the oil for about 5 minutes. Stir in the rice and cook for a further 2 minutes to toast the grains. Pour in the wine and cook until reduced right down.

FOOD&WINE test-kitchen tips

- We found readily available butternut squash to be a fine substitute for the pumpkin here. We used one small squash.

- If your rice isn't perfectly fresh (a common occurrence in the U.S.), it may be quite dried out and need longer cooking and more liquid than specified here by the English author. We cooked the risotto for 25 minutes, and used about 3$\frac{1}{2}$ cups liquid in all. The risotto really doesn't need any more chicken flavor, though. We just added hot water when we ran out of stock.

wine recommendation Rustic Italian flavors call for simple Italian wines. Bardolino or Valpolicella, both from the Veneto region of Italy, will be perfect partners for this homey risotto.

3 Now pour in one-fourth of the stock and stir well. Cook gently until the liquid has been absorbed, then stir in another ladleful of stock. Continue cooking and stirring, gradually adding the stock, until the rice grains are just tender and the risotto is creamy. The whole process should take about 15 minutes.

4 About 2 minutes before the end of the cooking, stir in the pancetta, mascarpone, and half the Parmesan. Check the seasoning, then serve in warmed bowls, sprinkled with the remaining Parmesan.

light chicken stock   Place 6½ to 7 pounds raw chicken carcasses or bony portions in a large stockpot. Add 5 quarts of cold water, 3 quartered onions, 2 chopped leeks, 2 large chopped carrots, 4 chopped celery stalks, 1 small head garlic (cut across in half), 1 large sprig fresh thyme, and 1 tablespoon sea salt. Bring slowly to a boil, skimming off any scum that rises using a large metal spoon (not slotted because the scum can drain through). Boil for 5 minutes, then turn the heat right down and simmer for 3 to 4 hours. Cool and allow the solids to settle. Line a colander with a sheet of wet cheesecloth and slowly pour the stock through. Cool and chill. This can be kept in the fridge for up to 3 days or frozen. It makes about 3 quarts of lovely stock.

thai fried rice

khao pad (from Thailand)

from *Hot Sour Salty Sweet*

SERVES 1

This is a simple, straightforward version of Thai fried rice, a dish we usually eat at least once a day in Thailand, and about half that frequently at home. While we like other versions of fried rice, for us it is the Thai version that is far and away the best. Maybe it is the combination of fish sauce, jasmine rice, and the taste of the wok. Maybe it is the squeeze of lime and fish sauce with chiles *(prik nam pla)* as condiments. Maybe it is the hundreds of different places where we've happily sat eating Thai fried rice, the totality of all those nice associations. Whatever it is, we love it. Thai fried rice is one of life's great simple dishes.

The following recipe is for one serving. If you have a large wok, the recipe is easily doubled to serve two; increase the cooking time by about 30 seconds. If you are serving more than two, prepare the additional servings separately. The cooking time is very short, so once all your ingredients are prepared, it is easy to go through the same cooking process—simply clean out the wok and wipe it dry each time. It is much easier to prepare *khao pad* when your wok isn't overly full. Total preparation time is about 8 minutes; cooking time is about 4 minutes.

2	tablespoons peanut oil
4 to 8	cloves garlic, minced (or even more if not using optional ingredients)
1 to 2	ounces thinly sliced boneless pork (optional)
2	cups cold cooked rice (preferably Thai jasmine)
2	scallions, trimmed, slivered lengthwise, and cut into 1-inch lengths (optional)
2	teaspoons Thai fish sauce, or to taste

garnish and accompaniments

About ¼ cup coriander leaves

About 6 thin cucumber slices

1	small scallion, trimmed (optional)
2	lime wedges
¼	cup Thai Fish Sauce with Hot Chiles (page 177)

Heat a large heavy wok over high heat. When it is hot, add the oil and heat until very hot. Add the garlic and stir-fry until just golden, about 20 seconds. Add the pork, if using, and cook, stirring constantly, until all the pork has changed color completely, about 1 minute. Add the rice, breaking it up with wet fingers as you toss it into the wok. With your spatula, keep moving the rice around the wok. At first it may stick, but keep scooping and tossing it and soon it will be more manageable. Try to visualize frying each little bit of rice, sometimes pressing the rice against the wok with the back of your spatula. Good fried rice should have a faint seared-in-the-wok taste. Cook for approximately 1½ minutes. Add the optional scallions, then the fish sauce, and stir-fry for 30 seconds to 1 minute.

Turn out onto a dinner plate and garnish with the coriander. Lay a row of cucumber slices, the scallion, and the lime wedges around the rice. Squeeze the lime onto the rice as you eat it, along with the chile sauce—the salty, hot taste of the sauce brings out the full flavor of the rice.

notes Once you've tossed the garlic into the hot oil, you can also add about ½ teaspoon red curry paste or Thai roasted chile paste *(nam prik pao).* It adds another layer of flavor and a little heat too.

Fried rice is very accommodating: If you have a little tomato or spinach or other greens, finely chop them and add after you've begun to stir-fry the rice.

Many people (we're among them) like to eat a fried egg on top of their fried rice. Wipe out your wok, heat about 2 teaspoons of oil, and quickly fry the egg, then turn it out onto the rice. It's delicious.

▼

other main dishes

FOOD&WINE test-kitchen tips

- This particularly delectable fried rice is a meal in itself, but we also like it, without the optional sliced pork, alongside a simple sautéed pork chop. As a side dish, the rice serves three or four people nicely.

wine recommendation A wine based on the aromatic Muscat grape will be a fabulous match for the exotic flavors of this dish. Look for a Gelber Muskateller from Austria or a Goldenmuskateller from northern Italy.

thai fish sauce with hot chiles *prik nam pla (from Thailand, Laos)* This common Thai chile sauce is our everyday condiment, almost as important in our house as salt. It keeps forever and brings to the table a reliable hit of salt and chile heat. It's not mild and subtle, like the Vietnamese *nuoc cham,* but brassy and forward and altogether unapologetic. Drizzle a little on fried rice or plain rice, or Thai or Lao food, or whatever you please, mouthful by mouthful.

We keep our *prik nam pla* in a plastic container in the refrigerator, topping it up with extra fish sauce as it runs low. Eventually the chiles too run low, and also lose their punch. Then it's time to top up the chiles (and then the sauce is *very* hot).

When handling bird chiles, you may want to wear rubber gloves to protect your skin. When you chop them, by hand or in the processor, you may find yourself coughing and sneezing as the capsaicin from the cut chiles hits the air. Don't worry, it passes soon. And this simple sauce is worth the effort.

MAKES JUST OVER 1 CUP SAUCE

½ cup bird chiles, stems removed
1 cup Thai fish sauce

Place the chiles in a food processor and pulse to finely chop (stop before they are a mush). Or, wearing rubber gloves to protect your hands, use a cleaver or sharp knife to mince the chiles on a cutting board.

Transfer the minced chiles (with their seeds) to a glass or plastic container and add the fish sauce. Cover and store in the refrigerator. The sauce will keep indefinitely, losing chile heat over time; top it up with extra chiles or fish sauce when it runs low. Serve in small individual condiment bowls.

other main dishes

vegetables
& side dishes

asian long beans with soy shallot vinaigrette

from *Tom Douglas' Seattle Kitchen*

MAKES 6 SERVINGS

We like Chinese long beans, which are often 12 inches or longer, for this dish, but of course you can use any type of fresh green bean. Blanching the beans and immediately chilling them in ice water to stop the cooking helps maintain the best color. You can leave the long beans whole and tie them in decorative knots for a dramatic presentation, or you can cut them into more manageable 3-inch lengths.

for the soy shallot vinaigrette

3	tablespoons sherry vinegar
3	tablespoons finely chopped shallots
4	teaspoons fresh lemon juice
2	teaspoons soy sauce
2	teaspoons Asian fish sauce
1	teaspoon Chinese chile paste with garlic
1	teaspoon sugar
½	teaspoon minced garlic
½	cup peanut oil

for the beans

1	pound Chinese long beans or green beans, ends trimmed
Kosher salt	
2	teaspoons sesame seeds, toasted

1 To make the vinaigrette, in a small bowl, combine the vinegar, shallots, lemon juice, soy sauce, fish sauce, chile-garlic paste, sugar, and garlic. Whisk in the peanut oil until well emulsified. Set the vinaigrette aside.

FOOD&WINE test-kitchen tips

- Though conceived as part of a bento box, these flavorful beans can be used any which way—as an appetizer, a salad, a side dish with simply cooked poultry or meat, or as part of a buffet.

- As an accompaniment, these are best with a simply prepared main dish, like grilled salmon, sautéed chicken, or roast beef.

2 Fill a large pot with lightly salted water and bring to a boil. Add the long beans and cook until tender, about 5 minutes. Drain the beans and immediately plunge them in a container of ice water. When the beans are chilled, drain them and pat off the excess water on kitchen towels. In a large bowl, toss the beans with the vinaigrette. Season to taste with kosher salt.

on the plate If you've used long beans, you can gather a few together and tie them in a knot. Long beans look nice stacked lengthwise in little bundles. If there's any extra vinaigrette in the bowl, drizzle it over the beans and sprinkle them with the toasted sesame seeds.

a step ahead The vinaigrette can be made a few days ahead and stored refrigerated, covered with plastic wrap. You can blanch the beans a few hours before needed and keep them, covered, in the refrigerator.

how to toast seeds and nuts Toast seeds and nuts by placing them in a heavy skillet over medium heat for a few minutes, tossing and stirring constantly until they brown lightly and give off a toasted aroma. You can also place seeds and nuts on a baking sheet in a preheated 350° to 375°F oven for 5 to 10 minutes (sesame seeds and pine nuts brown quickly, while large nuts like pecan halves take a bit longer). Stir the seeds or nuts occasionally and watch them carefully so they don't burn. Don't overcrowd the nuts. Try to keep them in a single layer whichever method you use.

Hazelnuts have thin brown skins. After roasting the nuts, remove most of the skins by rubbing the still-warm nuts against each other in a clean dish towel.

If you are using a food processor to chop toasted nuts, be sure to pulse off and on briefly so you don't turn them into a paste. Otherwise, just chop them with a sharp knife.

Nuts and seeds are high in oil and they turn rancid quickly. Buy the freshest, best-quality nuts and seeds you can find. For freshness, store nuts in the freezer; you can use them directly in the recipes without thawing.

marinated butternut squash

sapece di zuca

from *Holiday Food*

SERVES 8 TO 12

It is their simple way with seasonal vegetables that most amazes me about Italian cooks. This marinated squash dish is a lot more than the sum of its ingredients, for both flavor and presentation. You can make the whole dish in the morning; just hold the mint until the moment before serving.

As with almost all Italian vegetable dishes, a drizzle of your best extra-virgin olive oil, right before serving, will add infinitely to your pleasure.

2   medium butternut squash, skin on, seeded and cut crosswise into 1-inch slices
Kosher salt and freshly ground black pepper
½   cup extra-virgin olive oil
¼   cup red wine vinegar
½   medium red onion, sliced paper-thin
½   teaspoon hot red pepper flakes
1   tablespoon dried oregano
1   garlic clove, sliced paper-thin
¼   cup fresh mint leaves

Preheat the oven to 450°F.

Season the squash with salt and pepper, drizzle with ¼ cup of the olive oil, and arrange in a single layer on a cookie sheet or two. Roast until just tender, 18 to 20 minutes.

Meanwhile, stir together the remaining ¼ cup of oil, the vinegar, onion, pepper flakes, oregano, and garlic and season with salt and pepper.

FOOD&WINE test-kitchen tips

- For the marinade, about half a teaspoon of salt seemed to be the right quantity to us.

- Since the warm squash absorbs the marinade more readily than it would when completely cooled, we let the slices cool just a few minutes in the pan before transferring to a serving dish and pouring the marinade over them.

When the squash is cooled, immediately transfer to a dish and pour the marinade over them. Allow to cool in the marinade for at least 20 minutes. This dish can be made up to 6 hours in advance but should not be refrigerated. Sprinkle with the mint just before serving at room temperature.

zucchini-cheese patties
kolokythokeftedes

from *The Foods of the Greek Islands*

MAKES 6 TO 8 SERVINGS

Zucchini patties are a very common *meze* and are often served during Lent, when those who observe the Greek Orthodox religious traditions abstain from any foods derived from animals. You will find many variations of these patties throughout Greece: Some cooks, for example, prefer to boil the zucchini, then mash it and drain it in a cheesecloth bag before mixing it with sautéed onions and other ingredients. This recipe uses grated raw zucchini, scallions and plenty of fresh herbs. The cheese, which would be omitted during Lent, is optional.

These patties are adapted from a recipe that Kalliopi Delios makes at her taverna, Kastro, in Avgonima. To bind the patties, she uses cornstarch instead of flour, with the result that the patties are particularly light-textured.

4	cups grated zucchini (3 to 4 zucchini), drained in a colander for at least 1 hour
1	cup chopped scallions (white and most of the green parts)
1	cup chopped fresh flat-leaf parsley
1	cup grated hard myzithra, kefalotyri, pecorino Romano or Parmesan cheese (optional)
1	cup cornstarch
½	cup chopped fresh mint
1	tablespoon dried oregano, crumbled

Salt and freshly ground black pepper
Olive oil and safflower oil for frying

In a large bowl, combine the zucchini, scallions, parsley, cheese (if using), cornstarch, mint, oregano and salt and pepper to taste. Let stand at room temperature for 15 minutes.

FOOD&WINE test-kitchen tips

- As the recipe suggests, the patties can be served hot or allowed to cool to warm or even to room temperature. But we're willing to bet you won't want to wait to let them cool; they're so good hot out of the pan while they're still crisp.

- Though served as *meze*—the Greek equivalent of *tapas*—in their homeland, the patties make a delectable side dish with sautéed chicken breasts.

In a large, deep skillet, heat 1½ inches of a combination of olive and safflower oil over medium-high heat to 350°F. To make a test patty, stir the zucchini mixture and, using the spoon, scoop up an amount about the size of a golf ball. With the help of a second spoon, shape it into a patty and place it in the hot oil. Fry, turning once, until browned, about 3 minutes. Taste the patty and adjust the seasonings in the remaining zucchini mixture, if necessary. Shape and fry the remaining patties, in batches, and transfer to paper towels to drain. Serve hot, warm or at room temperature.

curried brussels sprouts

from *The Farmer's Market Cookbook*

YIELDS 6 SERVINGS

I have enjoyed brussels sprouts since I was a little kid, when I would peel each leaf from the vegetable and slowly consume them. Finding brussels on the branch is so exciting to me. I'm never sure if I want to pick off the vegetable or land the stalk in a vase as a floral display, so I usually buy two. The stalk itself is edible (like broccoli stalks). You just have to peel away the fibrous outer layer to expose the more tender inner flesh. Cut the stalks into the same size as the sprouts and add them to the mix. Of course, if the ones on branch are not available, use ones that have already been plucked for you.

1	branch of brussels sprouts (about 2 inches in length with well-developed sprouts)—yields approximately 3 cups
1	cup chicken stock
1	cup water
4	ounces unsalted butter—at room temperature
2	tablespoons curry powder

Salt and freshly ground black pepper to taste

Remove the brussels sprouts from the branch, discard any damaged external leaves, and, using a paring knife, place a light "X" on the bottom end of each sprout. Place the sprouts in an 8-inch highsided pan, in a single layer, more or less. Add the stock and water, and bring to the boil over a high heat. Reduce the heat to a simmer and cook for 15 minutes.

Combine the butter and curry together to make an amalgamated mass. Then add this into the sprouts and season with salt and pepper. Cook an additional 10 minutes to reduce the remaining liquid to glaze the brussels sprouts. Serve hot.

FOOD&WINE test-kitchen tips

- If you're not buying the sprouts by the branch, 1½ pints will be the right quantity for this recipe.

- We love these with steamed lobster, broiled salmon, or baked ham.

tempura with western vegetables

seiyo yasai no tempura

from *The Japanese Kitchen*

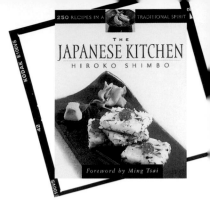

YIELDS 4 SERVINGS AS A SIDE DISH

Japanese vegetable tempura can employ any fresh vegetables, including sweet potato, carrot, burdock, lotus root, onion, green beans, shiitake mushrooms, okra, *kabocha* pumpkin, chrysanthemum leaves, eggplant, bamboo shoots, and shiso. Today asparagus, button mushrooms, and several other newcomers have joined this traditional group. Use any locally available, seasonal vegetables to enjoy this now very popular preparation.

The oil for tempura is a blend of vegetable oil and sesame oil, usually about 80 percent vegetable oil and 20 percent sesame oil. Increasing the proportion of sesame oil provides a deeper golden color and nuttier flavor to the fried items.

1	egg
1½	cups cake flour
1	zucchini, cut diagonally into ⅓-inch-thick slices
1	fennel bulb, cut into ⅓-inch-wide sticks
8	button mushrooms, stems removed
8	large dandelion leaves, stems removed

A blend of sesame oil and vegetable oil, for deep-frying

condiments

2	cups *tentsuyu* (tempura dipping sauce, page 189)
½	cup grated daikon

In a 2-cup measuring cup, beat the egg lightly, and add enough ice water to make ¾ cup liquid, about ½ cup. Transfer half of the egg liquid to a medium bowl, reserving the rest. Add ½ cup flour to the egg liquid in the bowl, and immediately give several big stirs with a pair of cooking chopsticks, a fork, or a whisk. Do not stir the batter thoroughly. Overmixing develops the gluten in the flour and produces a lumpy, bready, heavy crust when the batter is fried.

▼

vegetables & side dishes

Put ½ cup flour into a medium bowl for dredging the vegetables. In a large, deep skillet, heat 3 inches of oil to 340°F. Pick up one vegetable slice, and dredge it with flour. Shake off the excess flour, and dip the vegetable slice in the batter. Pull out the vegetable slice, and lightly shake off the excess batter. Carefully add the vegetable slice to the heated oil. This process—dredging and shaking the vegetable slice, dipping it in batter, then placing it in the hot oil—should take only a few seconds.

Cook all the vegetables in the same way, in small batches, three to five pieces at one time (depending on the size of the skillet), until the outsides are light golden and crisp and the vegetables are cooked through. Transfer the fried vegetables to a rack. When you've used half the vegetables, add the remaining egg liquid and ½ cup flour to the bowl, and stir. Use this batter to finish cooking the vegetables.

Serve the tempura immediately, with the dipping sauce and grated daikon in separate bowls on the side. Diners should add a little grated daikon to the sauce before dipping the fried items in it.

It is always best to eat tempura when it has just been removed from the oil. This makes it necessary for the cook to work without stopping and feed the diners continuously, until they say, "We have had enough!" At the risk of losing some crispiness, however, you can serve all the tempura on a large platter after you finish the frying. In this case, replacing a little of the flour in the batter with cornstarch will prevent the fried items from becoming soggy too soon.

FOOD&WINE test-kitchen tips

- Almost any vegetables can be used in tempura, as the author says. Dandelion greens were out of season when we tested this recipe. Frisee or curly endive both worked well as substitutes.

- With our oil at the recommended temperature, our cooking time was about two minutes a side for the zucchini, fennel, and mushrooms and one minute per side for the leafy green.

tempura dipping sauce *tentsuyu* Tentsuyu is a dipping sauce that is served with piping-hot fried foods, such as tempura. Dipping hot foods in *tentsuyu* cools them a little, and at the same time provides extra flavor. This sauce is served at room temperature.

YIELDS 2⅔ CUPS SAUCE

3 tablespoons *mirin* (sweet cooking wine)

2 cups *ichiban dashi* (first fish stock)

5 tablespoons *usukuchi shoyu* (light-colored soy sauce)

1½ tablespoons *shoyu* (soy sauce)

1½ tablespoons sugar

In a medium pot, bring all the ingredients to a boil. Remove the pot from the heat, and let the sauce cool to room temperature.

You can refrigerate the sauce for up to three days, covered. Before using it, heat it through and let it cool to room temperature.

vegetables & side dishes

roast tomatoes stuffed with bitter greens

from *Simple to Spectacular*

MAKES 4 SERVINGS

To reduce the bitterness of the greens, we cook

them quickly first; to keep them moist during roasting, we add a little goat cheese. The result is an assertive but creamy mixture that smacks of the farm. This variation is best hot or warm, rather than cold. Serve as a first course, as part of a buffet, or as a side dish.

4   firm but ripe tomatoes (about 6 ounces each)
Salt and freshly ground black pepper
¼   cup extra-virgin olive oil
½   cup chopped scallions
2   tablespoons minced shallots
About 4 cups mixed bitter greens (arugula, dandelion, radicchio, etc.), washed, dried, and roughly chopped
⅓   cup soft fresh goat cheese
2   tablespoons balsamic or sherry vinegar

1   Preheat the oven to 450°F. Cut a ¼-inch slice from the smooth end of each tomato (reserve these slices) and use a spoon to scoop out all of the insides, leaving a wall about ¼ inch thick. Sprinkle the inside of the tomatoes with salt and pepper. Discard the woody core and seeds; reserve the tomato pulp.

2   Place 2 tablespoons of the olive oil in a large skillet and turn the heat to medium-high. Add the scallions and shallots, with a large pinch of salt, and cook, stirring, for about 3 minutes, until they are wilted and translucent. Add the greens and cook, stirring, until they wilt, just a minute or two. Remove from the skillet and cool briefly.

▼

FOOD&WINE test-kitchen tips

- When you cut a ¼-inch slice from the tomato, it loses its bottom. Don't worry; the recipe works out just fine. Each stuffed tomato sits neatly on its top, which is less roly-poly than the bottom. And the open bottom becomes the top of the stuffed tomato.

- The cooked tomatoes are fragile. We found the best way to transfer them from the pan is with two large spoons.

3 Combine the greens with the tomato pulp and salt and pepper to taste. Fill the tomatoes about halfway, then spoon one-quarter of the goat cheese into each tomato. Finish stuffing the tomatoes with the remaining greens mixture and replace the top slices.

4 Spread 1 tablespoon of the olive oil in a shallow roasting pan that will allow for a little room between the tomatoes, then place them in the pan and drizzle with the remaining 1 tablespoon olive oil. Sprinkle with salt and pepper and place the roasting pan in the oven.

5 Roast for 30 to 40 minutes, until the tomatoes are shriveled and the stuffing is hot (pierce the stuffing to its center with a skewer and touch the skewer to your wrist or lip).

6 Transfer the tomatoes to a platter and place the roasting pan over high heat. Add the vinegar and cook, stirring, for just about 15 seconds. Drizzle the juices over the tomatoes and serve.

TIME: 1 HOUR

potato dumplings with pumpkin, hazelnuts, bacon, and brown butter

from *Wildwood*

SERVES 4 AS AN APPETIZER OR SIDE DISH

Field pumpkins are meant for carving, but sugar pumpkins make a nice soup or purée to go with a game dish. This recipe uses one of my favorite flavor combinations: pumpkin, bacon, sage, and brown butter. The dumplings can be made 1 day ahead.

potato dumplings

1½	pounds Yukon Gold potatoes, peeled and quartered
2	teaspoons chopped fresh sage
1	teaspoon salt
¼	teaspoon cayenne pepper
¼	teaspoon ground allspice
¼	teaspoon ground nutmeg
¼	teaspoon freshly ground black pepper
½	cup all-purpose flour
¼	cup semolina flour
1	large egg, beaten

1	sugar pumpkin (3 to 4 pounds), seeded and cut into 6 pieces
1	tablespoon olive oil
1¾	teaspoons salt
¾	teaspoon freshly ground black pepper
4	slices bacon
½	cup (1 stick) unsalted butter
2	tablespoons fresh lemon juice
½	cup hazelnuts, toasted, skinned, and chopped (page 195)
2	tablespoons chopped fresh flat-leaf parsley
¼	cup shaved Asiago or pecorino cheese

▼

To make the dumplings: Preheat the oven to 325°. In a large pot, cover the potatoes with water. Bring to a boil, reduce heat, and simmer for about 15 minutes, or until tender when pierced with a knife. Drain well and let stand at room temperature to dry for 5 minutes. When the potatoes are cool enough to handle, pass them through a food mill or grate them on the large holes of a box grater. Cover a large baking sheet with waxed paper or parchment paper. Spread out the grated potatoes on it, and place in the oven to dry out for 5 minutes. Place in the refrigerator to cool, about 15 minutes.

Put the potatoes in a large bowl. Form a well in the center and add the sage, salt, cayenne, allspice, nutmeg, and pepper. Add half of each of the flours and stir the mixture for 1 minute. Stir in the egg and the remaining flours. Transfer the dough to a lightly floured board and knead, working to incorporate all of the ingredients. Wrap in plastic wrap and refrigerate for 1½ hours or overnight.

Meanwhile, preheat the oven to 350°. Put the pumpkin or squash in a baking pan. Baste lightly with the olive oil and season with ¾ teaspoon of the salt and ¼ teaspoon of the pepper. Bake for 25 to 35 minutes, or until slightly soft. Leave the oven on. Let cool and cut off the skin. Cut the pumpkin or squash into ½-inch dice and set aside.

To form the dumplings, remove the dough from the refrigerator and cut into 4 pieces. Dust a board with semolina flour and roll each piece of dough into a rope ½ inch in diameter. Cut into 1-inch pieces and place on an oiled jelly-roll pan. (At this point, the dumplings can be refrigerated overnight.) Bake the dumplings for 20 to 25 minutes, or until lightly browned and cooked through.

FOOD&WINE test-kitchen tips

- This recipe makes a generous, restaurant-size portion. We cut the recipe in half and found that the quantity was just right for four.

- Since sugar pumpkins are hard to find in many parts of the country, we tested this recipe with butternut squash, which worked beautifully.

Just before the dumplings are ready, in a 12-inch skillet, cook the bacon until crisp. Transfer the bacon to paper towels to drain, then crumble. Discard the drippings and wipe out the pan. Add the butter and cook over medium heat until it begins to brown. Add the bacon, lemon juice, hazelnuts, parsley, diced pumpkin or squash, and the remaining 1 teaspoon salt and $\frac{1}{2}$ teaspoon pepper. Cook to heat through.

To assemble, spoon the dumplings into pasta bowls and top with the pumpkin brown butter sauce. Garnish with the cheese and serve.

toasting nuts Preheat the oven to 325°. Place the nuts on a large jelly roll pan, spreading them out so they don't touch. Toast in the oven for 20 minutes, or until lightly browned, occasionally shaking the pan so the nuts toast evenly.

If toasting hazelnuts, remove the nuts from the oven and wrap them in a dish towel to steam and cool them. Once they have cooled a bit, roll the hazelnuts around in the towel to remove the skins. Transfer the hazelnuts to a colander with medium holes and roll them around with your hands to knock off the remainder of the skins. As the hazelnuts are skinned, remove them from the colander.

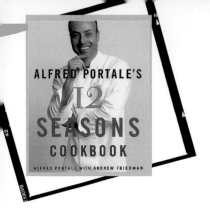

potato and butternut squash gratin with gruyère

from *Alfred Portale's 12 Seasons Cookbook*

MAKES 6 SERVINGS

Potato gratins can be enormously satisfying, especially as rich accompaniments to steaks, but they are also rather one-dimensional. In this recipe, the modest investment of adding butternut squash, and suffusing the cream with thyme and marjoram, pays huge dividends as the gratin assumes a more compelling and complex character with virtually no additional work.

2   pounds butternut squash

3   large russet potatoes

1   teaspoon chopped fresh thyme

1   teaspoon chopped fresh marjoram

1   teaspoon chopped fresh sage

Coarse salt and freshly ground white pepper to taste

3   cloves garlic, peeled and minced

About 2 cups heavy cream

4   ounces Gruyère cheese, coarsely grated

Preheat the oven to 375°F. Generously butter a 9-by-12-inch gratin dish.

Peel the squash and trim the top and bottom. Cut off the seed-filled bottom, halve it, and remove and discard the seeds. Slice the neck of the squash into ⅛-inch-thick rounds and slice the base into ⅛-inch-thick half circles. Peel the potatoes and cut them into ⅛-inch-thick slices. (A French or Japanese mandoline works very well for this.)

In a small bowl, combine the thyme, marjoram, and sage.

FOOD&WINE test-kitchen tips

- If you don't have a large gratin dish, a 9-by-12-inch Pyrex baking dish works perfectly well.

- A food processor makes quick work of the potato slicing.

Beginning with the half circles of squash (reserve the more attractive rounds for the top layers), layer about ⅓ of the squash slices in the gratin dish. Sprinkle with some of the herbs and season with salt and pepper. Layer ½ the potato slices over the squash layer. Sprinkle with some of the herbs and ½ of the minced garlic. Season with salt and pepper.

Spread another third of the squash slices on the potatoes. Sprinkle with some of the herbs and season with salt and pepper. Spread the remaining potatoes in another layer over the squash and sprinkle some of the herbs and the rest of the garlic. Top with the remaining squash and herbs, and season with salt and pepper.

While firmly pressing down on the squash and potatoes with a large spoon, spatula, or your fingers, slowly pour the cream over the top and down the sides of the dish. Add enough to just barely cover the vegetables when pressed. Too much cream will result in a soupy gratin. Too little cream will make it dry.

Cover the dish with foil and bake the gratin for 45 to 50 minutes. Remove the foil and sprinkle with the Gruyère. Continue to bake, uncovered, for 25 to 30 minutes, or until the vegetables are tender, the cream is nearly absorbed, and the top of the gratin is lightly browned. Let the gratin rest for about 10 minutes to absorb all the cream before serving.

potatoes in herbed cream

4 SERVINGS

Just homey scalloped potatoes, really, but with generous quantities of whole herb sprigs steeped in the cream. The technique of infusion works perfectly here. In addition to being fast, it allows just the right amount of flavor to be released into the cream, which in turn is absorbed by the potatoes, making them taste as if they were grown deep in an herb bed.

1	cup whole milk
½	cup heavy cream
4	cloves garlic
3	4-inch sprigs fresh marjoram or Italian oregano
2	4-inch sprigs fresh rosemary
3	4-inch sprigs fresh thyme
1	2-inch sprig fresh sage
6	fresh bay laurel leaves, torn, or 2 dried plus ¼ teaspoon ground nutmeg
¾	teaspoon salt
	Freshly ground black pepper to taste
2	tablespoons unsalted butter, softened
2	large russet (Idaho) potatoes (about 1½ pounds)

1 cream Place the milk and cream in a small saucepan over medium heat. Smash the garlic cloves with the side of a chef's knife and remove the peels. When the milk and cream are boiling, add the garlic, herb sprigs, bay leaves, salt, and pepper. Bring the mixture back to a boil, then immediately remove it from the heat, cover, and let steep for 30 minutes or longer while you prepare the potatoes.

FOOD&WINE test-kitchen tips

- The author suggests smashing the garlic cloves with the side of a chef's knife and removing the peels. This is a great trick for peeling garlic quickly. The easiest way to do it is to put the flat of the blade on the cloves and hit it sharply with your fist.

- As in the preceding recipe, the fastest way to slice the potatoes into even ⅛-inch-thick rounds is to use a food processor.

2 gratin Preheat the oven to 425°F. Butter a shallow 1½-quart baking dish with 1 tablespoon of the butter. Peel the potatoes, slice them ⅛ inch thick, and arrange them in the dish. Bring the herbed cream back to a simmer. Hold a large fine sieve over the baking dish and pour the cream through it and over the potatoes, coating all the slices. The liquid will not completely cover the potatoes at this point. Dot with the remaining 1 tablespoon butter. Bake until the top is nicely browned and the potatoes are tender, 30 to 35 minutes. Halfway through the cooking, use the back of a large spoon to lightly press down any potatoes that are not yet submerged into the cream.

variations You can omit the cream and use additional milk in its place, but the top won't brown quite as well. To forgo the dairy altogether, use a rich chicken stock, infusing it in exactly the same way as the milk.

herb substitutions

- You can omit any of the herbs listed above, for instance, adding only the thyme and bay leaves, or marjoram and rosemary.
- For a lavender-scented potato gratin, add 6 fresh English lavender sprigs and 3 3-inch sprigs fresh rosemary or thyme in place of the herbs listed above.

she-jump-up pot

from *My Mother's Southern Entertaining*

6 TO 8 SERVINGS

Mother remembers distinctly as a young girl with her daddy down in Georgia hearing a lady tell about how the black children on a rice plantation would come screaming, "She-jump-up! She-jump-up!" at the first sight of rice sprouting in the vast water beds. Rice and cotton were the very foundations of this wealthy society till the twentieth century when most of the industries shifted to Louisiana and other states in the Deep South, but to this day there are locals all over the Carolinas and Georgia who still refer to various rice stews, pots, and casseroles as "she-jump-up" this and that. Mother's not sure, but she thinks it might have been her grandmother, Sweet Maa, who began adding raisins and peanuts to the She-Jump-Up Pot we love to fix at the beach.

¼	cup (½ stick) butter
1	tablespoon bacon grease
1	medium-size onion, finely chopped
1	large celery rib, finely chopped
2	cups long-grain rice
3	cups chicken stock or broth
½	cup chopped golden raisins
½	cup crushed peanuts
1	teaspoon salt
¼	teaspoon cayenne pepper

FOOD&WINE test-kitchen tips

- If you don't keep bacon grease around, you'll need to fry two or three slices to get a tablespoon of rendered fat. Then you can crumble the strips and throw them into the rice along with the butter. Or you can just eat them.

- Rice varies a great deal. If yours isn't done in the 25 minutes allotted, add a few tablespoons of water and continue baking.

- To test whether or not rice is done, break a grain with your thumbnail and look inside. There should be no hard, opaque white core.

Preheat the oven to 350°F.

In a medium-size, heavy, flameproof pot, heat together 2 tablespoons of the butter and the bacon grease over moderate heat, then add the onion and celery and stir till soft, about 5 minutes. Reduce the heat to low, add the rice, and stir briefly till the grains are coated. Add the broth, raisins, peanuts, salt, and cayenne, stir well, cover, and bake till the rice is tender, 20 to 25 minutes. Add the remaining 2 tablespoons butter and, using a fork, fluff the rice till the butter has melted. Cover and keep warm till ready to serve.

creamed corn with smoky bacon, chanterelles, and thyme

from *Wildwood*

SERVES 6 AS A SIDE DISH OR LUNCH ENTRÉE

C r e a m e d   c o r n seems to have become a dish of the past, perhaps because we think of it as a canned food. This version of creamed corn, which combines fresh corn with herbs, heavy cream, and chanterelle mushrooms, and a bit of smoky bacon, bears little resemblance to its canned namesake. Serve this as a lunch entrée or as an accompaniment to roasted chicken or pork chops. Any mushroom will work in this recipe, although the flavors of the chanterelles and corn blend especially well together.

2	thick slices smoky bacon, cut into ¼-inch strips
	Kernels cut from 4 ears yellow or white corn (about 4 cups)
4	ounces chanterelle or portobello mushrooms, wiped clean and chopped into ½-inch pieces
½	yellow onion, chopped
1	cup heavy cream
1	tablespoon fresh lemon juice
1	teaspoon minced fresh thyme
1	teaspoon salt
½	teaspoon freshly ground black pepper
1	tablespoon minced fresh flat-leaf parsley

In a large skillet, cook the bacon over medium heat until crisp. Remove the bacon from the pan and drain on paper towels. Pour off the bacon drippings and reserve 1 teaspoon.

FOOD&WINE test-kitchen tips

- If you don't have fresh thyme, dried is okay here, since the leaves will rehydrate in the warm cream. Substitute about ¼ teaspoon dried.

- In addition to the serving suggestions given in the recipe, we'd like to add salmon. This side dish is *so* good with simple roasted, grilled, or sautéed salmon.

Add the reserved bacon drippings back to the skillet. Over medium heat, sauté the corn, mushrooms, and onion for 6 minutes, or until the mushrooms appear soft, stirring occasionally. Blend in the cream, lemon juice, thyme, salt, pepper, and bacon. Bring to a simmer and cook the cream to reduce until thick, 3 to 4 minutes. The starch in the corn will help thicken the cream. Add the chopped parsley. Ladle into bowls and serve.

barley with caramelized onions and mushrooms

from *The Farmer's Market Cookbook*

YIELDS 6 SERVINGS

The flavor of this nutty-earthy grain sends me back to my childhood and steaming bowls of my mother's famous mushroom barley soup. Here is a side dish that will pair fantastically with a roast, grilled fish, or a melody of vegetables. Or try this recipe as a stuffing for a whole chicken.

2	medium Vidalia onions
3	tablespoons olive oil
2	garlic cloves—diced
¼	pound wild mushrooms—cleaned and sliced thin
2	tablespoons thyme—leaves only
3	cups chicken stock (homemade or canned, low-sodium)
1	cup pearl barley

Salt and black pepper to taste

Slice the onions into very thin julienne strips. Heat a 2-quart saucepan over medium heat and add the oil. Add the onions and cook until golden, approximately 15 to 20 minutes, tossing constantly so the onions don't burn. Add the garlic and wild mushrooms and continue cooking for another 5 minutes. Add the thyme leaves and slowly pour in the chicken stock. Bring to a boil and then add the barley. Season with salt and pepper. Cover and reduce the temperature to low, simmering for another 20 to 25 minutes. Turn off the heat and let rest for 10 minutes, then fluff the barley with a fork. Serve warm.

FOOD&WINE test-kitchen tips

- When Vidalia onions aren't available, regular yellow onions will do—and nicely.

- If your barley has been around a while, it may be very dry, in which case this dish will take longer to cook. If it's not done in 25 minutes, just keep cooking it, adding a bit of water if needed so that the barley won't stick to the bottom of the pan.

etta's cornbread pudding

from *Tom Douglas' Seattle Kitchen*

MAKES 6 SERVINGS

Bread pudding was invented as a tasty way to use up old bread and it's usually served as a dessert. We've come to love these puddings so much that we bake different "breads" (like gingerbread or chocolate cake) just so we can put together a bread pudding. In another twist, we've created savory puddings to accompany our poultry and seafood dishes. We found ourselves baking special breads just to make them into pudding, in this case cornbread.

The cornbread pudding here is made with dry Jack cheese, which is nuttier and tangier than regular Jack cheese. Our favorite is Vella Dry Jack from Sonoma, California. Or use sharp Cheddar instead; while the flavor of the cornbread pudding would change, it would be equally delicious. We serve this luscious pudding with roasted salmon, but it would also be great partnered with roast chicken.

This recipe makes more cornbread than you need to make the pudding. You can freeze the extra cornbread for future batches or, if you're like us, you can snack on it while it's warm, spread with butter and honey.

for the cornbread

1	cup all-purpose flour
¾	cup medium-ground yellow cornmeal
½	cup grated pepper Jack cheese (1½ ounces)
1	teaspoon baking powder
1	teaspoon salt
2	large eggs
1	cup milk
3	tablespoons honey
¼	cup (½ stick) unsalted butter, melted, plus a little more for buttering the pan

▼

FOOD&WINE test-kitchen tips

- The excellent cornbread recipe is well worth making to eat on its own.

- Should there be any of this luscious pudding leftover, it reheats well in the microwave.

vegetables & side dishes

for the pudding

1	tablespoon unsalted butter, plus a little more for buttering the pan
1	cup thinly sliced onions (about ½ large onion)
¾	cup grated dry Jack cheese
2	teaspoons chopped fresh flat-leaf parsley
½	teaspoon chopped fresh rosemary
½	teaspoon chopped fresh thyme
2¼	cups heavy cream
4	large eggs
1	teaspoon kosher salt
½	teaspoon freshly ground black pepper

1 To make the cornbread, preheat the oven to 425°F. Butter an 8-inch square baking dish. Combine the flour, cornmeal, cheese, baking powder, and salt in a large bowl. In a mixing bowl, whisk together the eggs, milk, and honey. Add the wet ingredients to the dry ingredients, stirring until just combined. Add the melted butter and stir into the mixture. Pour into the prepared pan and bake until a toothpick comes out clean, 15 to 20 minutes. When cool enough to handle, cut into 1-inch cubes. You should have about 8 cups cornbread cubes, but you only need one third of the cornbread cubes (or 2⅔ cups) for this recipe.

2 To make the pudding, reduce the oven temperature to 350°F. Put the 2⅔ cups of cornbread cubes in a buttered 8-inch square baking dish. Set aside. Heat the 1 tablespoon butter in a sauté pan over low heat and cook the onions very slowly until soft and golden brown, at least 20 minutes, stirring occasionally. Remove from the heat. Scatter the onions, cheese, and herbs over the cornbread cubes. Whisk together the heavy cream and eggs with salt and pepper in a mixing bowl and pour over the cornbread cubes. Let sit for 10 minutes so the cornbread absorbs some of the custard. Bake until set and golden, about 40 minutes. Serve hot.

a step ahead You can make the cornbread and store it in the freezer, covered tightly in plastic wrap, for a few weeks until you are ready to make the cornbread pudding. The onions can be caramelized a day ahead and stored, covered, in the refrigerator. The cornbread pudding can be baked a day in advance and stored in the refrigerator, covered. Before serving, reheat the cornbread pudding, covered with aluminum foil, in a preheated 375°F oven until warmed through, 35 to 40 minutes.

fearrington house angel biscuits

from *My Mother's Southern Entertaining*

ABOUT 60 BISCUITS

One of Mother's favorite haunts anywhere is Fearrington House in Fearrington Village just outside Chapel Hill, North Carolina, without doubt one of the most distinguished restaurants in all the South—created, incidentally, by the same Jenny Finch with whom I went to high school in Charlotte. Mother loves virtually all the refined Southern food served there, but "I'd make the trip just to eat the angel biscuits they serve at every meal." High praise from a lady who's always said that no biscuit dough should ever be kneaded or contain a trace of sugar! Do note that this dough can be chilled in a greased, covered bowl up to four or five days.

1½ tablespoons active dry yeast

1 cup warm water

5 cups all-purpose flour

1 tablespoon baking powder

1 teaspoon baking soda

¼ cup sugar

1 tablespoon salt

2 cups Crisco vegetable shortening

2 cups buttermilk

In a small bowl, sprinkle the yeast over the water and let proof.

Sift together the flour, baking powder, baking soda, sugar, and salt into a large mixing bowl, then add the shortening and work the mixture with your fingertips till it resembles coarse meal. Add the yeast mixture and buttermilk and stir with a wooden spoon till the dough is smooth.

FOOD&WINE test-kitchen tips

- The dough should be quite moist and sticky, and so you'll need to keep dusting your work surface with flour as you knead and roll.

- When these are in the oven, watch them like a hawk. The sugar in the dough makes them go quickly from perfect to too dark.

On a lightly floured work surface, knead the dough for 2 to 3 minutes, then roll out ½ inch thick. Cut out biscuits with a 2½-inch biscuit cutter, place on one or two ungreased baking sheets, gather up the excess dough, and repeat the procedure. Cover the biscuits with a clean kitchen towel and let rise for 30 minutes.

Meanwhile, preheat the oven to 450°F. When the biscuits have risen, bake them till golden brown, about 12 minutes. Serve hot.

martha pearl advises When making biscuits, never add liquid to the flour mixture till you are ready to mix, since it activates the leavening. If you do so in advance, the biscuits will not be very fluffy.

vegetables & side dishes

desserts

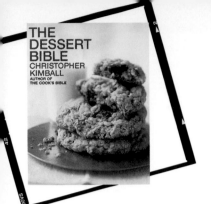

snipdoodles

from *The Dessert Bible*

MAKES 20 TO 24 COOKIES

According to James Beard, snickerdoodles were called by many different names, depending on the region of the country where the recipe was found. Along the Hudson River Valley they were called schnecken doodles, yet snipdoodles or snickerdoodles were also common names. I am partial to the name snipdoodles as well as to this recipe. I add a bit of nutmeg to the batter, which adds a gentle perfume to what is a very simple cookie. I tested them with Crisco instead of milk, and the cookies were flatter, more spread out, and a bit crispier. I prefer a more delicate, softer snipdoodle and therefore used the milk. The texture of these cookies is heavenly, light but with a nice chew. They bake up nice and thick, almost like a macaroon.

8	tablespoons (1 stick) unsalted butter, softened but still firm
1½	cups plus 3 tablespoons granulated sugar
2	large eggs
1	teaspoon vanilla extract
¼	cup milk
3	cups all-purpose flour
¾	teaspoon baking soda
1	teaspoon cream of tartar
½	teaspoon salt
½	teaspoon nutmeg
1	tablespoon cinnamon

1 Beat the butter and 1½ cups of the sugar in the bowl of an electric mixer or with a wooden spoon until creamy and smooth, about 3 minutes. Add the eggs and vanilla and beat until fully incorporated. Add the milk and stir to incorporate. In a separate bowl, whisk together the next 5 ingredients (flour through nutmeg) and then stir into the butter-sugar mixture. Chill dough for 2 hours. Heat oven to 350 degrees. Line a cookie sheet with parchment paper.

FOOD&WINE test-kitchen tips

- This recipe calls for parchment paper. We love the new reusable parchment paper that comes in sheets. You can just wipe it off and use it again.

- For speed, we used a large melon baller to scoop the dough into walnut-size rounds.

2 Shape dough into large, walnut-size balls, about 1¼ inches in diameter. Mix together the remaining 3 tablespoons sugar and cinnamon in a small bowl. Dip tops of dough balls in sugar-cinnamon mixture. Place balls 3 inches apart on lined baking sheet. Bake for about 12 minutes, rotating the baking sheet after 6 minutes. Cookies will appear undercooked when removed from the oven; the centers will still be very moist and light. Remove cookies to a rack; as they cool, they will firm up. Repeat with a new sheet of parchment paper until all the dough is baked.

what can go wrong?   This is an easy cookie to make, but just be sure not to overbake. They should appear undercooked when removed from the oven.

THE EASY WAY TO REMOVE
BAR COOKIES & BROWNIES

Line pan with two pieces of
parchment paper at right angles.

Simply lift
out paper
when
brownies
are done.

yoyos

from *Cookies Unlimited*

MAKES ABOUT 30 COOKIES

The recipe for this Australian sandwich cookie was sent to me simultaneously by two different friends from Down Under—food stylists Janet Lillie and Maureen McKeon. The following is a combination/distillation of the two recipes.

cookie dough

1⅓	**cups all-purpose flour**
⅓	**cup cornstarch**
½	**teaspoon baking powder**
12	**tablespoons (1½ sticks) unsalted butter, softened**
⅔	**cup confectioners' sugar**
1	**teaspoon vanilla extract**

lemon filling

6	**tablespoons (¾ stick) unsalted butter, softened**
1	**cup confectioners' sugar**
1	**tablespoon lemon juice**
2	**cookie sheets or jelly roll pans covered with parchment or foil**

1 Set the racks in the upper and lower thirds of the oven and preheat to 350 degrees.

2 Combine the flour, cornstarch, and baking powder in a bowl; stir well to mix.

3 In the bowl of a standing electric mixer fitted with the paddle attachment, beat together the butter and confectioners' sugar on medium speed until soft and light, about 3 or 4 minutes. Beat in the vanilla. Lower the speed and beat in the flour mixture.

4 Remove the bowl from the mixer and finish mixing the dough with a large rubber spatula.

FOOD&WINE test-kitchen tips

- It's not a bad idea to switch the pans in the oven halfway through the cooking time so that the cookies are sure to bake evenly.

- In our kitchen, the cookies kept well for three days.

5 Use a teaspoon measuring spoon or a small ice cream scoop to scoop up a piece of the dough. Roll each piece into a ball between the palms of your hands and place on the prepared pans, leaving about 2 inches around each cookie in all directions. Press each cookie with the back of a fork dipped in flour to flatten the cookies slightly, and make a crisscross pattern.

6 Bake the cookies for about 15 minutes, or until they are a uniform light golden color. Cool the cookies on the pans on racks.

7 While the cookies are cooling, prepare the filling. In the bowl of an electric mixer fitted with the paddle attachment, beat together the butter and confectioners' sugar on medium speed until very light, about 5 minutes. Beat in the lemon juice a little at a time, then continue beating until very light and smooth.

8 Turn half the cookies upside down so that the flat bottom side is uppermost. Pipe or spoon about ½ teaspoon of the filling on each. Cover with another cookie, bottom to bottom.

9 Store the finished cookies between sheets of parchment or wax paper in a tin or plastic container with a tight-fitting cover.

raspberry rectangles

from *The Dessert Bible*

MAKES **24** RECTANGLES

This recipe started out as an attempt to develop date squares, a common recipe from the forties and fifties in which the dough mixture used for the base is also used for a crumb topping. The filling is usually either jam or a cooked filling made from dried fruit. After reviewing a few recipes, I determined that the most common combination of ingredients was 1½ sticks butter, 1½ cups flour, 1½ cups oats, and 1½ cups granulated sugar. When I tested this recipe, I found that the bars were much too sweet, so I reduced the total sugar to 1 cup, using ½ cup of light brown sugar and ½ cup granulated. This was a marked improvement, with more flavor and a more balanced level of sweetness. I played with the nuts, preferring a pairing of sweet almonds with nutty pecans, although you can use either by itself if you like. I also added baking soda to the recipe to make the crust a bit lighter.

For the filling, I tested a variety of jams, including apricot, strawberry, and blackberry, none of which had the bright, strong flavor of raspberry, which stands up nicely to oats and nuts. The traditional date filling was dull and unappealing by comparison. These cookies are extremely rich and buttery and will need to cool completely before cutting. I suggest letting them sit for at least 2 hours before serving.

1¼	cups quick-cooking oats
1½	cups all-purpose flour
½	cup granulated sugar
½	cup packed light brown sugar
¾	teaspoon baking soda
¼	teaspoon salt
½	cup chopped pecans or almonds or a mixture
12	tablespoons (1½ sticks) unsalted butter, softened
1	cup raspberry preserves

FOOD&WINE test-kitchen tips

- We found that the easiest way to get these out of the pan is to remove the whole uncut batch at once with a large, flexible spatula. Run it around the edge and then slide it under the parchment paper. If you cut the rectangles in the pan, the first couple are bound to be messy. Of course, then you just have to eat them.

- Unusual among cookies, these were as good on the fourth day as they were fresh out of the oven.

1 Adjust oven rack to middle position and heat oven to 350 degrees. Butter a 9 x 9-inch baking pan and line with parchment (see illustration, page 213). In a large bowl, whisk together the first 7 ingredients (oats through nuts). Blend in the softened butter with a fork or with an electric mixer on slow speed for 3 to 4 minutes, or until the mixture is blended well and looks like wet sand. Place two-thirds of the mixture into the prepared pan and press onto the bottom. Spread with the preserves using a rubber spatula. Sprinkle the remaining crust mixture on top.

2 Bake for 30 minutes, turning pan front to back after 15 minutes. Completely cool before removing from pan and cutting.

what can go wrong? You do want to use the correct size baking pan; otherwise the cookies will be too thin or too thick and not bake up properly. You also want to be sure to leave enough of the mixture, roughly one-third, to use as a topping. Finally, when they are baked properly, the cookies should be neither raw and moist nor hard and dry. They should be firm but still moist.

desserts

mamoul
syrian and lebanese date-filled cookies

from *Cookies Unlimited*

MAKES ABOUT 30 COOKIES

This is a classic Middle Eastern pastry of a light dough wrapped around a rich filling. I first learned about *mamoul* from my friend Dahlia Bilger, who kept pressing me to make some with her when she was a student at the New York Restaurant School in the early eighties. Alas, in the intervening years I lost the recipe Dahlia and I concocted. This one is loosely based on a recipe in Claudia Roden's *A Book of Middle Eastern Food* (Knopf, 1972).

When you buy *mamoul* in Middle Eastern markets, they have usually been decorated with a kind of pastry pincer to make an attractive pattern of raised ridges on the surface of the dough. Presumably this is in order to hold the confectioners' sugar with which they are sprinkled. I find that pricking the tops with a fork in a regular pattern accomplishes the same thing.

date filling
- ½   pound pitted dates, finely chopped
- 3   tablespoons water

dough
- 1¾   cups all-purpose flour
- 12   tablespoons (1½ sticks) cold unsalted butter, cut into 20 pieces
- 2   teaspoons rose or orange flower water
- 2   tablespoons milk

Confectioners' sugar for finishing

- 2   cookie sheets or jelly roll pans covered with parchment or foil

1 For the filling, put the dates and water in a medium saucepan over low heat. Bring to a simmer, stirring occasionally, and reduce, stirring often, until the consistency is thick and jam-like. Spread the filling out on a plate or shallow bowl to cool.

FOOD&WINE test-kitchen tips

- Each cookie will hold about half a teaspoon of the date filling.

- Covered with foil and left at room temperature, these keep nicely for two days. Plastic wrap makes them soften too much.

2 When you are ready to make the cookies, set the racks in the upper and lower thirds of the oven and preheat to 350 degrees.

3 To make the dough, in the work bowl of a food processor fitted with the steel blade, place the flour. Add the butter and pulse about a dozen times, or until it is finely mixed in. Take the cover off the machine and sprinkle the flour and butter mixture with the rose water and milk. Replace the cover and pulse until the dough just forms a ball. Scrape the dough onto a floured work surface, then press it together and roll it into a cylinder 15 inches long. Slice the dough every ½ inch to make 30 pieces of dough.

4 To form a *mamoul*, roll a piece of dough into a sphere, then insert an index finger into the sphere to make a hole. Use your thumbs to enlarge the hole so that the dough becomes a little cup. Fill with a spoonful of the filling, then close the dough around the filling. Place each cookie seam side down on one of the pans. Leave about 1½ inches around in all directions.

5 Repeat with the remaining dough and filling. After all the *mamoul* have been formed, press each gently to flatten it, and use a fork to pierce the surface in a decorative design.

6 Bake the *mamoul* for about 20 to 25 minutes, making sure they remain very white. They should take on no color at all. Cool on the pans on racks. Dust heavily with confectioners' sugar just before serving.

7 Store the cooled cookies between sheets of parchment or wax paper in a tin or plastic container with a tight-fitting cover.

butterscotch delights

from My Mother's Southern Entertaining

2 TO 3 DOZEN SQUARES

The reason Mother created these butterscotch squares was simple enough: she got tired of serving brownies at her guild luncheon and wanted to come up with something like a brownie but with a different flavor and slightly different texture. You can, of course, substitute chocolate chips for the butterscotch ones, but whether for an informal luncheon, picnic, or pool party, these squares do make for a nice change. If the squares are too gummy and awkward to cut, Mother advises dipping the knife in warm water.

for the bottom layer

- ½ cup (1 stick) butter, softened
- 1 large egg yolk
- 2 tablespoons water
- ½ teaspoon pure almond extract
- 1¼ cups all-purpose flour
- 1 tablespoon sugar
- ¼ teaspoon baking powder

One 12-ounce bag butterscotch chips

for the top layer

- 2 large eggs
- ¾ cup sugar
- 6 tablespoons (¾ stick) butter, melted
- 1 teaspoon pure vanilla extract
- ½ teaspoon pure almond extract
- 1 cup finely ground walnuts

Preheat the oven to 350°F. Grease a large baking pan and set aside.

FOOD&WINE test-kitchen tips

- Don't pass this recipe by because you think it's just for the typical butterscotch brownie, or blondie. Believe us, it's not. A whole batch lasted about ten minutes in our test kitchen. But should you be surrounded by less eager eaters, the squares keep well for two to three days.

- Bake these squares on the middle rack in the oven so that they cook evenly on the top and bottom.

To make the bottom layer, beat the butter, egg yolk, water, and almond extract with an electric mixer in a medium-size mixing bowl till well blended. Add the flour, sugar, and baking powder and beat till well blended. Scrape the mixture into the prepared pan and pat evenly with your hands across the bottom. Bake for 10 minutes, then scatter the butterscotch chips over the top and bake till the chips melt, about 5 minutes longer. With a spatula, smooth the melted chips over the cake.

To make the top layer, wash and dry the mixer beaters and, in a small mixing bowl, beat the eggs till frothy. Add the sugar, melted butter, and extracts and beat till well blended and smooth.

Pour the mixture over the butterscotch layer, spread evenly, sprinkle the walnuts evenly over the top, and bake till lightly browned, 30 to 45 minutes. Let cool completely, then cut the cake into 1½- to 2-inch squares.

martha pearl advises I always grease pans and casseroles with vegetable shortening, since it doesn't burn and stick as much as butter.

peak-of-summer berry crisp

from *Tom Douglas' Seattle Kitchen*

MAKES 5 TO 6 SERVINGS

In the Northwest we're known for our berries—raspberries, strawberries, blueberries, blackberries, marionberries, salmonberries, huckleberries, boysenberries—the list seems endless at the peak of summer. Any combination of berries is fine in this recipe. You can make crisps all year-round, using whatever fruit is in season: rhubarb, apples, peaches . . .

We served this berry crisp one summer at the Bite of Seattle (a very large food event in the Seattle Center, near the Space Needle). It was voted best dessert of the Bite. Who knows how many hotel pans of crisp we made? The number was huge. We scrambled every night of the event to keep up with the demand, begging our produce purveyor for more berries, baking, baking, baking . . . and enjoying every sweet minute.

This very simple dessert, still warm from the oven, cries out for a scoop of homemade ice cream, and may be our favorite dessert of all.

for the crisp topping

- ⅔ cup old-fashioned oats
- ⅔ cup firmly packed brown sugar
- ⅔ cup all-purpose flour
- ½ teaspoon ground cinnamon
- 6 tablespoons (¾ stick) cold unsalted butter, cut into dice

for the berries

- 2 cups fresh raspberries
- 2 cups fresh blueberries, picked over for stems
- ½ cup granulated sugar (if berries are very sweet, you may want to use less sugar)
- 2 tablespoons all-purpose flour

FOOD&WINE test-kitchen tips

- We kept this at room temperature and ate it happily for breakfast two days after baking. It didn't start getting soggy until the third day.

- The combination of raspberries and blueberries is part of what makes this really special, but if this recipe becomes your favorite one for crisp, as it well may, you can also use it for peaches, apples, or pears. When not including the tart raspberries, add a bit of lemon juice to the fruit.

for garnish

Vanilla ice cream or sweetened whipped cream

1 Preheat the oven to 350°F. To make the crisp topping, combine the oats, brown sugar, flour, and cinnamon in a bowl. Add the diced butter to the dry ingredients and blend with a pastry blender or the tips of your fingers until crumbly. Set aside.

2 In another bowl, toss the berries with the sugar and flour, using a rubber spatula. Pour the berries into a 9-inch pie pan. Cover the berries with the crisp topping. Set the filled pie pan on a baking sheet to catch any juices, then place in the oven and bake until the topping is golden brown and the juices are bubbling, 40 to 45 minutes.

on the plate Spoon generous portions of the warm crisp into wide shallow bowls and top with scoops of ice cream or whipped cream.

a step ahead If you enjoy making crisps, make a large batch of crisp topping (double or triple the recipe) and keep it in an airtight container in the freezer.

in the glass Try an Auslese (Riesling) from Germany's Rhine or Mosel valleys.

desserts

pumpkin ginger crème caramel on spiced pumpkin cake with pecan shorts and toffeed pecans

from *The Olives Dessert Table*

SERVES 8

Pumpkin season, though much anticipated by pumpkin lovers, is very, very short: It has to be cold enough to feel like fall, but the day after Thanksgiving, no one wants to hear about them anymore. Maria Wharton, a member of our pastry team, loves pumpkin and likes heavier spicing than either Paige or Todd, who agree the flavor should be more delicate. Here, a subtly flavored pumpkin custard balances a more aggressively spiced pumpkin cake, accented by buttery cookies and crunchy nuts.

pumpkin ginger crème caramel French custard bathed in caramelized sugar syrup. Though we usually insist on doing things from scratch, here we use canned pumpkin. It's more consistent, more convenient, and less messy. The flavor and texture of the custard is lighter and creamier than traditional pumpkin pie. If you're serving this on its own, you can make it in a 9-inch pie pan. In that case, bake this custard at 300 degrees for 50 to 60 minutes.

¼	cup chopped fresh gingerroot
1	cup milk
2	cups heavy cream
1	cup sugar
2½	tablespoons water
2	large eggs
½	large egg yolk
1½	cups canned pumpkin purée (not pumpkin pie filling)
¼	teaspoon salt
⅛	teaspoon grated fresh nutmeg ▼

FOOD&WINE test-kitchen tips

- Because of the pumpkin, these are firmer than typical crème caramel. They're easier to unmold and hold their shape beautifully.

Preheat the oven to 325 degrees.

Place the gingerroot, milk, and cream in a medium saucepan and bring to a boil over medium-high heat. Set aside to steep for 1 hour. Pour through a strainer and discard the gingerroot and other solids.

While the ginger is steeping, prepare the ramekins: Place ½ cup of the sugar and the water in a small saucepan and cook over high heat, stirring occasionally, until the sugar is caramelized, about 8 minutes. Pour into 8 clean, dry 5-ounce ramekins. Tilt the cups so that the bottoms are evenly covered. Set aside.

Place the eggs, egg yolk, pumpkin purée, the remaining ½ cup sugar, salt, and nutmeg in a large bowl and mix to combine. Add the cooled, strained milk and mix to combine. Pour the custard into the prepared molds. Place the molds in a large baking pan and fill halfway with hot water. Transfer the pan to the oven and bake until the custards jiggle but do not ripple, about 30 to 40 minutes. Cool to room temperature and place plastic wrap directly on the surface. Refrigerate at least 12 hours and up to 2 days.

spiced pumpkin cake Used here as an underliner for the Crème Caramel, it's also a nice tea cake served alone.

5	tablespoons unsalted butter, at room temperature
¾	cup brown sugar
1	large egg
⅔	cup canned pumpkin purée (not pumpkin pie filling)
¼	cup apple cider
1	cup all-purpose flour
1	teaspoon baking powder
¼	teaspoon baking soda
½	teaspoon salt

FOOD&WINE test-kitchen tips

- The recipe states that you can keep this for two days. That's safe for sure. We wrapped the cake well and it remained moist and tempting for four days.

1 teaspoon ground cinnamon

1 teaspoon ground ginger

¼ teaspoon ground cloves

¼ teaspoon ground mace

½ cup toasted pecans, roughly chopped (see page 230)

Preheat the oven to 350 degrees. Grease and flour an 8-inch-square cake pan.

Place the butter and sugar in the bowl of a mixer fitted with a paddle and beat until fluffy. Add the egg and beat for 1 minute. Scrape down the sides, add the pumpkin purée and cider and mix well. It will look broken but don't worry. Add the remaining ingredients, and mix until just combined. Spread into the prepared pan and transfer to the oven. Bake until a toothpick inserted comes out clean, about 20 to 25 minutes. Cool in the pan. Wrap and store at room temperature up to 2 days.

pecan shorts

MAKES 2 TO 3 DOZEN COOKIES

¼ pound (1 stick) unsalted butter, at room temperature

⅓ cup confectioners' sugar, plus additional for tossing

½ teaspoon salt

1 teaspoon vanilla extract

1 cup all-purpose flour

⅓ cup finely ground toasted pecans (see page 230)

Preheat the oven to 350 degrees.

▼

FOOD&WINE test-kitchen tips

- The best-ever version of a typical holiday treat called butterballs or Mexican wedding cookies, these are great keepers. The recommended two days here is conservative. They retained their texture for four days in our kitchen, and we believe would have lasted much longer—if we'd been able to resist eating them.

desserts

Place the butter and sugar in a bowl and mix until creamy. Add the salt and vanilla and mix to combine. Add the flour and pecans and mix until just combined.

Form the dough into 1-inch balls (a no. 100 scoop is helpful) and place on an ungreased baking sheet. Transfer the sheet to the oven and bake until the bottoms are golden, about 10 to 12 minutes. Cool on the sheet. When they have cooled completely, toss with confectioners' sugar. Store at room temperature up to 2 days.

toffeed pecans Making these takes time and effort but it's well worth it. This makes a snappy, salty garnish for crème brûlée or a topping for coffee, caramel, or chocolate ice cream. This recipe makes more than you will need, but since they are so much work to make, we think it's best to make a large quantity and keep some in the freezer.

MAKES 5 CUPS

½   **pound plus 2 tablespoons (2¼ sticks) unsalted butter**
1¾   **cups plus 2 tablespoons sugar**
1   **tablespoon salt**
3½   **cups pecan halves**

Line a baking sheet with parchment paper.

Place the butter in a small saucepan over medium-low heat and cook until melted. Add the sugar and salt and stir briskly until the mixture comes together. Add the nuts and cook, stirring the nuts evenly and constantly, until the sugar caramelizes and coats the nuts, about 5 to 10 minutes.

FOOD&WINE test-kitchen tips

- Despite the name, this is more like crunchy toffee with pecans in it than like toffee-covered pecans. Whichever, it's an irresistible candy that could easily be served on its own.

- The time necessary to caramelize the sugar varies depending on your sugar and the exact heat over which you cook it. It took us 15 to 20 minutes of stirring before the sugar turned brown.

When the sugar has turned a beautiful oak brown, carefully pour the hot mass onto the prepared sheet and quickly separate the nuts with forks or tongs. When the nuts have cooled completely transfer to an airtight container and store for 3 to 5 days or freeze up to 2 weeks.

to finish and assemble

1 Cut the Spiced Pumpkin Cake into 9 portions. Eat one and place the remaining 8 on individual dessert plates.

2 Run a paring knife around the edge of each Pumpkin Ginger Crème Caramel and gently push on the edge of the custard to break the vacuum. Tip upside down and center over the pumpkin cake. Allow the crème caramel to drop onto the cake: The sauce will come out of the mold right behind the custard.

3 Divide the Pecan Shorts equally among the plates.

4 Garnish with a handful of Toffeed Pecans.

FOOD&WINE test-kitchen tips

- Let's face it, as incredibly delicious as this dessert is, few people will make the whole thing at home—crème caramel perched on top of a square of cake with a toffee garnish and cookies on the side? Whew! The good news is that the recipe for each of the elements that goes into this extravaganza is an especially delectable version of that individual thing. All our testers and tasters agreed that they'd make any of the components to stand alone.

- For the ambitious among you, note that nearly all the parts keep extremely well, so the work can be spread out over several days.

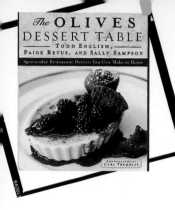
white chocolate banana bread pudding with caramel semi-freddo and boozy caramel sauce

from The Olives Dessert Table

SERVES 8 TO 10

The back room at Olives is used for private functions and meetings. More often than not, the size of the group grows or shrinks at the last minute. We needed an adaptable fall and winter dessert (ice cream is easy for summer): Our criteria were that it needed to keep for more than one day and be put together with no last-minute fussing. Without any real plan, we made batches and batches of banana bread. But now what? We made banana bread pudding—special but not quite special enough. When we added white chocolate to the custard, we felt that we were getting somewhere, but we still wanted to really wow our guests. A creamy Caramel Semi-Freddo was the perfect answer, especially when complemented by Boozy Caramel Sauce. We cook the sugar a bit longer than usual, giving it a lingering, smoky edge that is not as sweet as most caramels.

toasting nuts Preheat the oven to 350ºF. Place the nuts in a single layer on a baking sheet and bake until lightly toasted, about 15 to 20 minutes. Cool before using.

banana bread Inspired by a recipe by the mother of Linda Bedrosian, Paige's childhood friend, Paige has reworked the original recipe by reducing the amount of sugar and changing the method. Of course, you can make just the Banana Bread. Make two; it has a way of disappearing.

> 3 to 4 overripe bananas ("the nastier the better")
> 1¼ cups sugar
> ⅓ pound (1⅓ sticks) unsalted butter, melted and slightly cooled
> 2 large eggs, at room temperature
> 1 teaspoon vanilla extract
> 1½ cups all-purpose flour
> ½ teaspoon salt
> 1½ teaspoons baking soda
> ½ cup toasted walnuts (optional) (see above)

Preheat the oven to 350 degrees. Lightly grease an 8- to 9-inch loaf pan.

▼

Place the bananas and sugar in the bowl of a mixer fitted with a paddle or whisk attachment and whip the bejesus out of them, about 2 to 3 minutes.

Add the butter, eggs, and vanilla, beating well and scraping down the sides after each addition. Add the flour, salt, baking soda, and nuts, if using; mix to combine and scrape down the sides.

Place in the prepared pan and transfer to the oven. Bake until golden brown and firm in the center, about 1 hour. Set aside to cool for 10 to 15 minutes and then invert on a rack.

Wrap and store at room temperature up to 3 days or freeze up to 2 months.

white chocolate banana bread pudding Banana bread plus white chocolate custard makes banana bread pudding, which can stand alone: no caramel, no semifreddo. It's special enough for even a very significant dinner party. Or better yet, breakfast.

If you have leftover custard or simply want custard rather than bread pudding, you can place the custard mixture in small ovenproof dishes and bake them in a water bath at 325 degrees for about thirty minutes.

MAKES 8 TO 10 SERVINGS

2	cups milk
1	cup heavy cream
3	large eggs
2	large egg yolks
½	cup plus 2 tablespoons sugar
½	teaspoon salt
1	teaspoon vanilla extract
12	ounces white chocolate, melted
1	loaf Banana Bread (page 230), cubed (fresh, day old, or frozen)

FOOD&WINE test-kitchen tips

- The recipe suggests soaking the bread in the custard for 15 minutes to an hour. The longer the better, so that the liquid is fully absorbed and the bread distributes evenly throughout the pudding rather than floating on top.

Preheat the oven to 325 degrees. Lightly grease an 8-inch-square cake pan.

Place the milk and ½ cup of the cream in a saucepan and bring to a boil over medium-high heat. Place the eggs, egg yolks, ½ cup of the sugar, salt, and vanilla in a bowl and gradually add the milk mixture, whisking all the while. Add the melted chocolate and mix until it is fully incorporated.

Place the bread cubes in the prepared pan and pour the custard over it, pressing down to dunk them. Let rest at least 15 minutes and up to 1 hour.

Pour the remaining ½ cup cream over the top and sprinkle with the remaining 2 tablespoons sugar. Place in a hot-water bath and transfer to the oven. Bake until the pudding is firm and a knife inserted comes out clean, about 1 hour.

Serve warm or at room temperature as is, with Boozy Caramel Sauce (page 234), or sweetened whipped cream and sliced bananas.

caramel semi-freddo *Semifreddo* literally means "half frozen"; it's fluffy and aerated, and it has the same mouth feel but is lighter in texture than either ice cream or frozen mousse. It doesn't involve an ice cream machine, just a mixer and your freezer.

MAKES 1½ TO 2 QUARTS

- 3½ **cups heavy cream**
- 1½ **teaspoons vanilla extract**
- 1¾ **cups sugar**
- ½ **cup water**
- ½ **cup heavy cream**
- 5 **large eggs**
- 10 **large egg yolks**
- ½ **teaspoon salt**
- ¼ **cup prepared strong coffee**

▼

FOOD&WINE *test-kitchen tips*

- You get a lot of semi-freddo from this recipe. You can cut it in half. Or make the whole batch and figure on serving it on its own, or with the Boozy Caramel Sauce, later in the week.

In a large bowl, whip the cream and the vanilla until it holds stiff peaks. Set aside.

To make the caramel: Place the sugar and water in a saucepan and cook over medium heat until it turns a deep mahogany color, about 4 to 5 minutes. Do not stir. Gently swirl to even out the color. Slowly add the cream and stir very gently. Be careful, it will splatter. Set aside but keep warm.

Place the eggs, egg yolks, salt, and coffee over a hot-water bath and whisk until warmed. Add the caramel and whisk until the mixture is homogenous, thick, light in color, and has the consistency of soft whipped cream, about 4 to 5 minutes.

Immediately pour the mixture into the bowl of a mixer fitted with a whisk and whip on high speed until it cools to room temperature, about 5 to 8 minutes.

Fold in one quarter of the caramel-egg mixture to the reserved whipped cream. Add all the whipped cream to the caramel-egg mixture and gently fold to combine. Pour into a 6- to 8-cup freezer container and freeze at least 4 hours and up to 5 days.

boozy caramel sauce Great on any ice cream, drizzled on pound cake, or added to coffee, cappuccino, or milk. You can, if desired, omit the bourbon.

MAKES ABOUT 1 PINT

2	**cups sugar**
½	**cup water**
½	**teaspoon salt**
1	**cup heavy cream**
1	**tablespoon vanilla extract**
1	**tablespoon bourbon**

FOOD&WINE test-kitchen tips

- The authors of this book are wisely playing it safe by saying the sauce will keep for three days. We kept it for a week in the test-kitchen refrigerator, and it was still delectable.

Place the sugar, water, and salt in a small saucepan and bring to a boil over high heat. Cook without stirring until the mixture begins to color, about 4 to 5 minutes. When the mixture is tea-colored, stir lightly with a wooden spoon to even out the coloring. Continue cooking, stirring occasionally, until it turns a dark mahogany color, about 3 to 5 minutes.

Bubbles will rise and when they just start to break up, quickly and carefully drizzle in the cream. It will sputter and splatter and come to a boil at first, but just continue adding the cream slowly and steadily, stirring all the while. Off heat, add the vanilla and bourbon. Set aside to cool to room temperature. Cover and refrigerate at least 2 hours and up to 3 days.

Just before serving, gently reheat over low heat, stirring all the while.

to finish and assemble

1 Portion White Chocolate Banana Bread Pudding into 8 to 10 servings and garnish with sliced bananas, if desired.

2 Top with a generous scoop of Caramel Semi-Freddo.

3 Drizzle with Boozy Caramel Sauce.

desserts

FOOD&WINE test-kitchen tips

- As with the other recipe from *The Olives Dessert Table* (page 224), divide and conquer is the order of the day. You can spread out the preparation of the components of this elaborate dessert over several days.

- Also, to quote the introduction to this book, "It is not necessary to make any of these desserts in their entirety."

crème fraîche coffee cake

from *Nancy Silverton's Pastries from the La Brea Bakery*

YIELD: 10 TO 12 PIECES

Although this recipe was previously published in another book of mine, I would feel like I was gypping you if I didn't include it this time around. It's the ultimate morning coffee cake, screaming out for a hot cup of coffee or a big glass of ice-cold milk.

special item

10-inch, 14-cup-capacity bundt pan, lightly coated with melted butter

for the topping

1	cup (4 ounces) pecans
¼	cup plus 2 tablespoons light brown sugar, lightly packed
2	teaspoons ground cinnamon

for the batter

2	extra-large eggs
2	cups crème fraîche or sour cream
1	tablespoon pure vanilla extract
2	sticks (8 ounces) unsalted butter, chilled and cut into 1-inch cubes
1	tablespoon chopped lemon zest (about 1 lemon)
1	tablespoon baking powder
½	teaspoon kosher salt
2	cups granulated sugar
3	cups unbleached pastry flour or unbleached all-purpose flour

Adjust the oven rack to the middle position and preheat the oven to 325 degrees.

FOOD&WINE test-kitchen tips

- To be certain that the cake is cooked through, stick a skewer into the center. When it comes out clean, the cake is done.

- It's easy to get this out of the pan if you first run a knife around the edge between cake and pan.

To prepare the topping: Spread the pecans on a baking sheet and toast in the oven until lightly browned, about 10 to 12 minutes. Shake the pan halfway through to ensure that the nuts toast evenly. Cool and chop coarsely. In a small bowl, combine the nuts with the brown sugar and cinnamon, and set aside.

Turn the oven up to 350 degrees.

In a small bowl, whisk together the eggs, crème fraîche or sour cream, and vanilla extract.

In the bowl of an electric mixer fitted with the paddle attachment, cream the butter, lemon zest, baking powder, and salt on low, about 2 to 3 minutes, until softened. Add the sugar and turn the mixer up to medium for 3 to 4 minutes, until light and fluffy, scraping down the sides of the bowl as needed. Turn the mixer to low, add the egg mixture, a few tablespoons at a time, and mix until incorporated.

Add the flour to the butter mixture in 3 batches, turning the mixer off before each addition and mixing on low until just combined.

Pour half of the batter into the prepared pan and spread to even. Sprinkle half of the topping over the surface and pour the remaining batter over it, spreading evenly. Sprinkle the surface with the remaining topping.

Bake for about 1 hour, until firm to the touch.

chocolate chunk cookie cakes

from *Death by Chocolate Cakes*

MAKES 16 CAKES

½	pound (2 sticks) unsalted butter, cut into ½-ounce pieces; plus 1 tablespoon (melted)
2¼	cups plus 1 tablespoon all-purpose flour
1	teaspoon baking powder
¼	teaspoon salt
1	cup (8 ounces) tightly packed light brown sugar
¾	cup granulated sugar
3	large eggs
½	cup sour cream
1	tablespoon pure vanilla extract
12	ounces semisweet baking chocolate, chopped into ½-inch chunks

Preheat the oven to 350°F. Lightly coat the inside of each of 16 individual nonstick petite loaf pans with the 1 tablespoon of melted butter. Flour the insides of the individual loaf pans with the 1 tablespoon of flour. Shake out and discard the excess flour.

In a sifter combine the remaining 2¼ cups flour, 1 teaspoon baking powder, and ¼ teaspoon salt. Sift onto a large piece of parchment paper (or wax paper) and set aside until needed.

Place ½ pound butter, 1 cup light brown sugar, and ¾ cup granulated sugar in the bowl of an electric mixer fitted with a paddle. Mix on low speed for 1 minute, then beat on medium for 3 minutes, until soft. Scrape down the sides of the bowl and the paddle. Beat for an additional 3 minutes on medium until very soft and lighter in color. Scrape down the sides of the bowl. Add 3 eggs, one at a time, beating on medium for 30 seconds after each addition, and scraping down the sides of the bowl once all the eggs have been incorporated. Beat on medium for an additional 2 minutes until fluffy. Operate the mixer on low while gradually adding the sifted dry ingredients. Once they have been incorporated, about 1 minute, add ½ cup sour cream and 1 tablespoon vanilla extract and mix on low to combine, about 20 seconds. Remove the bowl from the mixer, add 12 ounces chocolate chunks, and use a rubber spatula to finish mixing the batter until thoroughly combined.

▼

Portion 4 slightly heaping tablespoons of the cake batter into each individual petite loaf pan. Spread the batter evenly. (If you are into a more tactile experience, you may use your well-washed index finger to spread the batter; otherwise use a rubber spatula.)

Place the units of petite loaf pans on the top and center racks of the preheated oven, and bake until a toothpick inserted in the center of one cake comes out clean, about 25 minutes. (Rotate the units from top to center halfway through the baking time, and turn each 180 degrees.) Remove the cakes from the oven and cool in the pans for 10 minutes at room temperature.

Invert the units to release the cakes. (If the cakes do not pop out of the pans by simply inverting them, use a small plastic knife to "cut" around the edges of each cake to free them from the pans without tearing the cakes.)

You don't have to ask permission to have a cookie cake, so you may reward yourself and enjoy one immediately. Or, invite the gang over and dispense with them forthwith. If the cakes are not immediately gobbled up, wrap each one individually in plastic wrap once it has cooled to room temperature. The cakes are good to go wherever and just about whenever at this point.

the chef's touch The plan here was for an unpretentious-looking cake that could withstand the rigors of being plopped into a lunch pail, squished in a brown paper bag, packed in a knapsack, or even stuffed in a tackle box. The cake would need to deliver an immediate, palate-pleasing reaction whether it was eaten moments after exiting the oven or several days later, when extricated from its lair to please a youngster at recess or reward the fanatic fisherman for perseverance and good luck. And, of course, this little cake would provide a chocolaty taste and texture that, although reminiscent of a favorite cookie, would actually transcend the genre of round and flat. I say, Mission Accomplished.

FOOD&WINE test-kitchen tips

- If you don't have the individual loaf pans called for here, we found the cakes turn out very nicely made in traditional muffin pans.

- As well as all the times to eat these cookie cakes suggested in the recipe, they'd be great for brunch.

Although the recipe calls for the chocolate to be chopped into $\frac{1}{2}$-inch chunks, I would suggest a nimble touch with the knife so as not to shatter the chocolate into small shards. Use a serrated cook's knife for this task, work carefully, and you will be rewarded with chunks that are distinctly obvious in the baked cake.

For quicker and more efficient portioning of the Chocolate Chunk Cookie Cake batter, use a #12 ice cream scoop rather than a tablespoon, and portion a level scoop into each individual petite loaf pan.

After the Chocolate Chunk Cookie Cakes have cooled to room temperature, individually wrap each cake with plastic wrap. They will stay remarkably fresh, for up to 4 days at room temperature, or for 1 week in the refrigerator. To avoid permeating the cakes with refrigerator odors, place the plastic-wrapped cakes in a large, tightly sealed plastic container. Allow refrigerated Chocolate Chunk Cookie Cakes to come to room temperature before serving.

Depending on the time of the year and the locale in which the cakes will be polished off, a chocolate-infused beverage—chocolate milk or hot chocolate—will make the break "a piece of cake."

chocolate chip goober gobble cupcakes

from _Death by Chocolate Cakes_

MAKES 18 CAKES

peanut chocolate chip cupcakes

1	cup all-purpose flour
½	teaspoon baking powder
½	teaspoon baking soda
½	teaspoon salt
1	cup (8 ounces) tightly packed light brown sugar
½	cup unsalted dry-roasted peanuts
½	cup Skippy creamy peanut butter
2	ounces (½ stick) unsalted butter, cut into ½-ounce pieces
2	ounces cream cheese
3	large eggs
¼	cup sour cream
2	teaspoons pure vanilla extract
½	cup semisweet chocolate chips

chocolate goober gobble

1	cup peanut butter
2	ounces semisweet baking chocolate, coarsely chopped and melted (page 245)

make the peanut chocolate chip cupcakes Preheat the oven to 325°F. Line 18 individual muffin tin cups with 2½-inch foil-laminated bake cups. Set aside.

In a sifter combine 1 cup flour, ½ teaspoon baking powder, ½ teaspoon baking soda, and ½ teaspoon salt. Sift onto a large piece of parchment paper (or wax paper) and set aside until needed.

Place 1 cup light brown sugar, ½ cup unsalted peanuts, ½ cup peanut butter, 2 ounces butter, and 2 ounces cream cheese in the bowl of an electric mixer fitted with a paddle. Mix on low speed for 1 minute, and then beat on medium for 3 minutes until combined.

Use a rubber spatula to scrape down the sides of the bowl. Add 3 eggs, one at a time, beating on medium for 30 seconds after each addition, and scraping down the sides of the bowl once all the eggs have been incorporated. Operate the mixer on low while gradually adding the sifted dry ingredients; mix until incorporated, about 30 seconds. Scrape down the sides of the bowl.

Add the ¼ cup sour cream and 2 teaspoons vanilla extract and mix on medium to combine, about 15 seconds. Remove the bowl from the mixer, add ½ cup chocolate chips, and use a rubber spatula to finish mixing the ingredients until thoroughly combined.

Portion 3 heaping tablespoons (about 2¼ ounces) of the cupcake batter into each bake cup. Place the muffin tins on the top and center racks of the preheated oven, and bake until a toothpick inserted in the center of the cupcake comes out clean, about 30 minutes. (Rotate the units from top to center halfway through the baking time, and turn each 180 degrees.) Remove the cupcakes from the oven and cool at room temperature in the tins for 10 minutes. Remove the cupcakes from the muffin tins (but not from the foil bake cups), and cool at room temperature for an additional 20 minutes prior to preparing the Chocolate Goober Gobble.

make the chocolate goober gobble Place 1 cup peanut butter and 2 ounces melted semisweet chocolate in the bowl of an electric mixer fitted with a balloon whip. Whisk on medium-high speed to combine, about 30 seconds. Scrape down the sides of the bowl. Whisk on high for an additional 30 seconds until very smooth and shiny.

assemble the cupcakes and serve Using a paring knife, make a 2-inch-in-diameter, circular cutout from the top of each Peanut Chocolate Chip Cupcake. To do this, insert the knife at a slight, inward angle about ½ inch away from the outside edge, and to a depth of about 1 inch, and cut all the way around the cupcake. Remove the cutout. (Wonder what the fate of those scrumptious cupcake scraps will be?) Portion a slightly heaping tablespoon of Chocolate Goober Gobble into each cupcake hollow. Serve immediately.

the chef's touch If the name Goober Gobble tickles your funny bone, wait until this peanut butter–chocolate duo tickles your palate. Somehow the Jerry Lewis and Dean Martin of confections couldn't be called something as mundane as "For Peanut Butter Lovers Only."

▼

FOOD&WINE test-kitchen tips

- If you resist the temptation to eat the cutout centers of these cupcakes immediately, you can always set them back on top of the Goober Gobble filling.

My mom (aka Mrs. D) has enjoyed Skippy brand creamy peanut butter since the early 1940s and started serving it to me shortly thereafter. (I arrived on the scene in 1945.) This may sound like an endorsement, but we tried two other well-known brands for this cupcake with not-so-delightful results. Mom knows best: Stick with Skippy for this one.

No need to chop the peanuts in this recipe if you use a table-model electric mixer. However, if you mix the cupcake batter by hand using a whisk, or if you use a hand-held electric mixer, coarsely chop the peanuts before adding.

I hesitate to suggest further embellishment of the Goober Gobble, but what the heck. To turn these fun cupcakes into a carnival, sprinkle one or more of the following over the Goober Gobble: chocolate chips, chocolate chunks, raisins, chopped peanuts, chocolate-covered peanuts, or peanut M&M's.

After assembly, you may keep the Chocolate Chip Goober Gobble Cupcakes covered in a tightly sealed plastic container for up to 48 hours at room temperature.

I can't imagine another liquid as effective in transporting the Gobble down the tummy as milk, and lots of it! That's what Mrs. D served the fledgling Guru of Ganache.

melting chocolate in a double boiler Melting chocolate for baking need not spoil your day. It's actually a cinch if just a couple of precautions are employed. First, set up the double boiler. (Make sure that the upper pan does not touch the water in the lower pan.) I recommend melting coarsely chopped chocolate slowly over medium heat while stirring frequently with a rubber spatula until the chocolate is completely melted and smooth. Melting it too quickly over high heat may render scorched, inedible chocolate. Avoid introducing any moisture into the melting or already melted chocolate; it may sieze (the chocolate stiffens into a coagulated mass, suitable only for the garbage disposal). Melted chocolate should stay that way for up to an hour, depending on the ambient temperature in your kitchen. If your kitchen is cool, keep the melted chocolate over warm water until ready to use, unless the recipe requires the chocolate to be chilled before using.

AMOUNT OF CHOPPED CHOCOLATE	APPROXIMATE MELTING TIME
1 to 2 ounces	2½ to 3 minutes
3 to 4 ounces	3½ to 4 minutes
5 to 6 ounces	4½ to 5 minutes
7 to 8 ounces	5½ to 6 minutes
9 to 16 ounces	6½ to 8 minutes

melting chocolate in a microwave oven I won't apologize for being such a late convert to microwaves, but I am now prepared to say that the microwave is a very efficient piece of equipment for melting and tempering chocolate. It's quick—about twice as fast as a double boiler—and it is relatively foolproof as long as you don't microwave for longer than necessary. (Just like a double boiler—too much heat and the chocolate will scorch.)

Microwave coarsely chopped chocolate in a glass bowl. After removing the chocolate from the microwave oven, use a rubber spatula to stir it until smooth. At Ganache Hill we use a Panasonic Model NN-S758, 1100-watt microwave oven, and we always use the medium setting for melting chocolate. Melted chocolate should stay that way for up to an hour, depending on the ambient temperature in your kitchen. If your kitchen is cool, keep the melted chocolate over warm water until ready to use, unless the recipe requires the chocolate to be chilled before using. The following melting times may vary, depending on the model, wattage, and power settings available on your microwave oven.

AMOUNT OF CHOPPED CHOCOLATE	APPROXIMATE MELTING TIME
1 to 3 ounces	1½ minutes
4 to 8 ounces	2 to 2½ minutes
9 to 16 ounces	2½ to 3 minutes

chocolate heart of darkness cakes

from *Death by Chocolate Cakes*

MAKES 12 CAKES

dark chocolate truffle hearts

8	ounces semisweet baking chocolate, coarsely chopped
¾	cup heavy cream

chocolate cocoa cakes

5	ounces unsalted butter, cut into ½-ounce pieces; plus 2 teaspoons (melted)
⅔	cup all-purpose flour
½	cup unsweetened cocoa powder
8	ounces semisweet baking chocolate, coarsely chopped
3	large eggs
2	large egg yolks
½	cup granulated sugar
1	teaspoon pure vanilla extract

make the dark chocolate truffle hearts Place 8 ounces chopped semisweet chocolate in a small bowl. Heat ¾ cup heavy cream in a small saucepan over medium heat. Bring to a boil. Pour the boiling cream over the chopped chocolate. Set aside for 5 minutes and then stir with a whisk until smooth. Pour the mixture (called ganache) onto a nonstick baking sheet and use a rubber spatula to spread the ganache in a smooth, even layer to within about 1 inch of the inside edges. Place the ganache in the freezer for 15 minutes, or in the refrigerator for 30 minutes, until very firm to the touch.

Line a 10- to 12-inch dinner plate with parchment paper or wax paper. Remove the firm ganache from the freezer or the refrigerator. Portion 12 heaping tablespoons (a bit more than 1 ounce each) of ganache onto the paper. Wearing a pair of disposable vinyl (or latex) gloves, individually roll each portion of ganache in your palms in a circular motion, using just enough gentle pressure to form a smooth orb. This is a traditional truffle. You should refrain from indulging in them now, since absence of a truffle in a cake will make the heart grow darker. Return each formed truffle to the paper-lined plate, and place in the freezer while preparing the cake batter.

▼

pp

make the chocolate cocoa cakes Preheat the oven to 325°F. Lightly coat the inside of each of 12 individual nonstick muffin cups (3 inches in diameter) with some of the 2 teaspoons melted butter. Set aside until needed.

In a sifter, combine ⅔ cup flour and ½ cup cocoa powder. Sift onto a large piece of parchment paper (or wax paper), and set aside until needed.

Melt 8 ounces chopped semisweet chocolate and 5 ounces of butter in the top half of a double boiler, or in a microwave oven (see page 245 for more details), and stir until smooth.

Place 3 eggs, 2 egg yolks, and ½ cup sugar in the bowl of an electric mixer fitted with a paddle. Beat on medium-high speed for 2 minutes until the mixture is slightly frothy. Add the melted chocolate and butter and mix on low speed to combine, about 15 seconds. Continue to operate the mixer on low while gradually adding the sifted dry ingredients. Once they have been incorporated, stop the mixer and scrape down the sides of the bowl. Add 1 teaspoon vanilla extract and mix on medium to combine, about 15 seconds. Remove the bowl from the mixer and use a rubber spatula to finish mixing the batter until thoroughly combined.

Portion 3 heaping tablespoons (about 2½ ounces) of the cake batter into each muffin cup. Place the muffin tin on the center rack of the preheated oven. Bake for 5 minutes. Remove the truffles from the freezer. Remove the muffin tin from the oven and, moving quickly, place a single frozen truffle in the center of each portion of cake batter, pressing the truffle about halfway down into the batter. Immediately return the muffin tin to the center rack of the oven and bake until a toothpick inserted into a cake (not the truffle) comes out clean, 17 to 18 minutes.

Remove the cakes from the oven and cool at room temperature for 20 minutes. To remove the cakes from the muffin cups, hold the top edge of a cake, and give the cake a slight jiggle to loosen it from inside the cup. Then insert the pointed tip of a knife into an outside edge of the top of the cake and loosen it so that you can gently pull the baked cake out of the cup. Serve immediately while still warm.

the chef's touch You are undoubtedly aware that chocolate has not only pleased palates but also increased libido since the Aztec emperor Montezuma quaffed a cold, spiced cocoa drink before engaging in corporeal activities of a passionate nature. In Montezuma's day, only the elite had the privilege of chocolate, and indeed, drinking it from a golden goblet was de rigueur. The masses remained uninformed about chocolate's virtues until the seventeenth century, when English Quakers popularized sweetened hot chocolate as an alternative to demon gin. Ever since that time, chocolate lovers have had a warm spot in their hearts for hot chocolate (even though gin has remained one of the more popular sins).

Which brings me to Chocolate Heart of Darkness. This warm, molten chocolate cake is so sensual it could be the eighth deadly sin. How appropriate that it was created by my sister Denise Yocum, a psychologist in Massachusetts. Whose lust was she analyzing when she developed this recipe?

If the racks in your oven slide out easily and are stable, instead of removing the muffin tin from the oven, slide the center rack out and quickly insert the truffles. Then return the rack to its place and finish the baking.

After the Chocolate Heart of Darkness Cakes have cooled to room temperature, you may keep them covered with plastic wrap for up to 24 hours at room temperature, or in the refrigerator for 3 to 4 days. Being a purist who is stuck in his ways, here is a revelation I hate to admit: The cakes may be rewarmed in a microwave oven, and they are extraordinary. Make sure the cakes are at room temperature, then heat them one or two at a time for 30 to 40 seconds in a microwave oven set on defrost power. The cake will be warm and moist, and the truffle center will be a hot ooze of ecstasy.

FOOD&WINE test-kitchen tips

- The recipe suggests wearing vinyl or latex gloves when shaping the ganache. Bare skin is too warm for the mixture, and you can end up with melted chocolate all over your hands. But we didn't have any gloves in the kitchen when we tested these, so we just cooled our hands by frequently holding them under cold running water and then drying them off.

- Don't worry about making perfectly smooth truffles with the ganache. They're just going to melt inside the cake anyway.

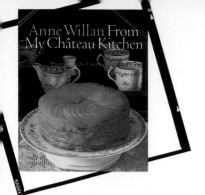

chocolate snowball

from *From My Château Kitchen*

SERVES 8 TO 10

You can keep the molded chocolate "ball" in the refrigerator up to three days, and it freezes well. Cover it with Chantilly cream as "snow" shortly before serving. One snowball serves at least eight to ten—it could hardly be richer!

½   lb/250 g dark chocolate, chopped

¾   cup/175 ml strong black coffee

1   cup/250 g butter, cut into pieces

1   cup/200 g granulated sugar

4   eggs, beaten to mix

8 to 10 mint sprigs, for decoration

for the chantilly cream

2   cups/500 ml heavy cream

1 to 2 tablespoons confectioners' sugar

1   teaspoon vanilla extract

A 1-quart/1-liter charlotte mold or deep bowl

Pastry bag and small star tube

Line the charlotte mold or bowl with a single piece of foil, pressing it to the sides as smoothly as possible but without tearing the foil. Heat the oven to 350°F/175°C. Heat the chocolate with the coffee in a small saucepan over medium heat, stirring until melted. Bring the chocolate to a boil and simmer until it thickens but still falls easily from the spoon. Add the butter and sugar and continue stirring over the heat until the mixture is melted and smooth. Bring it just to a boil and then remove it from the heat.

FOOD&WINE test-kitchen tips

- Use bittersweet chocolate for the best results.

- The decorative mint sprigs are pretty but in no way necessary. If you can't find fresh mint, a light dusting of cocoa over the top would work as well, or just serve this easy, do-ahead, and luscious dessert as is. It's a guaranteed hit.

Whisk the eggs into the chocolate mixture, adding them a little at a time and whisking steadily—the heat will cook and thicken them. Strain the mixture through a sieve and into the lined mold. Set the mold in a bain-marie and bring it to a boil on top of the stove. Transfer it to the oven and bake it until the chocolate mixture has risen and a light crust forms on top, 35 to 45 minutes. Take the mold from the bain-marie and let it cool—the snowball will shrink but don't worry. Cover and chill the mold until firmly set, at least 12 hours.

To finish the snowball, run a knife around the edge of the mold and turn the snowball onto a large flat serving plate. Peel off the foil—the chocolate will stick and be messy but this is no matter since it will later be completely concealed in Chantilly cream. If some chocolate sticks in the mold, simply scoop it out and reshape it.

For the Chantilly cream, beat the cream until stiff (it's best if the cream is rather cold to start with). Whisk in the confectioners' sugar and vanilla and continue whisking until stiff again—take care not to overbeat as the cream will stiffen further when it is piped through the small tube. Fill the piping bag with the Chantilly cream and completely cover the snowball with tiny rosettes so no chocolate is visible. Top it with a single large rosette of cream and dot the sides here and there with mint sprigs. Chill it until serving, then cut it in wedges like a cake.

desserts

golden anniversary chocolate chip brownie cake

from *Death by Chocolate Cakes*

SERVES 12

brownie cake

½	pound (2 sticks) unsalted butter, cut into ½-ounce pieces; plus 2 teaspoons (melted)
2	cups all-purpose flour
½	teaspoon baking powder
¼	teaspoon salt
2	cups (1 pound) tightly packed light brown sugar
3	large eggs
½	cup sour cream
2	teaspoons pure vanilla extract
1	cup semisweet chocolate chips

golden sugar

2	cups granulated sugar
1	teaspoon fresh lemon juice

caramel

2½	cups granulated sugar
1	teaspoon fresh lemon juice
1	cup heavy cream

caramel buttercream

1¼	pounds (5 sticks) unsalted butter, cut into ½-ounce pieces
½	cup granulated sugar
¼	cup light corn syrup
3	large egg yolks

make the brownie cake Preheat the oven to 325°F. Lightly coat the insides of two 9 x 1½-inch nonstick cake pans with some of the 2 teaspoons of melted butter. Line the bottoms of the pans with parchment paper (or wax paper); then lightly coat the paper with more melted butter. Set aside.

▼

In a sifter combine 2 cups flour, ½ teaspoon baking powder, and ¼ teaspoon salt. Sift onto a large piece of parchment paper (or wax paper) and set aside until needed.

Place 2 cups light brown sugar and ½ pound butter in the bowl of an electric mixer fitted with a paddle. Mix on low speed for 1 minute, then on medium-high for 4 minutes until soft. Use a rubber spatula to scrape down the sides of the bowl; then beat on medium-high for 2 more minutes. Scrape down the sides of the bowl again. Add 3 eggs, one at a time, beating on medium for 1 minute after each addition, and scraping down the sides of the bowl once all the eggs have been incorporated. Operate the mixer on low while gradually adding the sifted dry ingredients. Once they have been incorporated, about 45 seconds, add ½ cup sour cream and 2 teaspoons vanilla extract and mix on low speed to combine, about 20 seconds. Add 1 cup chocolate chips and combine on low for 10 seconds. Remove the bowl from the mixer and use a rubber spatula to finish mixing the ingredients until thoroughly combined.

Immediately divide the cake batter into the prepared pans (about 3 cups of batter in each pan), spreading the batter evenly. Bake on the center rack in the preheated oven until a toothpick inserted in the center of each cake layer comes out clean (spearing a chocolate chip doesn't count), about 40 minutes. Remove the cake layers from the oven and cool in the pans for 20 minutes at room temperature. Invert the cake layers onto cake circles or cake plates. (The cakes should readily release from the pans; if not, use a paring knife to cut around the inside edges of the pan before inverting.) Carefully peel the paper away from the bottoms of the cake layers and set aside at room temperature until needed.

make the golden sugar Place 2 cups sugar and 1 teaspoon lemon juice in a large saucepan. Stir with a whisk to combine. (The sugar will resemble moist sand.)

Caramelize the sugar for about 10 minutes over medium-high heat, stirring constantly with a whisk to break up any lumps. The sugar will first turn clear as it liquefies, then light brown as it caramelizes. Remove the saucepan from the heat. Immediately pour the caramelized sugar onto a nonstick baking sheet with sides and place in the freezer to harden, about 10 minutes. (If you are short on room in your freezer, you may harden the sugar in the refrigerator, about 20 minutes; the sugar will also harden in an air-conditioned room, about 30 minutes.)

Use the top edge of the blade of a cook's knife to strike and break the hardened caramelized sugar into smaller pieces. Pulse the pieces of golden sugar in a food processor fitted with a metal blade for about 45 seconds, until it is finely chopped. Sift the sugar in a medium-gauge strainer. Remove the chopped sugar from the strainer, and store it in a tightly sealed plastic container until ready to use for decorating the cake. (Save the finely sifted golden sugar to sweeten your coffee.)

prepare the caramel Place 2½ cups sugar and 1 teaspoon fresh lemon juice in a large saucepan. Stir with a whisk to combine.

Caramelize the sugar for about 12 minutes over medium-high heat, stirring constantly with a whisk to break up any lumps. Remove the saucepan from the heat. Slowly add 1 cup heavy cream to the bubbling hot sugar, whisking vigorously until smooth. (Adding the cream to the sugar creates very hot steam, so be careful to avoid a steam burn on your whisking hand.) Transfer the caramel to a medium bowl and set aside at room temperature.

make the caramel buttercream Place 1¼ pounds butter in the bowl of an electric mixer fitted with a paddle. Mix on low speed for 1 minute, then beat on medium for 2 minutes. Scrape down the sides of the bowl and the paddle. Beat on medium-high for 4 minutes until pale yellow in color and almost double in volume. Transfer the whipped butter to a medium bowl and set aside until needed.

Heat ¼ cup of the sugar and ¼ cup light corn syrup in a small saucepan over medium heat. Stir to combine and bring to a boil. Meanwhile place 3 egg yolks and remaining ¼ cup sugar in the bowl of an electric mixer fitted with a balloon whip. Whisk on high until pale yellow in color and slightly thickened, about 3 minutes. At this point the sugar syrup should be boiling and clear. Slowly drizzle the boiling syrup into the egg yolks while whisking on medium. Once the mixture is combined, increase the speed to high, and whisk for 5 minutes until thoroughly mixed. Scrape down the sides of the bowl. Add 1 cup of the caramel from the bowl and whisk on high for 5 more minutes. Add about half the amount of whipped butter and whisk on medium for 30 seconds, then add the remaining butter and whisk on medium for another 15 seconds. Scrape down the sides of the bowl. Now whisk on high for 5 minutes until the caramel buttercream is light and fluffy. Set aside at room temperature until ready to assemble the cake. (Cover the remaining caramel with plastic wrap and set it aside at room temperature as well.)

▼

assemble the cake   Transfer 1 cup of caramel buttercream to a pastry bag fitted with a medium star tip. Set aside.

Use a cake spatula to spread 1½ cups caramel buttercream evenly and smoothly over the top and sides of one of the inverted cake layers. Turn the second cake layer right side up, place it on top of the iced cake layer, and press down gently but firmly to level the layers. Smoothly spread the remaining caramel buttercream (excluding the buttercream in the pastry bag) over the top and sides of the cake. Pipe out a circle of stars (about 1 inch high and 1 inch wide), each one touching the next, along the outside edge of the top of the cake. Press the finely chopped golden sugar into the sides of the cake, coating evenly. Finally, pour the remaining caramel onto the top of the cake. (The caramel should spread over the top to the inside edges of the buttercream stars.)

Refrigerate for several hours before serving.

to serve   Heat the blade of a serrated slicer under hot running water and wipe the blade dry before cutting each slice. Place each slice onto a serving plate and keep at room temperature for about 30 minutes before serving. (This will allow the caramel to flow attractively and deliciously over the sides.)

the chef's touch   When my wife, Connie, told her parents that she and her four brothers and sisters were planning a fiftieth anniversary party for them, her parents said they did not want a party. The young-at-heart couple felt they weren't old enough to celebrate a fiftieth anniversary. Visions of a swarm of septuagenarians toasting the good old days was not their idea of fun. The siblings fell into their traditional childish roles, and disobeyed their parents by throwing an "Anti-versary" party. To appease, they promised the couple that they would be the oldest ones there, and pledged a night of celebratory decadence. Decadent indeed— especially the Chocolate Chip Brownie Cake that The Trellis's pastry chef, Kelly Bailey, created for the occasion. (P.S. The children were forgiven.)

FOOD&WINE test-kitchen tips

- A good chefs' trick: While frosting the cake, keep a container of hot water handy. Frequently dip your spatula into it and then wipe dry. The heat will help you to spread the buttercream smoothly.

- We found that the fully assembled cake kept beautifully, loosely wrapped with foil and refrigerated, for three days. We were amazed that all the textures—even the crunchiness of the golden sugar on the sides—were still perfect after that long a period.

Is caramel really burnt sugar? Not unless it is burnt caramel. Although caramel is easy enough to prepare, it's also fairly easy to burn if you don't give it your undivided attention.

If the caramel for the top of the cake becomes too stiff to pour, place the bowl of caramel in a container of hot water to warm until the caramel is free-flowing but not hot; otherwise, it will melt the buttercream.

The caramel on top of the cake must be very firm before the cake can be cut into perfect slices; otherwise, the caramel will drool down the sides of the piece of cake (an appealingly sexy alternative presentation). For a perfectly clean cut, refrigerate the cake for 24 hours before slicing.

The cooled Brownie Cake layers may be frozen for an extended period (up to 3 to 4 weeks). Be certain to thoroughly wrap the cakes in plastic wrap to prevent dehydration and to protect them from freezer odors. The Golden Sugar may also be stored in an airtight plastic container in the freezer for an indefinite period of time.

This cake may be prepared over 3 days. Day 1: Bake the Brownie Cake layers. Once cooled, cover each layer with plastic wrap and refrigerate until assembling the whole cake. Prepare the Golden Sugar, then store in an airtight plastic container in the freezer until needed. Day 2: Prepare the Caramel and the Caramel Buttercream, then assemble the cake and refrigerate until the next day. Day 3: Slice and serve the cake as directed.

Of course, a Golden Anniversary celebration would not be complete without champagne. To complement the rich textures and unrestrained sweetness of this cake, I would select a very dry but lively (lots of persistent bubbles) 1990 Perrier Jouët Fleur de Lis Champagne.

desserts

▼

credits & acknowledgments

Artisan

(a division of Workman
Publishing, Co., Inc.)
708 Broadway
New York, NY 10003
(212) 254-5900
www.workman.com

- **Hot Sour Salty Sweet** *A Culinary
Journey through Southeast Asia* by
Jeffrey Alford and Naomi Duguid.
Copyright © 2000 by Jeffrey Alford and
Naomi Duguid. Used by permission of
Artisan, a division of Workman Publishing,
Co., Inc.
location photographs copyright ©
2000 by Jeffrey Alford and Naomi
Duguid/Asia Access
studio photographs copyright © 2000
by Richard Jung

Broadway Books

(a division of Random House, Inc.)
1540 Broadway
New York, NY 10036
(212) 782-9000
www.broadwaybooks.com

- **How to Cook Without a Book** *Recipes
Every Cook Should Know by Heart* by
Pam Anderson. Copyright © 2000 by Pam
Anderson. Used by permission of
Broadway Books, a division of Random
House, Inc.

- **Simple to Spectacular** *How to Take
One Basic Recipe to Four Levels of
Sophistication* by Jean-Georges
Vongerichten and Mark Bittman.
Copyright © 2000 by Jean-Georges
Vongerichten and Mark Bittman. Used by
permission of Broadway Books, a
division of Random House, Inc.
photographs Gentl & Hyers

Clarkson Potter/Publishers

(a division of Random House, Inc.)
201 East 50th Street
New York, NY 10022
(212) 751-2600
www.clarksonpotter.com

- **Holiday Food** *Recipes for the Most
Festive Time of Year* by Mario Batali.
Copyright © 2000 by Mario Batali. Used
by permission of Clarkson Potter/
Publishers, a division of Random House,
Inc.
photographs copyright © 2000 by
Quentin Bacon

- **Anne Willan: From My Château Kitchen** by Anne Willan. Copyright © 2000 by Anne Willan, Inc. Used by permission of Clarkson Potter/Publishers, a division of Random House, Inc.
photographs copyright © 2000 by Langdon Clay

Doubleday Books

(a division of Random House, Inc.)
1540 Broadway
New York, NY 10036
(212) 782-9000
www.doubleday.com

- **Simply Tuscan** *Recipes for a Well-Lived Life* by Pino Luongo. Copyright © 2000 by Pino Luongo. Used by permission of Doubleday, a division of Random House, Inc.
photographs Jeff McNamara

- **Alfred Portale's 12 Seasons Cookbook** by Alfred Portale with Andrew Friedman. Copyright © 2000 by Alfred Portale. Used by permission of Doubleday, a division of Random House, Inc.
photographs Gozen Koshida

HarperCollins Publishers, Inc.

10 East 53rd Street
New York, NY 10022
(212) 207-7000
www.harpercollins.com

- **Savoring the Spice Coast of India** *Fresh Flavors from Kerala* by Maya Kaimal. Copyright © 2000 by Maya Kaimal. Used by permission of HarperCollins Publishers, Inc.
photographs copyright © 2000 by Zubin Shroff and John Bentham

- **Cookies Unlimited** by Nick Malgieri. Copyright © 2000 by Nick Malgieri. Used by permission of HarperCollins Publishers, Inc.
photographs copyright © 2000 by Tom Eckerle

The Harvard Common Press

535 Albany Street
Boston, MA 02118
(617) 423-5803
www.harvardcommonpress.com

- **The Japanese Kitchen** by Hiroko Shimbo. Copyright © 2000 by Hiroko Shimbo-Beitchman. Used by permission of The Harvard Common Press.

credits & acknowledgments

▼

Houghton Mifflin Company

215 Park Avenue South
New York, NY 10003
(212) 420-5800
www.hmco.com

- **The Foods of the Greek Islands**
*Cooking and Culture at the Crossroads
of the Mediterranean, Including Recipes
by New York's Acclaimed Molyvos
Restaurant* by Aglaia Kremezi. Used by
permission of Houghton Mifflin Company.
text and photographs
copyright © 2000 by Aglaia Kremezi

Hungry Minds, Inc.

909 Third Avenue
New York, NY 10022
(212) 884-5000
www.hungryminds.com

- **1,000 Jewish Recipes** by Faye Levy.
Copyright © 2000 by Faye Levy. Used by
permission of Hungry Minds, Inc.

Alfred A. Knopf

(a division of Random House, Inc.)
201 East 50th Street
New York, NY 10022
(212) 751-2600
www.randomhouse.com

- **Julia's Kitchen Wisdom** *Essential
Techniques and Recipes from a Lifetime
of Cooking* by Julia Child with David
Nussbaum. Copyright © 2000 by Julia
Child. Used by permission of Alfred A.
Knopf, a division of Random House, Inc.
photographs Paul Child

Little, Brown and Company

1271 Avenue of the Americas
New York, NY 10020
(212) 522-8700
www.littlebrown.com

- **The Dessert Bible** by Christopher
Kimball. Copyright © 2000 by Christopher
Kimball. Used by permission of Little,
Brown and Company, Inc.
illustrations Gary Hallgren

The Lyons Press

123 West 18th Street
New York, NY 10011
(212) 620-9580
www.lyonspress.com

- **The Farmer's Market Cookbook** *Seasonal Recipes Made from Nature's Freshest Ingredients* by Richard Ruben. Copyright © 2000 by Richard Ruben. Used by permission of The Lyons Press.

William Morrow and Company, Inc.

(a division of HarperCollins Publishers, Inc.)
10 East 53rd Street
New York, NY 10022
(212) 207-7000
www.harpercollins.com

- **Death by Chocolate Cakes** *An Astonishing Array of Chocolate Enchantments* by Marcel Desaulniers. Copyright © 2000 by Marcel Desaulniers. Used by permission of HarperCollins Publishers, Inc.
photographs copyright © 2000 by Duane Winfield

- **Tom Douglas' Seattle Kitchen** by Tom Douglas with Denis Kelly, Shelley Lance, and Duskie Estes. Copyright © 2000 by Tom Douglas. Used by permission of HarperCollins Publishers, Inc.
photographs Jan Cobb

- **My Mother's Southern Entertaining** by James Villas. Copyright © 2000 by James Villas. Used by permission of HarperCollins Publishers, Inc.
photographs copyright © 2000 by Dennis Gottlieb

- **Cracking the Coconut** *Classic Thai Home Cooking* by Su-Mei Yu. Copyright © 2000 by Su-Mei Yu. Used by permission of HarperCollins Publishers, Inc.
photographs copyright © 2000 by Alexandra Grablewski

▼

credits & acknowledgments

Scribner

(a division of Simon & Schuster)
1230 Avenue of the Americas
New York, NY 10020
(212) 698-7000
www.simonsays.com

- **The Herbfarm Cookbook** by Jerry Traunfeld. Text copyright © 2000 by Jerry Traunfeld. Used by permission of Scribner, a division of Simon & Schuster.
  photographs copyright © 2000 by Jonelle Weaver

- **Rick Bayless: Mexico One Plate at a Time** by Rick Bayless with Jeanmarie Brownson and Deann Groen Bayless. Text copyright © 2000 by Richard Lane Bayless. Used by permission of Scribner, a division of Simon & Schuster.
  black & white photographs copyright © 2000 by James Baigrie
  color photographs copyright © 2000 by Gentl & Hyers

- **50 Chowders** *One-Pot Meals—Clam, Corn & Beyond* by Jasper White. Text copyright © 2000 by Jasper White. Used by permission of Scribner, a division of Simon & Schuster.
  photographs copyright © 2000 by Gentl & Hyers

Simon & Schuster

1230 Avenue of the Americas
New York, NY 10020
(212) 698-7000
www.simonsays.com

- **The Olives Dessert Table** *Spectacular Restaurant Desserts You Can Make at Home* by Todd English, Paige Retus, and Sally Sampson. Copyright © 2000 by Todd English, Paige Retus, and Sally Sampson. Used by permission of Simon & Schuster.
  photographs copyright © 2000 by Carl Tremblay

Ten Speed Press

P.O. Box 7123
Berkeley, CA 94707
(510) 559-1600
www.tenspeed.com

- **Gordon Ramsay: A Chef for All Seasons** by Gordon Ramsay with Roz Denny. Text copyright © 2000 by Gordon Ramsay.
Used by permission of Ten Speed Press.
photographs copyright © 2000 by Georgia Glynn Smith

- **Wildwood** *Cooking from the Source in the Pacific Northwest* by Cory Schreiber. Copyright © 2000 by Cory Schreiber.
Used by permission of Ten Speed Press.
food photographs copyright © 2000 by Richard Jung
location photographs copyright © 2000 by Jerome Hart

Villard Books

(a division of Random House, Inc.)
201 East 50th Street
New York, NY 10022
(212) 751-2600
www.villard.com

- **Nancy Silverton's Pastries from the La Brea Bakery** by Nancy Silverton.
Copyright © 2000 by Nancy Silverton.
Used by permission of Villard, a division of Random House, Inc.

Workman Publishing Co., Inc.

708 Broadway
New York, NY 10003
(212) 254-5900
www.workman.com

- **Staff Meals from Chanterelle** by David Waltuck and Melicia Phillips. Copyright © 2000 by David Waltuck and Melicia Phillips. Used by permission of Workman Publishing Co., Inc.

credits & acknowledgments

photo & illustration credits

Photographs & Illustrations from Book Interiors

Jeffrey Alford and Naomi Duguid/Asia Access: 78, 117, 175; Quentin Bacon: cover (bottom), 150 (far left), 169, 178 (far right), 183; James Baigrie: 12 (second from left), 37; Edmund Barr: Pots and pans photos on 12, 44, 80, 114, 150, 178, 210; John Bentham: 67; Paul Child: 83, 146; Langdon Clay: 80 (left), 85, 119, 251; Jan Cobb: 114 (second from right), 143, 178 (second from right), 206, 210 (far left), 223; Roberto de Vicq de Cumptich: 14, 95; Tom Eckerle: 215, 219; Gentl & Hyers: 44 (far left and second from left), 48, 75, 114 (far left), 131, 178 (far left), 191; Dennis Gottlieb: 44 (far right), 60; Gary Hallgren: 213; Jerome Hart: 80 (right), 113; Richard Jung: 150 (second from left), 176, 203; Gozen Koshida: 12 (second from right), 28, 44 (second from left), 69; Aglaia Kremezi: 178 (second from left), 185; Jeff McNamara: 12 (far right), 33, 150 (second from right and far right), 163, 165; Jerry Ruotolo: 6, 287; Zubin Shroff: 80 (middle), 106; Georgia Glynn Smith: 114 (second from left and far right), 123, 135, 149; Elizabeth Traynor: 15, 94; Carl Tremblay: 210 (middle photos), 225, 231; Jonelle Weaver: 12 (far left), 23; Duane Winfield: 210 (far right), 239, 244, 247, 253.

Photographs & Illustrations from Book Jackets

Melanie Acevado: 34 (location photo), 124 (location photo), 184 (location photo)

Ruven Afanador: 61, 66, 107

Quentin Bacon: 168, 182

Amos Chang: 59, 70, 86, 120, 200, 208, 220

Langdon Clay: 84, 118, 250

Andrew Eccles: 27, 68, 104, 138, 196

Tom Eckerle: 214, 218

FPG and ©Photodisc: 186, 204

Alexandra Grablewski: 98, 159

Gentl & Hyers: 26, 36, 46, 52, 56, 74, 87, 109, 128, 154, 156, 190

Jerome Hart: 24, 112, 193, 202

Lisa Hubbard: 212, 216

Richard Jung: 77, 116, 132, 152, 174

Gozen Koshida: 27

Michael McLaughlin: 39, 82, 144

Jeff McNamara: 32, 163, 164

Maria Robledo: 101, 136

Steven Rothfeld: 18, 236

Ellen Silverman: 34 (food photo), 124 (food photo), 184 (food photo), 92, 126, 187

Brian Smale: 16, 29, 42, 72, 140, 162, 166, 180, 205, 222

Georgia Glynn Smith: 122, 133, 147, 172

Carl Tremblay: 224, 230

Jonelle Weaver: 20, 22, 198

Duane Winfield: 238, 242, 246, 252

index

Page numbers in boldface indicate photographs.

Index

Index

Index

Index

Hundreds of recipes are rigorously tested and tasted to select those worthy of the distinction "best of the best." Sampling a winning dish are Judith Hill (left), editor in chief of FOOD & WINE Books, and Dana Speers, *Best of the Best* project manager.